Drink, Power, and Society in the Andes

UNIVERSITY PRESS OF FLORIDA

Florida A&M University, Tallahassee
Florida Atlantic University, Boca Raton
Florida Gulf Coast University, Ft. Myers
Florida International University, Miami
Florida State University, Tallahassee
New College of Florida, Sarasota
University of Central Florida, Orlando
University of Florida, Gainesville
University of North Florida, Jacksonville
University of South Florida, Tampa
University of West Florida, Pensacola

Drink, Power, and Society in the Andes

Edited by Justin Jennings and Brenda J. Bowser

University Press of Florida

Gainesville Tallahassee Tampa Boca Raton

Pensacola Orlando Miami Jacksonville Ft. Myers Sarasota

First cloth printing, 2009
First paperback printing, 2020

25 24 23 22 21 20   6 5 4 3 2 1

Library of Congress Cataloging-in-Publication Data
Drink, power, and society in the Andes / [edited by] Justin Jennings
and Brenda J. Bowser.
p. cm.
Includes bibliographical references and index.
ISBN 978-0-8130-3306-8 (alk. paper) | ISBN 978-0-8130-6838-1 (pbk.)
1. Indians of South America—Alcohol use—Andes Region. 2. Indians of South
America—Andes Region—Social life and customs. 3. Chicha—Andes Region—History.
4. Drinking of alcoholic beverages—Andes Region—History. 5. Drinking customs—
Andes Region—History. 6. Andes Region—Social life and customs. I. Jennings, Justin.
II. Bowser, Brenda J., 1957–
F2229.D75 2008
394.1'3098—dc22   2008038634

The University Press of Florida is the scholarly publishing agency for the State University System of Florida, comprising Florida A&M University, Florida Atlantic University,
Florida Gulf Coast University, Florida International University, Florida State University,
New College of Florida, University of Central Florida, University of Florida, University
of North Florida, University of South Florida, and University of West Florida.

University Press of Florida
2046 NE Waldo Road
Suite 2100
Gainesville, FL 32609
http://upress.ufl.edu

Contents

Tables

Figures

1

Drink, Power, and Society in the Andes

An Introduction

Justin Jennings and Brenda J. Bowser

The Inca at his table
Quaff'd it in his mirth
And thus we are all able
To prove its ancient worth
Who one cup has tasted
Soon will want another
To drink it, nothing wasted
To his chief or brother.

Fill the cup with chicha,
Patriots, to the brink;
Drain it to the bottom:
Liberty we drink!

—An English explorer's loose translation of a drinking song
  sung in a Peruvian tavern in 1823 during the war of independence

Alcohol is perhaps the most ancient, the most widely used, and the most versatile drug in the world (Dudley 2002; Heath 1976: 41), and its production, exchange, and consumption have long structured individuals' relationships with society, the environment, and the cosmos throughout the world (Douglas 1987a). For example, the production of millet beer in Africa defines gender roles, determines irrigation schedules, and dominates household rhythms (Holtzman 2001). Exchange of wines in ancient Egypt led to the development of an elite cuisine, and drinking *pulque* in Mesoamerica brought imbibers closer to the divine (Joffe 1998; La Barre 1938).

In the Andes, people's participation in the production, distribution, and consumption of alcohol has woven them into their social, economic, and political structures for millennia.

Drinking, like other aspects of culture, can act as a force of both social stability and change. Individuals in the Andes or elsewhere are not trapped within a culture's social structure, but instead, these structures are actively maintained, negotiated, and at times transformed as people live their lives (Bourdieu 1977; Giddens 1979). For example, traditional gender roles are reinforced when a woman serves beer to her husband. By spilling the beer, or even forcing him to drink too much, however, a wife can punish her husband for infidelity without breaking social norms (see Bowser 2004; Weismantel, this volume). The flow of alcohol through society helps to reveal the tension between social structure and personal agency that creates identities, channels power, and fires social change (see, e.g., Sahlins 1985).

This volume presents nine chapters from scholars using ethnographic, historical, and archaeological approaches to study how alcoholic beverages have been integrated into Andean societies over the last fifteen hundred years. The authors consider how alcohol has maintained gender roles, kinship bonds, status hierarchies, ethnic identities, exchange relationships, and production regimes that form communities. At the same time, the authors consider how shifts in alcohol production, exchange, and consumption have precipitated social change. By bringing together scholars from diverse theoretical, methodological, and regional perspectives, we hope to demonstrate the pivotal role that alcohol has long played in the Andes.

Alcohol Studies

Fermentation is a natural process that humans have long manipulated to enrich their diet, preserve surpluses, detoxify food, and decrease cooking times (Steinkraus 1996: 3–4). One of the common by-products of fermentation is ethanol, and people in the Andes have long made alcoholic beverages out of a rich variety of cereals, roots, fruits, and seeds (Goldstein, Coleman Goldstein, and Williams, this volume). These indigenous beverages are commonly called chicha, with corn beer (*chicha de maíz*) being perhaps the most common of these beverages consumed today. In recent decades, chicha consumption has declined as distilled liquors, such as the cheap, plentiful, and strong *trago* made from sugarcane, and commercial barley and wheat beers have become more popular.

Although few anthropologists initially go into the field with a research focus on alcohol (Wilson 2005a: 5), the importance of alcohol to culture has been recognized since at least the 1940s (Bunzel 1940; Horton 1943). This early work tried to move past simple psychological explanations for drinking as pathological and toward more nuanced understandings that placed drinking patterns within their cultural contexts. Since that time, fieldwork throughout the world has steadily increased our knowledge of the complex role that beer and wine play in structuring societies (see, e.g., de Garine and de Garine 2001; Douglas 1987b; Everett et al. 1976; Heath 2000; Marshall 1979; Pittman and Snyder 1962; Wilson 2005b). This work has clearly demonstrated that the production and consumption of alcohol are central to the creation of identity, the construction and maintenance of power, the functioning of social networks, and the practice of religions (see, e.g., Dietler 2006; Heath 2000).

The Andes was one of the first regions of the world that came under study by scholars specifically interested in the role of alcohol in society. This work began in the 1950s with Dwight Heath's ethnographic work on ritual drunkenness among the Camba people of eastern Bolivia (1962) and John Murra's historical work on the role of corn (predominately in the form of corn beer) in the Inca Empire (1960). Since this pioneering work, many articles have explored alcohol production and use in the Andes (e.g., Bray 2003a; Doughty 1971; Goldstein 2003; Morris 1979; Simmons 1962; Valdez 2006), and several influential books have discussed the role of alcohol in the region (e.g., Allen 2002; Bastien 1978; Cummins 2002; Isbell 1978; Weismantel 2001).

Of particular note are four books that focus exclusively on the role of alcohol in the Andes. The first of these, *Borrachera y memoria: La experiencia de lo sagrado en los Andes*, is an edited volume that explores the ritual dimensions of chicha consumption from the colonial period to the present (Saignes 1993). The volume's principal focus is on drunkenness—explaining why drinking is fundamental to traditional religions in the Andes and why the Catholic Church has long been opposed to these practices. The second book, entitled *Maíz, chicha y religiosidad andina*, also looks at chicha's role in ritual, but has greater time depth (Cavero Carrasco 1986). After devoting eight pages of text to the uses of chicha in pre-Inca cultures, the book explores Inca production and consumption of alcohol through historical records. He then turns to the social, political, and ritual aspects of chicha drinking in the Andes today.

The last two books are ethnographies. *Chicha de maíz: Bebida y vida del pueblo Catacaos* (Camino 1987) discusses the complex role placed by corn beer in Catacaos, a town on the far north coast of Peru. The book looks in particular at how cultural identity is formed through the process of making and drinking beer. The final book, *Holy Intoxication to Drunken Dissipation: Alcohol among Quichua Speakers in Otavalo, Ecuador*, discusses how the role of beer in Ecuadorian society has changed since the Spanish Conquest (Butler 2006). In particular, the book focuses on how drinking practices in the community of Huaycopungo radically changed as villagers rethought long-standing traditions in the aftermath of an earthquake.

In this volume, the authors build on previous scholarship to consider the role of alcohol in the Andes over the long term. The chapters cover a wide variety of topics, but touch on three themes of long duration in the region. The first theme, *reciprocity and power*, looks at how the production and consumption of alcohol create a dynamics of power that brings people together into interlocking reciprocal obligations. The second theme, *identity and society*, explores the ways in which fermented beverages (and, in Allen's case study, carbonated drinks) create, and occasionally challenge, gender roles, social networks, community structures, and ethnic identity. The final theme, *continuity and change*, centers on how drinking regimes have remained stable or changed over time and the implication of these shifts on the social system.

Reciprocity and Power

The Indians do not obey us, we cannot finish the communal sowing or build the community center because it is by the means of chicha that the Indians obey us. (Testimony of local lords in 1566 against a recent ban on the distribution of alcoholic beverages.[1])

It is he who loves us, expressing (his love) with one or perhaps two bottles. (The mayor of Chuschi's response to a question about how friends helped him with the fiesta of Yarqa Aspiy in 1970.[2])

Reciprocity is the backbone of the traditional Andean economy (Alberti and Mayer 1974; Allen 2002: 49, and in this volume; Isbell 1978: 167; Mayer 2002; Weismantel, this volume), and alcohol is emblematic of the hospitality through which reciprocal obligations are performed. The most common form of exchange today is delayed reciprocal labor exchange between small networks of family and friends in a community. In these exchanges, often called *ayni* (Aymara) or *mita* (Quechua), the sponsor of the event is generally responsible for providing food and drink for invited laborers. People come in part for camaraderie and for a good meal, but they provide their labor in order to ensure that the host will return the favor at a later date (Mayer 2002: 109).

In larger communal projects, or for work for the church or state, a sponsor is not obligated to repay workers with labor at a later date. Instead, the host must throw a feast for the workforce as payment for its labor (Allen 2002: 72–74; Isbell 1978: 167–177; Mayer 1974, 2002: 108–112). Unlike ayni, these *minka* (or *minga* in Quechua) exchanges are asymmetric, since labor is not later returned (Mayer 2002: 110). In many cases, people enter into minka exchanges in order to perform tasks that cannot be easily performed by a small group of villagers, such as the construction of a house, or to complete communal duties like canal cleaning. In other cases, minka exchanges are part of long-standing relationships between social unequals (Mayer 2002: 116).

Power can be defined as the ability to coerce or persuade people to behave in a certain manner (after Stanish and Haley 2004: 56). It is created and maintained through social relationships (see, e.g., Bourdieu 1977; Foucault 1979), and the food and drink that accompany minka exchanges are integral to these relationships in at least three ways. First, the feasts reify social positions by the ways in which goods are served, whom they are served to, and how they are served (Allen 2002: 96–98; Bowser 2000: 228–229; Bowser 2004; Colloredo-Mansfeld 1999: 150–159; Jennings and Chatfield, this volume). The social order is recapitulated at the event (see, e.g., Lincoln 1989: 88), and the host family accrues considerable social prestige. Second, these exchanges provide the opportunity to reassert social position by ostentatious displays of wealth. Offering jar after jar of beer to one's guests is generous, but it is also a presentation of power, since the guest may be unable to reciprocate (see, e.g., Mauss 1990). Finally, a laborer provides more work than the labor-equivalent cost of the food and drink that he or she consumes at the minka feast (Mayer 2002: 116). While couched in an idiom of reciprocity, this imbalance not only is recognized by all but also provides a labor surplus that can be used to pursue the goals of the host family (Jennings 2005; Mayer 2002: 116).

Minka exchanges also curtail power, however, because of the demands that the feast places on a host. The organization of a major feast is a daunting task that few in the community would choose to pursue. If a sponsor fails to provide sufficient food and drink, the workers will not work as hard, and may not work at all (Isbell 1978: 177). Since food and drink were traditionally prepared within the community, hosts have long relied on family, friends, and exchange partners to help in organizing the feast (Jennings 2005). One's generosity is therefore dependent on the participation of others, and thus elite ambitions must be balanced with a concern for maintaining strong relationships with one's neighbors and kin (Jennings and Chatfield, this volume).

Minka exchanges have long been significant in the Andean political economy, and the consumption of chicha has been an essential beverage at these events (Allen 2002; Cavero Carrasco 1986; Hastorf and Johannessen 1993; Morris 1979; Murra 1960; Saignes 1993). Reciprocity was *the* structuring principle of Inca political economy, and the passing of a drink from host to guest was perhaps the most widely recognized metaphor for this relationship (Cummins 2002; Ramírez 2005; Weismantel, this volume). Historical documents describe the consumption of chicha made from maize, manioc, peanuts, and molle (the fruit of the pepper tree) in the Inca Empire both at large public events and within households (Bray, this volume; Cavero Carrasco 1986; Goodman-Elgar, this volume; Hastorf and Johannessen 1993; Morris 1979; Murra 1960; Saignes 1993). The shared consumption of beer linked the Inca leader, the cosmos, and the people through its reciprocal flow (Cummins 2002; also see Bray, Goodman-Elgar, and Weismantel, this volume).

The Spanish chroniclers were especially interested in the large amounts of chicha that were prepared at great feasts held by the state (Bray, this volume; Goodman-Elgar, this volume; Hastorf and Johannessen 1993; Morris 1979; Murra 1960). Excessive drinking was encouraged, and, as Bernabé Cobo suggests of these feasts, "the principal activity is to drink until they cannot stand up" (1979: 28). At these events, the Inca emperor was able not only to fulfill his reciprocal duties for the labor rendered to the state but also to reaffirm his position of power by putting laborers in his debt by the sheer quantity of food and chicha that he provided (Bray 2003a: 18–19; Hastorf and Johannessen 1993: 118–119; Moore 1989: 685; Morris 1979: 32). To underwrite these events, the empire invested heavily in expanding maize production by opening up new areas to cultivation, improving preexisting agricultural lands, and demanding maize as tribute from outside areas (Murra 1960). The Inca also centralized chicha production by assigning brewing responsibilities for state feasts to the *mamacuna*, the sequestered "chosen women" who labored exclusively for the state (Morris 1979).

As it was in other regions of the world (Sherratt 1995: 12–13), alcohol was likely of long-standing importance in the pre-Inca world and may have operated in a similar idiom of reciprocity (Weismantel, this volume). There are, however, no written records that precede the Spanish Conquest that can be used to study earlier chicha use. In other areas of the world, scientists have found increasing success in identifying alcoholic beverages by the residues that are left behind in vessels (McGovern 2003; Samuel 2000). Unfortunately, similar research in the Andes is only beginning to be done and has yet to be fully published. Without these direct methods, archaeologists have attempted to find archaeological correlates that can be used to indirectly identify chicha production and consumption in the prehistoric Andes (see, e.g., Moore 1989; Goldstein, Coleman Goldstein, and Williams, this volume).

After his work at the Inca administrative center of Huanacopamapa, Craig Morris was the first archaeologist to attempt to rigorously identify beer-making facilities by correlating his findings on the ground, in this case, extensive concentrations of large jars and rocker grinding stones, to ethnographic and historical accounts of brewing (Morris 1979; Morris and Thompson 1985).

Jerry Moore (1989) and Rafael Segura Llanos (2001) built on Morris' work by outlining these archaeological correlates in greater detail. These authors suggest that, despite considerable variability, all corn chicha brewed in the Andes today goes through the following production steps: maize grain selection; removal of kernels; soaking of corn; germination or mastication; drying; grinding; cooking; straining; and fermentation (Moore 1989: 687; Segura Llanos 2001: 134–135). They then consider what material correlates from each stage might be recoverable. For example, they suggest that the drying phase of chicha production could be identified by the presence of drying mats, *jora* (dried sprouted maize kernels), and open patios. One could document the straining phase by finding sieves and chicha dregs (known as *alfrecho*).

The existence of multiple material correlates provides strong evidence for past chicha production in the Chimú state on Peru's north coast (AD 900–1470) (Moore 1989) and in Middle Horizon levels (AD 600–1000)

at the urban site of Cajamarquilla on Peru's central coast (Segura Llanos 2001). Clear chicha production has also been demonstrated by Izumi
Shimada (1994) for late Moche (AD 500–600), by Joan Gero (1990, 1992)
in Early Intermediate Period Recuay (AD 200–600), by Ryan Williams
and his colleagues for the Middle Horizon Wari state (AD 600–1000)
(Goldstein, Coleman Goldstein, and Williams, this volume; Moseley et
al. 2005), and by Paul Goldstein for Middle Horizon Tiwanaku (AD 500–
1100) (2003; 2005).

The archaeological correlates for chicha production tend to favor specialized production facilities in areas with good preservation. For example,
a row of large fermenting jars would not be found in the home of a small-
scale producer, and jora would decompose rapidly on the moist eastern
slopes of the Andes. Domestic production in the highlands is therefore
more difficult to document using these indicators. Archaeological correlates, moreover, have been detailed solely for maize beer production (but
see the discussion of Goldstein, Coleman Goldstein, and Williams, this
volume, on the correlates for molle beer production).

Another way that chicha consumption has been studied is through the
isotopic analysis of human bone. Carbon isotope analysis can be used to
track changes in maize consumption by measuring the amount of plants
with C_4 photosynthetic pathways that were consumed. With little access to
marine foods and no other major C_4 subsistence crop, the Andes is an ideal
location for the study of carbon isotopes (Hastorf 1991: 148–152; Hastorf
2001: 174–176; Larsen 2000: 272). Christine Hastorf (1991) was among the
first scholars to extensively use carbon isotopes as part of her study of the
Late Intermediate to Late Horizon transition in the Upper Mantaro Valley
of southern Peru. She has demonstrated that maize consumption increased
overall after the Inca Conquest of the region, and that men were consuming more maize than women during the Late Horizon. Hastorf argues that
this pattern was the result of men's privileged access to the Inca feasts,
where large amounts of chicha were consumed.

Interestingly, carbon isotopic analysis of individuals in Moquequa has
revealed a similar trend of high maize consumption among males in the
Tiwanaku state (Goldstein 2003: 164). The marked maize consumption in
these cases contrasts with the much lower levels of maize consumption,
even among elites, at the important site of Chavín de Huántar during the
Early Horizon (900–200 BC) (Burger and Van Der Merwe 1990). Isotope
studies measure maize consumption, but do not necessarily indicate that
the maize was consumed in the form of chicha. The potential of chemical

studies of human bone to detect plants that were used to make nonmaize chicha remains unexplored.

The identification of chicha production and consumption in the pre-Columbian past, of course, does not mean that we should assume that the political economy operated through similar ethoses of reciprocity (see continuity and change discussion below, and Hayashida, this volume). We do know, however, that drinking was important. Drinking vessels can be identified ichnographically in the ancient Andes, and the *kero*, or drinking cup, seems to have been particularly important in the Wari, Tiwanaku, and Inca polities (Bray 2003a; Cummins 2002; Cook and Glowacki 2003; Goldstein 2005).

While we can be reasonably sure that the Inca cups were used for corn beer, it is difficult to make a strong case for what similar vessels contained in earlier cultures except through historical and ethnographic analogies to more recent Andean cultures. In a similar manner, high percentages of serving vessels at sites are one of several lines of evidence that have been used for evidence of widespread feasting in the ancient Andes (Bray 2003a, 2003b, 2003c; Costin and Earle 1989; Cook and Glowacki 2003; Goldstein 2003, 2005; Lau 2002). Among these vessels are *keros* and bowls that were likely used to hold drinking liquids. Without residue analyses on these vessels, however, we cannot say for certain that they were used for the drinking of fermented beverages.

Identity and Society

> Taking a seat at the far end of the banquet, Paria Caca sat there like a poor miserable stranger. . . . Only one man finally offered him a drink . . . that one man . . . was spared. (From an early-seventeenth-century tale of the mistreatment of a Peruvian deity and his subsequent wrath.[3])

> Would that were all one needed to know! . . . the server can choose a plain or fancy serving cup, asua [corn beer], trago, a mix of two, or even a beer; a tiny sip or a large serving; an outpouring of flowery phrases of honor or a perfunctorily extended hand. (An ethnographer expresses her confusion over how guests are served in Otavalo, Ecuador.[4])

As in other areas of the world (Bowser 2000, 2004; Douglas 1987a; McDonald 1994; Partanen 1991; Wilson 2005b), the production and consumption of alcohol in the Andes are used to define gender, faction, ranking, and ethnicity. Reciprocal obligations not only are about political power but also form the core of Andean cosmology. In the central Andes, reciprocity is couched within an overarching cosmology that frames a world composed of circulating currents. Through these currents, the essence of life, in some regions called *sami* or *enqua*, flows through the world and ultimately turns back on itself, creating a closed ring (Allen 2002: 36; Bolin 1998: 232). In order to receive sami, one must offer it to other people, places, and objects (Allen 1982: 194). If one's relationships with kin, labor partners, nature, and the gods are in order, then one will be infused with sami (Greenway 1989: 9, as quoted in Ackerman 1991: 73). The flow of sami therefore depends on proper conduct. Since shirking one's responsibility as a woman, a leader, or a community member invites divine retribution on all (Bode 1990), so-cial roles, and the reciprocal obligations commensurate with these roles, have long been communally enforced (Ramírez 2005). The proper flow of chicha, between the gods, the dead, and the living, is a fundamental part of the flow of sami.

One of the primary ways that social roles are displayed in this region is through cuisine (Goldstein, Coleman Goldstein, and Williams, this volume). As Mary Weismantel notes (1988: 194), the cooking and eating of food is "a means of expressing what a people think of themselves." Food is not simply a passive signal of one's gender, status, and ethnicity; it is also often creatively used to advance social change (Weismantel 1988). Both central to the reciprocal obligations that structure interactions and infused with *sami* through the fermentation process (Allen 2002; Weismantel, this volume), alcohol is central to identity creation in the Andes. Through mak-ing, offering, and drinking beer, identities are "actively constructed, em-bodied, performed, and transformed" (Dietler 2006: 235).

Men are associated more with the consumption of alcohol than are women in the Andes. While both sexes drink, a man's relationship with other men is affirmed through drinking. His ability to hold his liquor marks him as a man, and, through alcohol, "friendships and agreements are sealed and kinship is acknowledged" (Weismantel 1988: 188).

Women are most closely associated with chicha production. Although men and children sometimes help in the brewing process (Allen 2002: 152; Valderrama Fernández et al. 1996: 55), women control the process (Cutler and Cárdenas 1947: 37; Hayashida, this volume; Orlove and Schmidt 1995: 276; Perlov, this volume). The preparation and serving of chicha, as with all food, is central to women's identity (Weismantel 1988: 28), and for women who sell chicha (*chicheras*) the drink offers "considerable social power and autonomy," which they aggressively defend (Perlov, this volume).

Chicha is the customary offering to one's guests, and women are often the ones who serve it (Weismantel, this volume). To serve no drink, or to serve a drink of poor quality, is an affront to the guest. Chicha, therefore, is in constant demand, and a woman is traditionally responsible for maintaining a ready supply of the beverage (see Bowser 2004 for similar practices in the Amazon). Since chicha takes days to make and often spoils quickly (Jennings 2005; Perlov, this volume), it is constantly being prepared in the home. The various pots for making it dominate household assemblages (Holmberg 1971; Simmons 1962), and chicha production is often used to symbolize the proper domestic arrangement (Allen, this volume).

The social order is also expressed through drinking. When people get together to drink in small groups, there is usually just a single cup. As Allen explains (2002: 119–122), the manner of drinking expresses both social solidarity and difference. Solidarity is expressed by the host's passing a drink to each guest. The guest toasts the host and other members of the group and sometimes shares his or her cup with several people. At the same time, social difference is expressed through the host's unreciprocated gift. Moreover, the order in which the drinks are given, the phrase used in offering the drink, and the quantity of drink can signal social ranking.

Serving nuances are particularly important for women's political power. At public events, women and men often sit apart. The women usually cluster around the bundles of food and jars of drink that they prepared, and the men assemble in lines sometimes facing each other (Allen 2002: 142; Bolin 1998: 190). While men and women may rank individuals during the course of highly formalized conversations, women tend to be less vocal at these gatherings (Allen 2002; Bastien 1978; Gose 1994; Isbell 1978). They do the bulk of the serving, however, and thus are able to define, and often manipulate, social rank through differences in the way that drinks are served (see Bowser 2000, 2004, for an Amazonian example; Butler 2006). Serving thus provides a more subtle and less confrontational means of ranking individuals that may run counter to the public discourse supported by men.

The idea of reciprocity and the cosmic flow of energy also structured Andean cosmology at the time of the Inca (Allen 1984: 152; Ossio 1996; Ramírez 2005). The offering of chicha to the earth, for example, was integral to agricultural fertility (Goodman-Elgar, this volume), and a shared toast between the Inca and local lords reaffirmed their relationship (Cummins 2002: 98; Weismantel, this volume). Inca feasts often lasted several days, and drinking, not eating, was the core activity (Cummins 2002: 110). An imperial drinking culture, typified by the *aríbalo* serving vessel (Bray, this volume), spread across the Andes and helped to create an "imagined community" during the short-lived Inca Empire (see, e.g., Anderson 1991).

The Andes was more linguistically and culturally diverse during the Inca Empire and preceding periods, and drinking likely played a significant role in defining local identities as well (Goldstein, Coleman Goldstein, and Williams, this volume). The few documents that we have on local customs, such as the Huarochirí manuscript (Salomon and Urioste 1991), hint at the integral role that drinking played in local cosmologies, and early chroniclers describe the great variety of indigenous beverages across the Andes. Although archaeologists are becoming increasingly interested in identity issues (see, e.g., Reycraft 2004), there have been few attempts to critically examine pre-Inca "drinking cultures" (after Wilson 2005a) in the Andes. With few exceptions (e.g., Knobloch 2000; Moore 1989), the Inca have been used as an analogy to explain drinking production and consumption in past cultures. The chapters in this volume by Anderson and Goldstein, Coleman Goldstein, and Williams attempt to move away from this analogy by examining how drinking may have functioned differently in the Tiwanaku and Wari states of the Middle Horizon.

Continuity and Change

When they drank, they would wet their fingers with the chicha in the tumbler from which they were drinking. They then would spatter the chicha toward the Sun or toward the Earth or toward the Fire; in doing this they would pray for peace, life, and contentment. (A seventeenth-century account by a Spanish priest of a traditional drinking custom in the Andes.[5])

No alcohol, no getting drunk—but an ordeal nonetheless. We chugged down cup after cup of the sticky sweet liquid, night fell, the big fireless room grew cold, the drinks made us shiver, but no one left until the bottles were empty. (An ethnographer's description of a Pentecostal fiesta in Sonqo, Peru, where Coca-Cola, Fanta, and Sprite, instead of chicha, were consumed.[6])

Substantial changes have occurred in the Andes since the Spanish Conquest. The clash of cultures brought the region for the first time into contact with the Western world, and Andean people were decimated by disease and warfare. Entire villages were deserted, people relocated (often against their will) to new areas, and many languages and customs were lost. Indigenous and creole uprisings followed in the eighteenth century and led to the breakup of the Spanish Empire and the founding of the modern Andean nation-states.

Yoked to European interests in guano, silver, and other resources, the new states were economically volatile and politically unstable. By the twentieth century, political juntas were replaced by elected democracies, and the states were being transformed by mass migration, new technologies, and global cultures (Cook 1998; Klarén 2000; Spalding 1984).

These changes have fundamentally transformed Andean society, and it would be naïve to think that drinking regimes have remained unaffected. As Hayashida notes in her chapter in this volume, Spanish attempts to regulate chicha consumption, the campaign to stamp out native religion, and the catastrophic population decline would have reshaped beer production and consumption in the sixteenth century alone.

There have been other significant changes as well. In terms of production, for example, cane sugar, introduced after the conquest, was used to increase alcohol content in chicha (Cutler and Cárdenas 1947), and Old World cereals like oats, barley, and wheat were combined with traditional ingredients to form new chichas (such as *chicha de siete semillas* [seven-seed chicha]). One of the most significant examples of consumption change occurred as the result of a virulent campaign to demonize chicha in the first half of the twentieth century. The campaign linked imbecility and violence to chicha drinking and stigmatized chicha drinkers as lazy, poor, uneducated, and dangerous country dwellers (Bejarano 1950).

The pace of change in Andean alcohol production and consumption is increasing today. Home-brewed beer is steadily being replaced by commercial beer in many areas (Orlove and Schmidt 1995), and *chicherías*, the small brewery/taverns that were once ubiquitous (Perlov, this volume), are becoming rare. Potent *trago* is being increasingly consumed, and alcoholism is tearing at the fabric of families (Allen 2002; Butler 2006). A variety of changes, including religious conversions, emigration, and agricultural reform, are breaking down the reciprocal bonds that traditionally held communities together (Allen 2002, this volume; Bolin 1998; Butler

2006). At the same time, chicha is now being embraced as a marker of Andean ethnicity by protesters, writers, and politicians (Weismantel, this volume).

These drastic changes must be acknowledged by archaeologists (Hayashida, this volume). Archaeologists need to further develop direct measures of chicha production and consumption, such as residue and isotopic analysis (discussed earlier), as well as elaborate on the archaeological signatures of beer production, distribution, and consumption (see, e.g., Hayden 2001: 40–41). We should not presuppose that a cup was used to drink beer—we need to demonstrate it.

There is nonetheless a danger of retreating from exploring the dimensions of prehistoric chicha in order to wait for technological and methodological solutions. Residue analyses, for example, have typically yielded only a very coarse-grained understanding of the plant remains left in pots, and our ability to accurately determine subtle isotopic differences in corn or other plants as they are transformed into chicha remains far out of reach. Despite our best efforts, our understanding of alcohol in the ancient Andes may continue to be derived primarily from ethnographic and historical sources from the region (e.g., Stahl 1993). Does this mean, then, that any study of pre-Columbian alcohol production based on analogies is fatally flawed?

Despite the many changes that have occurred over the last five hundred years, there may be considerable continuity in some aspects of Andean society. Every culture has certain key symbols that are integral to its structural organization (Ortner 1973). In many cases, key symbols are remarkably durable, surviving political, economic, and social changes over hundreds of years (Geertz 1980: 134; Sahlins 1981: 17; Sahlins 1996: 421). These symbols can become part of a culture's "structures of the long term," which order social life in fundamental ways and become naturalized within a society (Bourdieu 1977: 164; Sahlins 1996: 395). These key symbols, of course, are not necessarily constant through the years, and Andean scholars must be careful about assuming a timeless Andean way of doing things (Isbell 1995, 1997). Sometimes personified as "lo andino" (Andeanness), this assumption can lead to the uncritical projection into the past of an array of social arrangements from Inca, early colonial, and modern examples (Quilter 1996: 308). Nonetheless, some core concepts of Andean society arguably have remained remarkably stable despite the massive changes over the last 500 years (Allen 1984: 152; Arnold 1991:

45–47; Karttunen 1992: 241; Quispe 1984: 607–608; Urton 1981). Material correlates for some aspects of Andean culture suggest that some of these concepts, like the *ayllu* and the worship of mountain peaks, may extend deeper into the past (Haas et al. 2003; Isbell 1997; Quilter 1990; Reinhard 1985a, 1985b; Sallnow 1987).

Some aspects of drinking, like the role of fermented beverages within reciprocal obligations, might also be core concepts (see Weismantel, this volume). The dependency today of village leaders on the distribution of alcohol, for example, echoes that of the local lords of the north coast of Peru during the mid-sixteenth century, and the tradition of flicking chicha to the gods remains prevalent in many villages today. We know that alcohol was fundamental to Inca rule, and the detritus of cups, serving vessels, and storage jars of earlier cultures may point to the important role of drinking deeper in the Andean past.

The biochemical characteristics of alcohol can also be the basis for arguing for some degree of continuity with earlier practices. There are, for example, fundamental steps that need to be taken to create an alcoholic beverage. The transformation of alcohol can take up to two phases. In the first phase, saccharification, nonfermentable starches are broken down into sugars by amylases and other enzymes. In the second phase, fermentation, a variety of bacteria, fungi, and molds convert the sugars into alcohol. Alcohol made from grains or other starchy substances must be saccharified before fermentation can occur (Soni and Sandhu 1999).

Most common Andean beverages, with the possible exception of molle chicha (Goldstein and Coleman 2004), go through both production phases. The production sequences used in small-scale chicha production in the Andes today are in part the result of the demands of the properties of the material being processed—there are fundamental biochemical steps that need to be taken in order to produce a palatable alcoholic beverage (see, e.g., Edmonds 1990: 57; Mahias 1993: 162; Narotzky 1997: 19). In a similar manner, there are physiological effects from alcohol that are universal to all humans. Although different groups have different tolerances and interpret drunkenness in different ways, we have a sense of the phenomenological effects that alcohol would have on people living in the ancient Andes. (See Moore [2005] for an example of how a phenomenological approach can inform our interpretation of past Andean cultures.) These biochemical aspects of alcohol, when combined with chicha's possible function as a long-term structure of meaning, provide support for the tentative use of ethnographic and historical analogies for understanding the role of alcohol in the ancient Andes (see Hayashida, this volume, for a counter-argument).

Drink in the Andes

The essays in this volume attest to the long importance of alcohol in the Andean world. The chapters combine ethnographic, historical, and archaeological data from the present to the first millennium AD and range across the Andes from Ecuador to northern Chile and Argentina. The volume begins with two ethnographic studies. First, Catherine Allen explores the radical changes in ritual drinking in a small Peruvian community since 1975. She looks at how chicha forms an important structuring metaphor in the community and how cane alcohol, carbonated drinks, and agricultural reform have played off and transformed this metaphor as lifeways have changed.

Diane Perlov's chapter is the second ethnographic study in the volume. Perlov analyzes women's work, power, and educational mobility among the chicheras in rural Bolivia. In particular, she looks at how some women gain significant economic and social independence through brewing but yet tend to favor the educational advancement of their sons over their daughters because of the labor that the girls provide in the chicherías.

Melissa Goodman-Elgar offers the first of two chapters that focus on the Inca. She suggests that terraced fields were an important site of Inca rituals that linked corn, chicha, and the Inca elite to the productive cycle. She then outlines a means to archaeologically study the use of terraces in feasts. In the following chapter, Tamara Bray considers the distribution of the aríbalo, a jar used to serve corn chicha, throughout the Inca Empire. While the form was standardized, variation in the size, design, and archaeological context of aríbalos speaks to the role of drinking in the Inca political economy.

The chapters by Goldstein, Coleman Goldstein, and Williams and Anderson bring us deeper into Andean prehistory. David Goldstein, Robin Coleman Goldstein, and Patrick Ryan Williams look at the use of chicha de molle at the Wari site of Cerro Baúl (AD 600–1000) in southern Peru. Through paleobotanical analysis of excavated areas, they demonstrate how molle was used as both an indicator of social rank within the site and a marker of Wari ethnicity that differentiated the people living in Cerro Baúl from others living in the valley. Anderson looks at the spread of the Tiwanaku drinking culture (AD 600–1100) by considering shifts in the drinking cup assemblages found at sites in the Cochabamba Valley of highland Bolivia. Drinking behavior changed radically as it became widespread during the period of Tiwanaku influence and transformed again after that influence waned.

The final three chapters are diachronic. Jennings and Chatfield consider the relationship between increasing pot size in the archaeological record and the curtailment of women's power. By looking at how pots were made, chicha was brewed, and parties were thrown within the traditional domestic economy of the twentieth century, the authors suggest that we can get a sense of the consequences of the supplanting of domestic production of ceramics and brewing by specialists.

Frances Hayashida's chapter is a caution on the uncritical use of ethnographic and historical analogues. She takes a critical look at how changes over the last 500 years may have affected alcohol production and consumption in the Andes and questions attempts to project chicha production and consumption regimes into the pre-Columbian world.

In the final chapter, Mary Weismantel moves from today's Ecuadorian Amazon to the Moche culture of Peru's north coast (AD 100–700) to consider how alcohol's enduring importance in the Andes may relate to its importance as a gift shared by both friends and rivals. She suggests that chicha has been used through the centuries to express the tension between inequality and shared identity that is found in all societies.

These chapters all touch on and extend the three themes of reciprocity and power, identity and society, and continuity and change that have been outlined in this Introduction. Fermented beverages have long brought the Andean world together by linking people not only with each other but with the cosmos. Through alcohol production and consumption, people define who they are and who they want to be. Even as beer and spirits structure the world, they also provide a means to transform it.

Through the lone drunkard or the sly server, alcohol provides openings for social change that can be incrementally slow or revolutionarily transformative. Drinking patterns are changing rapidly across the Andes as smaller communities break down and commercial alcohol replaces indigenous home brews (Allen, this volume; Weismantel, this volume). By providing a long-term perspective on drink in the Andes, we hope that this volume helps us grapple with our changing world as we continue into the twenty-first century.

Notes

Epigraph. In November of 1823, Robert Proctor encountered the proprietor of a tavern in the village of Cocoto on the central coast of Peru. The man sang for him a song sympathetic to the revolutionary war that was being fought against the Spanish. The quotation is the second verse of the song and the refrain (Proctor 1825: 331–332). Proctor's translation is a liberal one, and the Spanish text in his book for the same quotation reads as follows:

El Inca la usaba
Es su regia mesa
Con que ahora no impieza
Que es inmemorial.
Bien puede el che acaba
Pedir se renueve
El poto en que bebe
O su caporal.

Patriotas, el mate
De chicha llenad
Y alegres brindemos
Por la libertad!

1. In 1566, Dr. González de Cuenca, a colonial administrator on the north coast of Peru, forbade the distribution of alcoholic beverages to Indians. The decree had an immediate impact on the power of local lords, who mobilized against this new proclamation. Sensing that this threat to local rule also jeopardized Spanish tribute demands, Dr. Cuenca rescinded the ban five days later (Anonymous 1961, quoted in Moore 1989: 685).

2. The Yarqa Aspiy is the annual canal-cleaning ritual that takes place in September. In 1970, Billie Jean Isbell interviewed the mayor of the lower neighborhood of the town of Chuschi, who was responsible for hosting the feast after the ritual. The bottles that he refers to held trago, or cane alcohol (Isbell 1978: 170).

3. This quotation comes from the Huarochirí manuscript, a document recording local beliefs in the Huarochirí Valley of the Peruvian sierra. Paria Caca was a local god who became human to visit his people. Their lack of hospitality at the banquet led him to unleash a violent wind that swept the people out of the valley (Salomon and Urioste 1991: 125)

4. This quotation from Barbara Butler's ethnography (2006: 99), describes a few of the complex ways that female servers can represent, and occasionally reconfigure, the social order when large groups of people come together.

5. Father Bernabé Cobo completed a book on the Inca and early colonial Andes in 1653. This quotation describes the customary form of drinking chicha during this period (Cobo 1979: 119). The Sun and Earth were major gods.

6. Catherine Allen's drinking description comes from a house-raising party that

she attended in 2000. The builders were from a Pentecostal group that drank carbonated beverages instead of alcohol but that still participated in minka exchanges (Allen 2002: 229).

References Cited

Ackerman, Raquel
1991 The Despacho: Analysis of a Ritual Object. *Journal of Latin American Lore* 17(1): 71–102.
Alberti, Giorgio, and Enrique Mayer (eds.)
1974 *Reciprocidad e intercambio en los Andes peruanos*. Lima: Instituto de Estudios Peruanos.
Allen, Catherine J.
1982 Body and Soul in Quechua Thought. *Journal of Latin American Lore* 8(2): 179–196.
1984 Patterned Time: The Mythic History of a Peruvian Community. *Journal of Latin American Lore* 10(2): 151–173.
2002 *The Hold Life Has: Coca and Cultural Identity in an Andean Community*. 2nd edition. Washington, D.C.: Smithsonian Institution Press.
Anderson, Benedict
1991 *Imagined Communities: Reflections on the Origin and Spread of Nationalism*. New York: Verso.
Anonymous
1961 [1720]. Información anónima sobre la vida y costumbres del pueblo de Virú, Provincia de Trujillo, Departamento de la Libertad. Con un recetario criollo del maestro barbero Don Feliciano de Bergara. Siglo XVIII. Año 1720. *Revista del Archivo Nacional del Perú* 25(1): 5–25.
Arnold, Denise
1991 The House of Earth-Bricks and Inka-Stones: Gender, Memory, and Cosmos in Qaqachaka. *Journal of Latin American Lore* 17: 3–69.
Bastien, Joseph W.
1978 *Mountain of the Condor: Metaphor and Ritual in an Andean Ayllu*. Prospect Heights: Waveland Press.
Bejarano, Jorge
1950 *La derrota de un vicio: Origen e historia de la chicha*. Bogotá: Editorial Iqueima.
Bode, Barbara
1990 *No Bells to Toll: Destruction and Creation in the Andes*. New York: Scribner's.
Bolin, Inge
1998 *Rituals of Respect: The Secret of Survival in the High Peruvian Andes*. Austin: University of Texas Press.
Bourdieu, Pierre
1977 *Outline of a Theory of Practice*. Cambridge: Cambridge University Press.

Bowser, Brenda

2000 From Pottery to Politics: An Ethnoarchaeological Study of Political Factional-ism, Ethnicity, and Domestic Pottery Style in the Ecuadorian Amazon. *Journal of Archaeological Method and Theory* 7(3): 219–248.

2004 The Amazonian House: A Place of Women's Politics, Pottery, and Prestige. *Expedition* 46(2): 18–23.

Bray, Tamara L.

2003a Inka Pottery as Culinary Equipment: Food, Feasting, and Gender in Imperial Design. *Latin American Antiquity* 14(1): 3–28.

2003b The Commensal Politics of Early States and Empires. In *The Archaeology and Politics of Food and Feasting in Early States and Empires*, Tamara L. Bray, ed., pp. 1–13. New York: Kluwer Academic/Plenum.

2003c To Dine Splendidly: Imperial Pottery, Commensal Politics, and the Inca State. In *The Archaeology and Politics of Food and Feasting in Early States and Empires*, Tamara L. Bray, ed., pp. 93–142. New York: Kluwer Academic/Plenum.

Bunzel, Ruth

1940 The Role of Alcoholism in Two Central American Cultures. *Psychiatry* 3: 361–387.

Burger, Richard L., and Nikolaas J. Van Der Merwe

1990 Maize and the Origins of Highland Chavín Civilization: An Isotopic Perspec-tive. *American Anthropologist* 92(1): 85–95.

Butler, Barbara

2006 *Holy Intoxication to Drunken Dissipation: Alcohol among Quichua Speakers in Otavalo, Ecuador.* Albuquerque: University of New Mexico Press.

Camino, Lupe

1987 *Chicha de maíz: Bebida y vida del pueblo Catacaos.* Piura: Centro de Investi-gación y Promoción del Campesinado–Piura.

Cavero Carrasco, Ranulfo

1986 *Maíz, chicha y religiosidad andina.* Ayacucho: Universidad Nacional de San Cristóbal de Huamanga.

Cobo, Bernabé

1979 [1653] *History of the Inca Empire: An Account of the Indians' Customs and Their Origin Together with a Treatise on Inca Legends, History, and Social Institu-tions.* Translated and edited by Roland Hamilton. Austin: University of Texas Press.

Colloredo-Mansfeld, Rudi

1999 *The Native Leisure Class: Consumption and Cultural Creativity in the Andes.* Chicago: University of Chicago Press.

Cook, Anita G., and Mary Glowacki

2003 Pots, Politics, and Power: Huari Ceramic Assemblages and Imperial Admin-istration. In *The Archaeology and Politics of Food and Feasting in Early States and Empires*, Tamara L. Bray, ed., pp. 173–202. New York: Kluwer Academic/ Plenum.

Cook, David Noble

1998 *Born to Die: Disease and New World Conquest*. New York: Cambridge University Press.

Costin, Cathy, and Timothy Earle

1989 Status Distinction and Legitimation of Power as Reflected in Changing Patterns of Consumption in Late Prehispanic Peru. *American Antiquity* 54(4): 691–714.

Cummins, Thomas B. F.

2002 *Toasts with the Inca: Andean Abstraction and Colonial Images on Quero Vessels*. Ann Arbor: University of Michigan Press.

Cutler, Hugh C., and Martín Cárdenas

1947 Chicha, a Native South American Beer. *Botanical Museum Leaflets* (Harvard University) 13(3): 33–60.

de Garine, Igor, and Valerie de Garine

2001 *Drinking: Anthropological Approaches*. New York: Berghahn.

Dietler, Michael

2006 Alcohol: Anthropological/Archaeological Perspectives. *Annual Review of Anthropology* 35: 229–249.

Doughty, Paul L.

1971 The Social Uses of Alcoholic Beverages in a Peruvian Community. *Human Organization* 30(2): 187–197.

Douglas, Mary

1987a *Constructive Drinking: Perspectives on Drink from Anthropology*. New York: Cambridge University Press.

1987b A Distinctive Anthropological Perspective. In *Constructive Drinking: Perspectives on Drink from Anthropology*, Mary Douglas, ed., pp. 3–15. New York: Cambridge University Press.

Dudley, Robert

2002 Fermenting Fruit and the Historical Ecology of Ethanol Ingestion: Is Alcoholism in Modern Humans an Evolutionary Hangover? *Addiction* 97: 381–388.

Edmonds, Mark

1990 Description, Understanding, and the Chaine Operatoire. *Archaeological Review from Cambridge* 9(1): 55–70.

Everett, Michael W., Jack O. Waddell, and Dwight W. Heath

1976 *Cross-cultural Approaches to the Study of Alcohol: An Interdisciplinary Perspective*. The Hague: Mouton.

Foucault, Michel

1979 *Discipline and Punish: The Birth of a Prison*. New York: Random House.

Geertz, Clifford

1980 *Negara: The Theatre State in Nineteenth-century Bali*. Princeton: Princeton University Press.

Gero, Joan M.

1990 Pottery, Power, and . . . Parties! *Archaeology* 43(2): 52–56.

1992 Feasts and Females: Gender Ideology and Political Meals in the Andes. *Norwegian Archaeological Review* 25: 15–30.

Giddens, Anthony

1979 *Central Problems in Social Theory: Action, Structure, and Contradictions in Social Analysis.* Berkeley & Los Angeles: University of California Press.

Goldstein, David, and Robin Christine Coleman

2004 *Schinus Molle L.* (Anacardiaceae) Chicha Production in the Central Andes. *Economic Botany* 58(4): 523–529.

Goldstein, Paul

2003 From Stew-Eaters to Maize-Drinkers: The Chicha Economy and the Tiwanaku Expansion. In *The Archaeology and Politics of Food and Feasting in Early States and Empires*, Tamara L. Bray, ed., pp. 143–172. New York: Kluwer Academic/Plenum.

2005 *Andean Diaspora: The Tiwanaku Colonies and the Origins of South American Empire.* Gainesville: University Press of Florida.

Gose, Peter

1994 *Deathly Waters and Hungry Mountains: Agrarian Ritual and Class Formation in an Andean Town.* Toronto: University of Toronto Press.

Greenway, Christine

1989 Self and Spirit Loss in Quechua Healing Rites. Paper presented at the American Anthropological Association Annual Meeting, Washington, D.C.

Haas, Jonathon, Winifred Cremer, and Álvaro Ruiz

2003 Gourd Lord. *Archaeology* 56(3): 7.

Hastorf, Christine A.

1991 Gender, Space, and Food in Prehistory. In *Engendering Archaeology: Women and Prehistory*, Joan M. Gero and Margaret W. Conkey, eds., pp. 132–159. Cambridge: Blackwell.

2001 Agricultural Production and Consumption. In *Empire and Domestic Economy*, Terence N. D'Altroy and Christine A. Hastorf, eds., pp. 155–178. New York: Kluwer Academic/Plenum.

Hastorf, Christine A., and Sissel Johannessen

1993 Pre-Hispanic Political Change and the Role of Maize in the Central Andes of Peru. *American Anthropologist* 95(1): 115–138.

Hayden, Brian

2001 Fabulous Feasts: A Prolegomenon to the Importance of Feasting. In *Feasts: Archaeological and Ethnographic Perspectives on Food, Politics, and Power*, Michael Dietler and Brian Hayden, eds., pp. 23–64. Washington, D.C.: Smithsonian Institution Press.

Heath, Dwight B.

1962 Drinking Patterns of the Bolivian Camba. In *Society, Culture, and Drinking Patterns*, David J. Pittman and Charles R. Snyder, eds., pp. 22–36. New York: John Wiley & Sons.

1976 Anthropological Perspectives on Alcohol: An Historical Review. In *Cross-cultural Approaches to the Study of Alcohol: An Interdisciplinary Perspective*,

Michael W. Everett, Jack O. Waddell, and D. W. Heath, eds., pp. 41–101. The Hague: Mouton.

2000 *Drinking Occasions: Comparative Perspectives on Alcohol and Culture.* Philadelphia: Bruner/Mazel.

Holmberg, Alan

1971 The Rhythm of Drinking in a Peruvian Coastal Mestizo Community. *Human Organization* 30(2): 198–202.

Holtzman, John

2001 Food of Elders, the "Ration" of Women: Brewing, Gender, and Domestic Processes among the Samburu of Northern Kenya. *American Anthropologist* 103(4): 1041–1058.

Horton, Donald

1943 The Functions of Alcohol in Primitive Societies: A Cross-cultural Survey. *Quarterly Journal of Studies on Alcohol* 4: 199–320.

Isbell, Billie Jean

1978 *To Defend Ourselves: Ecology and Ritual in an Andean Village.* Prospect Heights, Ill.: Waveland Press.

Isbell, William H.

1995 Constructing the Andean Past, or "As You Like It." *Journal of the Steward Anthropological Society* 25(1–2): 1–12.

1997 *Mummies and Mortuary Monuments: A Postprocessual Prehistory of Central Andean Social Organization.* Austin: University of Texas Press.

Jennings, Justin

2005 La Chichera y el Patrón: Chicha and the Energetics of Feasting in the Prehistoric Andes. In *Foundations of Power in the Prehispanic Andes*, Christina A. Conlee, Dennis Ogburn, and Kevin Vaughn, eds., pp. 241–259. Archaeological Publications of the American Anthropological Association, vol. 14. Washington, D.C.: American Anthropological Association.

Joffe, Alexander H.

1998 Alcohol and Social Complexity in Ancient Western Asia. *Current Anthropology* 39(3): 297–322.

Karttunen, Frances

1992 After the Conquest: The Survival of Indigenous Patterns of Life and Belief. *Journal of World History* 3: 239–256.

Klarén, Peter Flindell

2000 *Peru: Society and Nationhood in the Andes.* New York: Oxford University Press.

Knobloch, Patricia J.

2000 Wari Ritual Power at Conchopata: An Interpretation of *Anadenanthera colubrina* Iconography. *Latin American Antiquity* 11(4): 387–402.

La Barre, Weston

1938 Native American Beers. *American Anthropologist* 40: 224–234.

Larsen, Clark Spencer

2000 *Bioarchaeology.* New York: Cambridge University Press.

Lau, George

2002 Feasting and Ancestor Veneration at Chinchawas, North Highlands of Ancash, Peru. *Latin American Antiquity* 13(3): 279–304.

Lincoln, Bruce

1989 *Discourse and the Construction of Society*. New York: Oxford University Press.

Mahias, Marie-Claude

1993 Pottery Techniques in India: Technical Variants and Social Choice. In *Technological Choices: Transformation in Material Cultures since the Neolithic*, Pierre Lemonnier, ed., pp. 157–180. New York: Routledge.

Marshall, Mac

1979 *Beliefs, Behaviors, and Alcoholic Beverages: A Cross Cultural Survey*. Ann Arbor: University of Michigan Press.

Mauss, Marcel

1990 *The Gift: The Form and Reason for Exchange in Archaic Societies*. New York: W. W. Norton.

Mayer, Enrique

1974 Las reglas de juego en la reciprocidad andina. In *Reciprocidad e intercambio en los Andes peruanos*, Giorgio Alberti and Enrique Mayer, eds., pp. 37–65. Lima: Instituto de Estudios Peruanos.

2002 *The Articulated Peasant: Household Economies in the Andes*. Boulder: Westview Press.

McDonald, Mary (ed.)

1994 *Gender, Drinking, and Drugs*. Oxford: Berg.

McGovern, Patrick

2003 *Ancient Wine: The Search for the Origins of Viniculture*. Princeton: Princeton University Press.

Moore, Jerry

1989 Pre-Hispanic Beer in Coastal Peru: Technology and Social Context of Prehistoric Production. *American Anthropologist* 91(3): 682–695.

2005 *Cultural Landscapes in the Ancient Andes: Archaeologies of Place*. Gainesville: University Press of Florida.

Morris, Craig

1979 Maize Beer in the Economics, Politics, and Religion of the Inca Empire. In *Fermented Food Beverages in Nutrition*, Clifford F. Gastineau, William J. Darby, and Thomas B. Turner, eds., pp. 21–34. New York: Academic Press.

Morris, Craig, and Donald E. Thompson

1985 *Huánuco Pampa: An Inca City and Its Hinterland*. New York: Thames and Hudson.

Moseley, Michael E., Donna J. Nash, Patrick Ryan Williams, Susan D. deFrance, Anna Miranda, and Mario Ruales

2005 Burning Down the Brewery: Establishing and Evacuating an Ancient Imperial Colony at Cerro Baúl, Peru. *Proceedings of the National Academy of Sciences* 102(48): 17264–17271.

Murra, John V.

1960 Rite and Crop in the Inca State. In *Culture in History: Essays in Honor of Paul Radin*, Stanley Diamond, ed., pp. 393–407. New York: Columbia University Press.

Narotzky, Susana

1997 *New Directions in Economic Anthropology.* Chicago: Pluto.

Orlove, Benjamin, and Ella Schmidt

1995 Swallowing Their Pride: Indigenous and Industrial Beer in Peru and Bolivia. *Theory and Society* 24: 271–298.

Ortner, Sherry B.

1973 On Key Symbols. *American Anthropologist* 75: 1338–1356.

Ossio A., Juan M.

1996 Symmetry and Asymmetry in Andean Society. *Journal of the Steward Anthropological Society* 24: 231–248.

Partanen, Juha

1991 *Sociability and Intoxication: Alcohol and Drinking in Kenya, Africa, and the Modern World.* Helsinki: Finnish Foundation for Alcohol Studies.

Pittman, David J., and Charles R. Snyder

1962 *Society, Culture, and Drinking Patterns.* New York: John Wiley & Sons.

Proctor, Robert

1825 *Narrative of a Journey across the Cordillera of the Andes, and of a Residence in Lima, and Other Parts of Peru, in the Years 1823 and 1824.* London: Archibald Constable.

Quilter, Jeffrey

1990 The Moche Revolt of Objects. *Latin American Antiquity* 1(1): 42–65.

1996 Continuity and Disjunction in Pre-Colombian Art and Culture. *RES* 29/30: 303–317.

Quispe, Ulpiano

1984 La "chupa": Rito ganadero andino. *Revista Andina* 2: 607–628.

Ramírez, Susan Elizabeth

2005 *To Feed and Be Fed: The Cosmological Bases of Authority and Identity in the Andes.* Stanford: Stanford University Press.

Reinhard, Johan

1985a Sacred Mountains: An Ethnoarchaeological Study of High Andean Ruins. *Mountain Research and Development* 5: 299–317.

1985b *The Nazca Lines: A New Perspective on Their Origins and Meaning.* Lima: Editorial Los Pinos.

Reycraft, Richard Martin (ed.)

2004 *Us and Them: Archaeology and Ethnicity in the Andes.* Los Angeles: Cotsen Institute of Archaeology, University of California.

Sahlins, Marshall

1981 *Historical Metaphors and Mythical Realities: Structure in the Early History of the Sandwich Islands.* Ann Arbor: University of Michigan Press.

1985 *Islands of History.* Chicago: University of Chicago Press.

1996 The Sadness of Sweetness: The Native Anthropology of Western Cosmology. *Current Anthropology* 37: 395–428.

Saignes, Thierry (ed.)

1993 *Borrachera y memoria: La experiencia de lo sagrado en los Andes.* Lima: Instituto Francés de Estudios Andinos.

Sallnow, Michael J.

1987 *Pilgrims of the Andes: Regional Cults in Cuzco.* Washington, D.C.: Smithsonian Institution Press.

Salomon, Frank, and George L. Urioste

1991 *The Huarochirí Manuscript: A Testament of Ancient and Colonial Andean Religion.* Austin: University of Texas Press.

Samuel, Delwen

2000 Brewing and Baking. In *Ancient Egyptian Materials and Technology*, Paul T. Nicholson and Ian Shaw, eds., pp. 537–576. Cambridge: Cambridge University Press.

Segura Llanos, Rafael

2001 *Rito y economía en Cajamarquilla: Investigaciones arqueológicas en el conjunto arquitectónico Julio C. Tello.* Lima: Pontificia Universidad Católica del Perú.

Sherrat, Andrew

1995 Alcohol and Its Alternatives: Symbol and Substance in Pre-Industrial Cultures. In *Consuming Habits: Drugs in History and Anthropology*, Jordan Goodman, Paul E. Lovejoy, and Andrew Sherratt, eds., pp. 11–46. New York: Routledge.

Shimada, Izumi

1994 *Pampa Grande and the Mochica Culture.* Austin: University of Texas Press.

Simmons, Ozzie G.

1962 Ambivalence and the Learning of Drinking Behavior in a Peruvian Community. In *Society, Culture, and Drinking Patterns*, David J. Pittman and Charles R. Snyder, eds., pp. 37–47. New York: John Wiley & Sons.

Soni, S. K., and D. K. Sandhu

1999 Microbiology of Fermentation. In *Biotechnology: Food Fermentation*, V. K. Joshi and Ashkot Pandey, eds., pp. 25–85. Calcutta: Educational Publishers and Distributors.

Spalding, Karen

1984 *Huarochirí: An Andean Society under Inca and Spanish Rule.* Stanford: Stanford University Press.

Stahl, Ann

1993 Concepts of Time and Approaches to Analogical Reasoning in Historical Perspective. *American Antiquity* 58(2): 235–260.

Stanish Charles, and Kevin J. Haley

2004 Power, Fairness, and Architecture: Modeling Early Chiefdom Development in the Central Andes. In *Foundations of Power in the Prehispanic Andes*, Christina A. Conlee, Dennis Ogburn, and Kevin Vaughn, eds., pp. 53–70. Archaeological Publications of the American Anthropological Association, vol. 14. Washington, D.C.: American Anthropological Association.

Steinkraus, Keith H.
1996 Introduction to Indigenous Fermented Foods. In *Handbook of Indigenous Fermented Foods*. 2nd edition. Keith H. Steinkraus, ed., pp. 1–5. New York: Marcel Dekker.

Urton, Gary
1981 *At the Crossroads of the Earth and the Sky: An Andean Cosmology*. Austin: University of Texas Press.

Valderrama Fernández, Ricardo, Carmen Escalante Gutiérrez, Paul H. Gelles, and Gabriela Martínez Escobar
1996 *Andean Lives: Gregorio Condori Mamani and Asunta Quispe Huamán*. Austin: University of Texas Press.

Valdez, Lidio M.
2006 Maize Beer Production in Middle Horizon Peru. *Journal of Anthropological Research* 62: 53–80.

Weismantel, Mary J.
1988 *Food, Gender, and Poverty in the Ecuadorian Andes*. Philadelphia: University of Pennsylvania Press.

2001 *Cholas and Pishtacos: Stories of Race and Sex in the Andes*. Chicago: University of Chicago Press.

Wilson, Thomas M.
2005a Drinking Cultures: Sites and Practices in the Production and Expression of Identity. In *Drinking Cultures: Alcohol and Identity*, Thomas M. Wilson, ed., pp. 1–24. New York: Berg.

2005b *Drinking Cultures: Alcohol and Identity*. New York: Berg.

2

"Let's Drink Together, My Dear!"

Persistent Ceremonies in a Changing Community

Catherine J. Allen

"Drinking together" is one of the most common human strategies for expressing and manipulating social bonds (Fig. 2.1). Andean societies, past and present, are no exception to this rule; indeed, drinking partnerships were a structuring feature of the Inca state (see, e.g., Cummins 2002). In this chapter, I examine the deep, pervasive (and often problematic) role of ritual drinking in a small Quechua-speaking community from the time I first encountered it in 1975 up to the present. Unlike the other authors in this volume, I focus upon a high-altitude context (3,200–4,000 meters) where corn will not grow.

The community, Sonqo, is a rural ayllu (corporate group based on kinship and shared connection to place deities) located in the District of Colquepata (Paucartambo Province) in the Department of Cuzco in southern Peru. Dispersed over 1,825 hectares of almost treeless tundra (*puna*), the community's approximately eighty-five households raise potatoes and herd sheep and camelids. Chicha is produced rarely, and always for a special occasion. In 1975, the more common alcoholic drink was trago, a distilled spirit produced from mashed sugarcane; during the 1990s *trago* was largely replaced by cheaper *alkul*, plain watered-down alcohol, and, to a lesser extent, by bottled commercial beer (*cerveza*). The 1990s also saw significant conversion to evangelical Protestantism. Converts foreswear alcoholic beverages in favor of carbonated soft drinks (*gaseosas*).

As the chapters in this volume abundantly demonstrate, the central role of chicha in Andean social and ritual life has deep historical roots reaching through Inca times at least into the Middle Horizon. Even in communities like Sonqo, where chicha is rare, it still provides the baseline for

Figure 2.1. A son serves his mother *chicha* in a wooden goblet-shaped *kero*. They are drinking in the corral to honor their sheep on the Feast of Saint John (June 24) in Sonqo. Photo by the author.

understanding the practices and beliefs, including those that originated in Europe, associated with alcoholic beverages. My chapter therefore addresses persistent continuities as well as transformations and disruptions that characterize Sonqo's drinking traditions.

The first part of this chapter is located in an "ethnographic present," namely, Sonqo as I came to know it between 1975 and 1985. I begin with a folktale that reveals—albeit indirectly—the meaning that chicha production carries in a puna community where maize is hard to come by. In this context, chicha production is an infrequent and festive event, an honorable duty incumbent on a festival sponsor, whose household mobilizes a network of social relations to get the job done. I go on to describe the highly formalized distribution and extravagant consumption of chicha at communal celebrations, a ritual process which manifests the ayllu as a complex articulation of hierarchical and egalitarian tendencies. I compare and contrast chicha with trago, as the two beverages perform similar ritual and social functions but involve residents of Sonqo (Sonqueños) in different kinds of economic and social relationships outside the ayllu.

The second part of the chapter moves through the 1990s to the present. Over that period many changes took place as Sonqo's orientation shifted from subsistence farming to cash crops, and from local, rather insular, concerns to more urban, cosmopolitan aspirations. I focus on two developments in this period—alcoholism and Protestant conversion. I discuss possible causes of the rise in problem drinking, including the weakening of the ritual framework within which heavy drinking was both meaningful and controlled. I go on to explore the relationship between alcoholism and the conversion of about half the community to Pentecostal Protestantism during the late 1990s. Conversion, I suggest, provides a sort of local version of Alcoholics Anonymous, as reforming alcoholics and their families provide each other support, discipline, and encouragement. Interestingly, the ceremony of drinking—its formal distribution and extravagant consumption—continues to be as strong and central as ever among Sonqo's Protestants. The drinks, however, are nonalcoholic gaseosas. Libations and invocation directed to the local earth deities, formerly an integral part of the ritual, are no longer practiced. Inebriation is "spiritual," as participants strive to speak in tongues. Thus, even as conversion to fundamentalist Protestantism is banishing alcohol consumption altogether, nonalcoholic beverages like soft drinks continue to play social and ritual roles that are rooted in the practices and ideology of chicha.

Chicha, Ayllu, and Trago

How the Chicha Was Ruined

One evening in 1975, I sat sharing shot glasses of *trago* with Don Erasmo Hualla, a ritual specialist and wonderful raconteur, and he told me this story. Although I have condensed and paraphrased the Quechua narrative, I follow his rendition fairly closely:

> In an isolated rural homestead there lived a married couple with their little child. One day, the husband had to travel and left his wife and child alone. His wife was in the process of preparing chicha in the large pot they call *raki*, and, as she had no one to help her, it was hard work. Then she saw another woman passing by, plying threads on a spindle as she walked along. Little did she realize that this stranger was a *condenado*, a damned soul.

"Come in, Mamáy," she called to the passerby, "and help me prepare the chicha." The stranger turned aside and entered the house. But far from helping, she sat silently on the threshold, and the woman had to continue doing all the work herself. Cordially, the woman offered a plate of food, but the guest didn't eat it. As she put the plate aside, the woman—to her horror!—saw a worm crawl out of the stranger's nose. Finally, she realized that she had invited a condenado into her house.

Night was falling. The woman wanted to go outside to tend her cows, but the condenado blocked the way. Finally, they agreed that the woman could go out tethered to a long rope, held firmly by the condenado. As soon as she was out of sight, the woman tied her end of the rope around a big stone, and when the condenado tugged on the rope to pull her in, she didn't return. Finally, the condenado came out to investigate—and found the rope tied around the stone. The woman had hidden under a cow and was nowhere to be seen. Enraged, the condenado rushed back inside the house.

"That goddam woman tricked me!" She seized the little child. "I'm going to eat you in your mother's stead!" (Mamayki rantita mikhusqayki!")

The child let out a terrible scream—and then there was silence, for the condenado had devoured the poor little thing. Its clothes and hair lay in a pile on the floor, and the chicha was red with its blood—*ruined*!

The condenado stuck her head out the door. "Come back, come back!" she called. "Your child fell into the raki." But the woman stayed out all night, hidden under the cow. At last the condenado gave up and walked off into the darkness, howling threats.

Morning came and the woman returned to the house. There were her child's clothes and hair on the floor and, floating in the *raki*, its little head and hands. The chicha was ruined, all red, undrinkable.

"What shall I do? My husband will be home soon!"

He returned that very day, and the woman told him the whole story. There, indeed, was their child, dead, and the chicha all bloody. The two of them began to fight like crazy. The raki got smashed. The chicha was ruined. And that's the end.

This story is not ostensibly about chicha at all, and yet chicha runs through it like a leitmotif. The tragic dissolution of the household is epitomized in the final comment, "The chicha was ruined." I begin with this story because it shows how chicha's deep significance touches a kind of cultural nerve even in contexts where chicha is a rarity.

The narrative introduces the couple as living in a lonely homestead. Many of Sonqo's far-flung households approximate this description. Only since 1995 have some families (particularly Protestant converts) begun to settle in clusters along a recently constructed road. Many families, furthermore, spend weeks or months of each year in secondary households located in the highest and most solitary pastures. Isolation and the scarcity of practical assistance are chronic problems. While the local economy depends on relationships of reciprocity, distances make communication difficult.[1] Labor exchanges have to be decided far in advance and have a way of falling through if, for example, one of the parties falls ill or is delayed while traveling. Yet isolated life in a sparse environment makes these relationships all the more necessary.

To a local listener in this context, the woman's chicha making will seem incongruous; an isolated homestead is an unlikely location for this activity. Making chicha is a complicated process involving several carefully timed steps (see Jennings and Chatfield, this volume). It requires the cooperation of at least two people (see Perlov, this volume), and, perhaps because the task is so labor-intensive and time-consuming, chicha is always made in quantity. It is improbable that a household of two adults would prepare chicha simply for their own consumption.

Erasmo did not say *why* the woman was making chicha, but a listener would probably assume that she was preparing to fulfill a *cargo* (civic responsibility) of some sort. Where, as in Sonqo, the altitude is too high for maize cultivation, chicha is prepared only for distribution at communal events like saints' festivals or major work parties. Ayllu-wide celebrations express and reproduce the unity of this dispersed, far-flung community, and cargo holders for these events go to great lengths to procure corn and organize the workforce necessary to prepare chicha. The wife of a cargo holder will call upon a network of kinswomen, particularly sisters-in-law, to help with chicha preparation.

If the woman in our story was preparing chicha for a cargo, she should have been joined by a work party of kinswomen. Yet she is alone. In other words, the woman's attempt to make chicha single-handedly in an isolated location makes no sense and is doomed to failure. Chicha making is a group enterprise; its production activates the bonds of mutual obligation that make up the social fabric of a rural ayllu. In our story, the attempt to perform this task in isolation has tragic consequences, for it leads the overburdened woman to call on a random passerby for help.

The condenado's arrival underscores the destructive irrationality of solitary chicha making. On one level, the message is simple: Be wary of strangers! Yet there is another, more complex, level of meaning here, for instead of hosting a party of kinswomen whose assistance she will later repay in kind, the woman invites in a creature who epitomizes the violation of reciprocity norms. Condenados are not just evil strangers; they are cannibalistic living-dead, individuals whose disregard for kinship bonds and reciprocity obligations has left them unable to die properly. The worst such offense is incest, but even minor dereliction of duty adds to the burden of violated obligation. After death, the flesh is unable to separate from bones, and condenados wander the isolated mountainsides in wormy, rotting bodies.

In the absence of mutual-aid relations, the woman has opened her door to a creature of endless consumption. Ravenous cannibalism is another aspect of condenado damnation. Denial of reciprocity in life finds expression, in death, as an insatiable appetite for human flesh. The condenado of our story sits in the doorway waiting for a cannibalistic feast, unwilling even to let her intended victim leave the house untethered.

So far, we have seen that the story emphasizes, through counterexample, the collaborative and collective nature of chicha production. The story itself, however, is not *about* chicha, but rather, uses chicha as a vehicle through which to express the moral and social dilemmas encountered by isolated households. Chicha is associated with the viability and reproduction of the household; ruined chicha epitomizes its disintegration.

As the story builds to its sorry close, the child's life and the chicha seem intrinsically linked. First the condenado tries to lure the mother back by yelling that the child fell in the chicha pot. Then comes a description of the little head and hands floating in the bloody pot, followed by the emphatic declaration that the chicha was ruined: "Aqha luyta perdiyachipun, yawar puka tiniyapun. Manan aqhatapas tomapunkuchu" (All the chicha was ruined, dyed red with blood. They [couldn't] drink that chicha). Ruined chicha might seem like the least of their troubles, yet Don Erasmo chose to reemphasize the point. We are left with an image of the estranged couple fighting in a pool of bloody chicha amid the shards of the broken raki.

The image points to a symbolic association between the household and the raki, and between the production of chicha and the perpetuation of the household through its children. The child's blood mixing with the chicha expresses an exaggerated introversion of family relations, resonating with the incest theme associated with condenados. Told in a puna setting, the narrative poignantly underscores the point that households cannot exist and reproduce in isolation.[2]

Chicha and Ayllu

Because the story addresses problems of isolation and introversion, it does not take us beyond the household. But what would have happened if our story couple had prepared chicha properly for its appropriate purpose?

First, they probably would have moved temporarily to a less isolated location, nearer to the central locale where festivities were to take place. Households in dispersed communities often have more than one domicile; they shift residence according to season, crop and pasture rotations, and social demands. If our couple did not have a more convenient residence, they would probably have called upon a kinsman or *compadre* (fictive kinsman) to lend his house for the purpose. The husband would have obtained the corn from another kinsman or compadre in a corn-growing community, or he would have purchased the corn with money in the Cuzco market. Male kinsmen would have cut large quantities of firewood from thorny bramblebushes and carried it laboriously to the site of chicha production. The wife would have been joined by the wives of her brothers (real and classificatory) and other available kinswomen. Their collective effort would bring about fermentation; this remarkable transformation of sprouted corn mash into spirits would take place right before their eyes and noses, and under their (hopefully) skilled hands. Finally, all these workers would expect to be fed a hearty soup and to receive several handfuls of coca leaves.

On the day of the festival, the chicha would have been transferred from the raki to an *urpu* and carried into the churchyard (or other location, depending on the occasion being celebrated; see Allen 2002a: 150–173).[3] It would have been placed next to a table covered with a finely woven sack (*kustal*), on which were placed two wooden cups called *keros*, a flat ceramic bowl called a *puchuela*, and a three-pronged whip symbolizing the ayllu's authority. The husband, as cargo holder, would sit behind the table, flanked by previous cargo holders and other senior men in the community. Two barefoot young men, ideally, the husbands of the cargo holder's sisters or daughters would sit in front of the table facing him, ready to serve the drinks according to his directions. (In Fig. 2.2, the Ukuku, or Bear Dancer, a kind of ritual clown, has stepped in to take over this role.)

If the husband were presiding over an event like Carnival as *alkaldi* (i.e., alcalde, mayor), his wife would join him. She would sit on the ground in front of the table, next to the chicha, with another set of three drinking vessels. I describe such an event in my ethnography of Sonqo (2002a: 115–116). Sonqo's Carnival as I witnessed it in 1976 should be understood as a kind of ethnographic present:

> The Alcalde rises to serve chicha. The youths fill the goblets and place them on the table. He surveys the gathering and . . . summons the oldest male among them.
>
> "Taytay Inocencio, hamuy aha uxyaq" (Father Inocencio, come drink some chicha). Inocencio approaches, hat in hand.
>
> The Alcalde holds out a q'ero, saying "Uxyayukuy, Taytáy," "Please drink, Father."
>
> Inocencio accepts with thanks: "Yusulpayki, diospagarasunki Taytay Alcalde."
>
> He dribbles some chicha onto the corners of the table. Then he pours some onto the ground for the Earth, and flicks some into the air for the mountain deities.
>
> Then he offers the q'ero back to the Alcalde, saying "Uxyakusunchis," "Let's drink together."
>
> The Alcalde takes a tiny sip and returns the q'ero with thanks. Inocencio may go on to offer sips to other people before he drinks down the remaining chicha in a single gulp and returns the q'ero to the Alcalde, thanking him profusely.
>
> But the Alcalde presents him with another q'ero-full of chicha, and after that with the low clay bowl, the puchuela. Only after having downed the third drink does Inocencio return to his place . . . and the ritual repeats. . . . Meanwhile the Alcalde's wife has been calling over the visiting women and presenting them with chicha in the same manner. . . .
>
> When all the newcomers have received chicha, the Alcalde and wife begin distributing handfuls of coca leaves, following much the same procedure used in offering chicha except that recipients of coca do not chew their leaves while standing at the ceremonial table. Each . . . carries the leaves back to his or her place and [chews] coca quietly and privately. . . . After about half an hour the women break

Figure 2.2. An Ukuku dancer in Sonqo serves *trago* (along with some off-color jokes) to community elders during festivities for Corpus Christi. On the table is a pair of *keros* already filled with *chicha*. The object next to the *keros* is a three-pronged whip. The *puchuela* is not visible in this photo. Photo by the author.

out the food and the coca wads are discreetly discarded. The young men carry dinner plates to the guests, and when the meal is eaten the whole process begins again.

After two rounds of food, the drinking continues. The Alcalde turns the distribution of chicha over to his two assistants. . . . Some of the older men begin to play long deep-voiced flutes, snare drums and the bombo (base drum). One couple begins to dance and then another and another. . . . The sky clouds over, the rain pours down and the people keep drinking and dancing.

Three aspects of this ceremony stand out with striking clarity.[4] First, *chicha distribution expresses, redefines, and validates social bonds.* The beverage is one element in a fairly complex distribution that includes coca leaf and cooked food. For all three—chicha, coca, and food—the order of distribution articulates a hierarchical configuration within the households composing the ayllu. The chicha distribution in particular emphasizes this hierarchy, as each recipient downs his three drinks standing formally before the assembled company. During Carnival celebrations, the separate distribution to the women by the alcalde's wife expresses the ayllu as gendered, consisting of parallel yet interdependent sets of men and women who drink separately but join together to dance as the festival progresses. The pair of keros manifests the pervasive duality characteristic of Andean social and ritual organization. (I'll return to the third "excess" drinking vessel below.)

Second, *communication is with a chthonic deity.* The living Earth and Sacred Places constantly receive offerings as long as the drinking continues. To pour chicha onto the ground or flick it into the air is called *saminchay,* "to offer sami." Sami is a kind of ebullient, nourishing spirit inherent in alcohol, coca leaves, food, and medicinal substances. Personal evidences of *sami* are talent, grace, force of personality, and good luck. Through repeated offerings of chicha, the powerful and omnipresent Earth and sacred places are satisfied, placated, and drawn into the festivities. Their participation is crucial to the perpetuation of the ayllu, which consists of people and land together in an interactive relationship (see Allen 2002a: 75–101).

Third, *collective intoxication* is an important aspect of the event.[5] While the formal distribution of chicha articulates hierarchy, its intoxicating effects produce an exhilarating relaxation of this very hierarchy in a drunken experience of *comunitas* (Turner 1969). Excessive drinking is what makes the ritual "work," for this collective outpouring of spirits animates and gladdens the living Earth. This is where the third drinking vessel comes into play. The low clay bowl is called a puchuela, a word derived from *puchu* (enough, or too much). While the obligatory two *keros* are a proper and complete pair, this "extra" third drink tips the recipient into a state of inebriation.

On some occasions, animals are drawn into this collective intoxication as well. In the annual celebration of the llamas of early August, llamas are force-fed "medicine" (*hampi*) consisting of chicha mixed with trago, soup broth, barley mash, and medicinal herbs (Fig. 2.3). Then the animals are doused with libations of chicha while their human keepers continuously sing and drink chicha. The surrounding hills are awakened by all the commotion and are said to dance together with the people and llamas.[6]

A similar ceremony takes place in July or August, when the freeze-dried potatoes called *ch'uñu* are moved into the storehouses. Men, drinking con-

Figure 2.3. In early August, a llama in Sonqo gets its "medicinal" dose of *chicha* mixed with *trago*, soup broth, barley mash, and special herbs. Photo by the author.

tinuously and pouring libations onto the ch'uñu, pour the ch'uñu into bins made of straw while their wives serve them chicha and sing continuously. They say that if this were not done, the ch'uñu would run out before the new potatoes ripened in February.

It is important to realize that this kind of intoxication has a purpose and occurs within a ritual framework. This framework is protective in two respects: it keeps the emotional and physiological turbulence of drunkenness within a well-defined context; it also protects the participants from dangers entailed by contact with supernatural beings. There is strength not only in numbers, but in the ritual process that unites ayllu members and sacred places according to positive and appropriate rules of behavior. By drinking with companions, one avoids the vulnerability of a lone human being in contact with the supernatural.

Our condenado story illustrates well the perils of this vulnerability. It also suggests that chicha production itself—perhaps due to the transformative process of fermentation—creates a similar state of vulnerability.[7] People need to gather together to work and drink appropriately to ward off these dangers and harness powerful beings in a positive way. Chicha is the most appropriate beverage for this purpose, but since it is rarely available, trago and other beverages come into play.[8]

Making Do with Rotgut Rum

Sugarcane was introduced to South America in the sixteenth century and rapidly became an important crop in Peruvian coastal and warm highland valleys. Although trago presumably has long been familiar to rural inhabitants of Paucartambo, the history of trago consumption in this region has not, as far as I know, been studied. When I arrived in Sonqo in 1975, trago was the obligatory stand-in for chicha on ritual occasions and was often offered to guests or shared among friends as a gesture of hospitality.[9] For example, during a house-raising party, the workers (kin and fictive kin of the householder) would take a break to rest:

> The host (let's call him Don Luis) gives each helper a handful of coca and then produces a bottle and a single shot glass. He pours a shot and offers it to Don Inocencio, the most senior person present, with the phrase, "Tomakusunchis" (Let's drink together). This word, appropriate for trago, is based on the Spanish root *toma*—rather than the Quechua root *uxya*, "Uxyakusunchis"—appropriate for the native chicha.
>
> As he does with chicha, Inocencio pours few drops of trago on the ground for the new Wasitira (House Earth, a manifestation of Pachamama), flicks some drops into the air for the Mountain Lords, and then, with the same courteous formality, offers sips to a few of his companions.
>
> After snarfing down the rest of the drink, Inocencio returns the shot glass to Luis, his host, who moves on to the next person in the status hierarchy. Status is roughly calculated in terms of age (age trumps youth) and gender (male trumps female); any real situation, of course, calls for calculated adjustments, as individual accomplishments and personal relationships come into play. In this hypothetical example, Luis next offers the shot to his elder sister, bypassing for the time being his middle-aged but lackluster neighbor, Valentino.

All social drinking follows this basic pattern. The only exceptions are hot beverages like tea or coffee, which are treated like food. While trago, beer, and soft drinks are served from a single glass to one person at a time, food and hot beverages are distributed more or less simultaneously to everyone present (though the order of service reflects the relative standing of the participants).

From ceremonial expressions of the ayllu to intimate family gatherings, drinking etiquette imposes a structure on the group of individuals that gathers around a bottle and shot glass. As it is rare for anyone to serve drinks without sharing coca leaves, the group is, simultaneously, subject to a different etiquette that imparts a contrasting and counterbalancing structure. Each person shares coca leaves with every other person, producing an egalitarian structure composed of symmetrical dyadic interchanges. This contrasts with the structure of drinking etiquette, which is asymmetrical and expresses a power differential between the recipients and the host who controls the hierarchical distribution of drinks. Thus, coca and alcohol counterbalance each other.[10]

As I returned to Sonqo several times over almost three decades, I observed changes in the kind of beverages consumed. By the late 1990s, trago (distilled sugarcane mash) had largely been replaced by alkul (straight alcohol), which is relatively cheaper and more accessible. Alkul is consumed straight, watered down, or mixed with gaseosas like Fanta (a carbonated orange drink). Beer still appears infrequently but is no longer the rarity it was in 1975.

Drinking etiquette, however, has not changed. Drinks are still doled out sequentially by one server with a single glass and shared with the same courteous phrases. Only in vocabulary did I observe a slight shift of emphasis: rather than reserving "uxyakusunchis" for chicha and "tomakusunchis" for other drinks, the two words now often are used interchangeably.

Drinking into Debt

Although Sonqueños bemoan their lack of chicha, *trago* has advantages in a cold environment. Its "firewater" quality produces a feeling of warmth, and its quick effects provide a kind of anesthetic against the chronic aches and pains produced by a life of hard labor in a harsh environment. Its pungent aroma is thought to ward off malign influences of the sort one might encounter, for example, while digging a grave. Trago's great disadvantage is that it has to be purchased with money from a mestizo middleman, either in the district capital or in the city of Cuzco. Transportation in quantity is difficult. And, because money is always in short supply, buying trago on credit has led many a household into a debt peonage relationship with mestizo shop owners in the district capital (Mayer 1988).

Although trago has a strong alcoholic sami and can substitute for chicha in ritual contexts, its association with debt and dependency contrasts strongly with chicha's deep association with hearth, home, and community.

Trago's cultural value is impoverished relative to that of chicha. It would be inconceivable, for example, to substitute trago for chicha in the story that begins this chapter. Chicha's cultural value arises fundamentally from the interactive social relations made manifest in the production process and in its ceremonial distribution. To make chicha is to make an ayllu. One doesn't make trago; one goes into debt buying it.

Changing Lives

In the Wake of Reform

Following the Agrarian Reform of the 1970s, the early 1980s saw a period of optimism, expansion, and turning from old ways to new opportunities. Enormous changes occurred very quickly. Sonqueños dropped their old system of sectoral fallowing in favor of planting cash crops like barley and oats and replaced animal manure with chemical fertilizers. A road, under construction off and on starting in 1974, was finally finished around 1990, putting Sonqo on the shortest route between Cuzco and Paucartambo.

The late 1980s and the early 1990s, however, also brought political upheaval and economic collapse. Sonqo was spared the kind of violence that wracked much of the Peruvian highlands, but the national instability put an abrupt stop to Sonqueños' high hopes. Transportation became unreliable and prohibitively expensive, rendering the new road useless. Cash crops failed and left farmers in debt. Sonqueños had to retrench and fall back on their old subsistence strategies, but there was really no going back. The old communal system of crop rotation was irrevocably gone; new aspirations were frustrated but not forgotten.

When I visited Sonqo in 2000 and 2003, I found the community significantly altered. The political and economic situation of the country had improved and development projects had come to Sonqo, supplying building material for "modern" two-story multiroom houses, as well as a system of piped water. In 2003, electricity had come to the few households that could afford to pay for it, and TV antennas sprouted from some of the new tile roofs. Today (to generalize about a complex process of change), the orientation and the aspirations of Sonqo's inhabitants are increasingly urban.[11]

The orientation has changed, but life still is gratingly hard, for cash income is exceedingly hard to come by.[12] In 2003, potato prices were too low for farmers to break even in many cases. The Spanish phrase "Nuestro trabajo no vale" (Our work has no value) often made its way into our Quechua conversations. Ironically, the "opening up" of this hitherto rather insular community intensified the inhabitants' sense of marginalization, utter poverty, and—most demoralizing of all—social and economic impotence. In other words, the orientation toward urban values runs in exact opposition to the actual circumstances of people's lives.

Alcoholism on the Rise

The 1990s saw a marked increase in alcoholism. By the year 2000, chronic drinking interfered to a far greater extent than before with work, family life, and social relations.[13] As I settled into conversations about the changes in the community, Sonqueños lamented the increase in *machaq runas* (drunks) and pointed to alcoholism as a problem. I was saddened to observe that my own generation had been hit particularly hard. Not coincidentally, this was the generation that came into adulthood in the late 1970s and, with great optimism, turned its energies to new opportunities opened by the Agrarian Reform. By the year 2000 they were past middle age, tired and disillusioned, with little or nothing to show for their initiative and hard work. The increase in alcoholism has to be understood in the context of these roller-coaster years of frustrated hopes and cancelled opportunities.

Other factors contributed to alcoholism as well. As long as Sonqo was a hinterland community, off the road and with a minimal cash economy, the trago supply was limited. Writing about Sonqo between 1975 and 1985, I described Sonqueños as "opportunistic" rather than chronic drinkers (Allen 2002a: 124): "When alcohol is available they like to drink it, and they often continue drinking for as long as the supply lasts. . . . As long as opportunities to drink are limited, the situation contains its own check; when the booze runs out everything returns to normal." As Sonqueños traveled more, with more access to cash and credit, the availability of alcohol increased—and opportunistic drinking turned to chronic drinking.

Yet "opportunistic" was perhaps an unfortunate word choice, as it implies a greedy lack of self-control that is misplaced in this Andean context. Drinking to excess has to be understood in terms of the deep cultural value placed on collective intoxication as a mode of communication with deities and an expression of shared identity. Although the drinking practices I describe above encourage and indeed require that participants drink "too much," they also provide a highly structured framework within which inebriation not only is meaningful and ritually effective, but is controlled, limited, and, in a word, "safe."

Sonqo Ayllu has largely collapsed as a unified entity, and community-wide celebrations no longer take place (see Allen 2002a: 203–247). The ritual framework has weakened while the habit of "too much" drinking persists as strongly as ever. Social drinking still follows the conventions I describe, but small transitory gatherings more easily turn into aimless drinking binges.

In 2000, I heard, for the first time, reports of people who drank in solitude. For example, my friend Doña Elvira,[14] who died an alcoholic in her late forties, had taken to the bottle during the long, cold days she spent herding sheep in the high pastures. I was told that she often came home drunk—quite a change from the quiet young woman I knew twenty years earlier as a superb weaver who actually disliked trago.

The Pentecostal Solution

Between my visits in 1995 and 2000, another remarkable change took place in Sonqo, a change related, among other things, to Sonqo's drinking problem. Close to half of Sonqo's households joined the Maranatas, a Pentecostal sect that originated in Sweden in the 1950s. The conversions began in 1994, when a young man who had lived in Cuzco for several years returned to Sonqo as a Seventh-Day Adventist. He married, and his extended family gradually followed him into Adventism.

Like other fundamentalist sects, Adventism forbids the consumption of alcohol, a welcome prohibition for families of abusive drinkers. The alcoholics themselves welcomed the moral support and discipline they found in the congregation. The downside of Adventism for Sonqueños was its proscription of practices that converts were less willing to give up, like chewing coca and eating *cuy* (guinea pig). Switching from Adventism to the Maranata sect, which prohibits alcohol but allows coca and other traditional practices, provided a solution to this dilemma.

Converts foreswear alcohol but not the familiar ceremony of drinking. Any special occasion—as when guests are received, contracts sealed, or new houses completed—calls forth the obligatory bottle and glass. Now, however, the bottle is a two-liter container of a carbonated beverage like Coca-Cola, Fanta, or Inca Kola (a very sweet corn-based soft drink with the flavor of bubble gum). The glass is a thick tumbler with a capacity of approximately eight ounces. The host fills the glass and doles out drinks one after the other in order of seniority. The drinking goes on until the bottles are empty.

Back in the 1980s, I was told that the bubbles in soft drinks and beer

were manifestations of strong sami, and that Protestants sometimes substituted soft drinks for alcohol in offerings to the Earth. This did not prove
true of the Maranatas, however, who bypass the offerings completely. In
other words, they continue to practice the etiquette that expresses social
bonds and group hierarchy, but no they longer share the substance of their
drinks directly with earth deities. Similarly, converts continue to share
coca leaves according to the old ritual forms, but they no longer blow on
the leaves to share their *samincha* with chthonic beings.

For traditionalists in Sonqo, omitting the samincha is a serious matter. Without the offerings, the Earth and sacred places get hungry, sad,
and angry; luck turns bad, animals die, and crops fail. With this in mind, I
asked a convert, son of my late friend Don Erasmo, the storyteller, whether
the Sonqueños had forgotten about Mother Earth and Sacred Places. He
emphatically replied, *"No!* We haven't forgotten them! But it's spiritual!"
(¡*Manan!* ¡Manan qunquruykuchu! ¡Pero es espiritual!) This may indicate
another reorientation, away from the profound concreteness of native Andean religion, in which matter and spirit are never completely separable.

Conversion is a recent development, and it remains to be seen how these
Andean converts develop this new "spirituality." Given the value placed on
ritual intoxication, it is not surprising that converts have embraced a Pentecostal denomination. Maranata practices include a strong charismatic
element expressed in revivalist singing and speaking in tongues (Coleman
2000: 89). The Maranata sect, moreover, favors local congregational independence, so Sonqo's congregation manages itself, and local converts lead
meetings.

While I did not have an opportunity to attend the Maranata religious
meetings, the group prayer that I witnessed at a house-raising party in
2003 was ecstatic and intense. Before the drinking (of gaseosas) began, the
maternal uncle of the host rose to lead the party in prayer. Bit by bit, as
intensity built, the other guests joined in, standing with raised arms, their
prayers blending into each other in a babble of voices. Although they did
not reach the point of speaking in tongues, the rush of words from many
voices praying simultaneously rendered the Quechua unintelligible.

I believe—based on this experience and subsequent conversations—that
ritual structure has undergone a significant transformation: the ecstatic,
trancelike aspect of communal celebration has split off from ritual drinking. It manifests itself instead through a different inebriation of spirit—
intense group prayer. Distribution of drinks continues to express social

bonds and to structure the group around the host or cargo holder. Interestingly, it also retains its bingelike character. This brings out more clearly a persistent element of collective binge drinking: it enforces commitment to, and participation in, the event that is being celebrated.

Disillusioned with old ways that no longer seem to serve them in the twenty-first century, Sonqueños are eager to find new ways of integrating themselves into a wider world. The ayllu that was Sonqo is breaking down into neighborhood-based "sectors" inhabited by either traditionalists or Protestants. Although with improved transportation it would be easier to obtain maize, chicha is produced, if anything, less frequently, because the ayllu-wide celebrations no longer take place. Traditionalists and Protestant converts alike are looking to build their lives around that ever-elusive cash income.

Nevertheless, old forms, time-honored styles of interaction, and modes of structuring group activities, persist. Protestants have deliberately turned to a sect that allows them to maintain many of the customs (coca chewing in particular) that they consider essential to their way of life. While forbidding alcohol, Maranata practices nevertheless produce an experience of ecstatic comunitas reminiscent of ritual intoxication. The Maranata sect, moreover, allows for local autonomy, so converts have a sense of charting their own course into the future.

Conclusion

As I have passed through three decades, my focus in this chapter has moved from chicha to trago/alkul to gaseosas. Each move has entailed a significant reorientation. Chicha production is local and depends on the networks of reciprocal-aid relationships (ayni) characteristic of traditional Andean communities. Both genders are critical to chicha production, for men obtain the maize and firewood, while women do the actual preparation. Once prepared, chicha is distributed according to ritual forms that delineate community structure and integrate the community with an animate landscape of guardian places. Drinking in these contexts is obligatory and deliberately excessive in order to produce an almost trancelike experience of "oneness" among the participants.

Trago, although usually consumed within smaller group settings, performs many of the same social and ritual functions as chicha; its distribution structures the participants as a group while its inebriating sami joins them to earth deities. However, the dimension of production (not to mention food value) is completely different. Trago arrives ready-made in markets and shops and has to be purchased with money or on credit. Women are, by and large, cut out of the picture, for it is generally men who perform these market transactions.

Manufactured far from Sonqo and purchased with money, gaseosas bear much the same relationship as trago to household and community economy. Moreover, when gaseosas are substituted for trago (or alkul), the landscape disappears as a living participant in drinking ceremony. Protestant converts no longer share their drinks with Mother Earth and Sacred Places. Rather, they pour forth their prayers to God the Father and find a kind of inebriation in prayer rather than in alcohol. Without intoxicating effects, drinking is no longer a vehicle for communication with the deity. It remains, however, a vehicle for integrating—indeed, enforcing—group interaction according to traditional social forms.

The big, colorful bottles filled with lively, sugary beverage carry a special glamour. Radio, television, and tourists in Cuzco make it abundantly clear that these very drinks are consumed across the globe. They are part of the greater world. From a critical perspective, gaseosas could be seen as an epitomizing symbol of the deceptive allure of global economy—deceptive because these Andean farmers operate in a context that seems to doom them to debt, dependency, and despair.

Such a perspective would see capitalism as a metaphorical *condenado* hovering in the doorway, watching hopeful Protestants twist open their big bottles of soda pop.[15] Like the condenado in Erasmo's story, this visitor would be a creature of endless consumption, but (more like a *pishtaco*; see, among others, Weismantel 2001) he would look like a friendly peddler or truck driver; and he would devour his victims little by little, imperceptibly, from within. By the time the people recognized their extractive guest for what he was, he would be a household fixture, hunkered down immovable next to the threshold. Then—weary and anxious, listless, pimple-faced, and toothless—what could they do but keep on drinking? The condenado would never leave, and the people would never stop drinking gaseosas.

But I am not entirely convinced by this dismal prophecy. Rural Andean farmers are, by and large, resourceful and smart; they may develop local strategies to resist and even exploit extractive forces. Whatever happens, this is how I leave Sonqueños in the ethnographic present of 2003. Their attitude is hopeful as they fill and refill their glasses, for they have changed their lives.

Notes

1. On Andean reciprocity, see Mayer (2002).

2. Variants of the same basic narrative might speak as well to other contexts, like that described by Perlov in this volume, in which mestiza chicheras need their daughters to keep their household business intact.

3. An urpu is a large, narrow-mouthed jar with small handles. It is strapped on the carrier's back and used for carrying chicha. In archaeological parlance, this vessel is usually called an aríbalo, a term derived from the Greek vessel with a similar shape. See the articles in this volume by Anderson, Bray, Goodman-Elgar, and Jennings and Chatfield.

4. I provide a more extended analysis of drinking ritual in Allen (2002a, 2002b).

5. Also see Gose (1994), Jennings (2005), Jennings et al. (2005), Weismantel (1991).

6. During the Feast of St. James (July 28), horses receive the same treatment.

7. Peter Gose provides an especially careful and sensitive analysis of chicha's conceptual relationship with death in *Deathly Waters and Hungry Mountains* (1994; especially see chap. 4).

8. Curiously, Andean peoples never invented a fermented potato beverage.

9. Trago is one of the perils of ethnographic research in Andean mountain communities. For the ethnographer, belting down one shot of trago after the other, "participant-observation" takes on an oxymoronic character. And be forewarned: Nobody, not even the most avid drinker, would claim that *trago* tastes good (though eventually one does get used to it). Fortunately, there are ways to cut down on alcohol consumption considerably: make your libations generous and share many sips of your drink. (This is much better than trying to surreptitiously pour the trago down your shirt.)

10. The counterbalancing effect of coca (a stimulant) and alcohol (a depressant) is both physiological and social-structural. For a more extended analysis, see Allen (2002a: 118–122).

11. I discuss these changes in detail in the afterword to the 2002 revised edition of *The Hold Life Has* (2002a).

12. See Mayer's (2002: 224) discussion of the relationship between subsistence and market economies in potato-farming households.

13. I did not gather statistical data on alcohol consumption. My generalization is based on extensive conversations in Sonqo along with observations of extended families I had known well for over two decades. By "alcoholism" I mean chronic obsessive drinking that interferes with work, health, family life, and social relations.

14. A pseudonym.

15. See Taussig (1980).

References Cited

Allen, Catherine J.

2002a *The Hold Life Has: Coca and Cultural Identity in an Andean Community*. 2nd edition. Washington, D.C.: Smithsonian Institution Press.

2002b The Incas Have Gone Inside: Pattern and Persistence in Andean Iconography. *RES: Aesthetics and Anthropology* 40: 180–203.

Coleman, Simon

2000 *The Globalization of Charismatic Christianity: Spreading the Gospel of Prosperity*. Cambridge: Cambridge University Press.

Cummins, Thomas B. F.

2002 *Toasts with the Inca: Andean Abstraction and the Images on Quero Vessels*. Ann Arbor: University of Michigan Press.

Gose, Peter

1994 *Deathly Waters and Hungry Mountains: Agrarian Ritual and Class Formation in an Andean Town*. Toronto: University of Toronto Press.

Jennings, Justin

2005 La Chichera y el Patrón: Chicha and the Energetics of Feasting in the Prehistoric Andes. In *Foundations of Power in the Prehispanic Andes*, Christina A. Conlee, Dennis Ogburn, and Kevin Vaughn, eds., pp. 241–260. Archaeological Publications of the American Anthropological Association, vol. 14. Washington, D.C.: American Anthropological Association.

Jennings, Justin, Kathy L. Antrobus, Sam J. Atencio, Erin Glavich, Rebecca Johnson, German Loffler, and Christine Luu

2005 "Drinking Beer in a Blissful Mood": Alcohol Production, Operational Chains, and Feasting in the Ancient World. *Current Anthropology* 46(2): 275–303.

Mayer, Enrique

1988 De hacienda a comunidad: El impacto de la reforma agraria en la provincia de Paucartambo, Cusco. In *Sociedad andina, pasado y presente: Contribuciones en homenaje a la memoria de César Fonseca*, Ramiro Matos Mendieta, ed., pp. 59–100. Lima: FOMENCIAS.

2002 *The Articulated Peasant: Household Economies in the Andes*. Boulder: Westview.

Taussig, Michael

1980 *The Devil and Commodity Fetishism in South America*. Chapel Hill: University of North Carolina Press.

Turner, Victor W.

1969 *The Ritual Process: Structure and Anti-Structure*. Ithaca: Cornell University Press.

Weismantel, Mary J.

1991 Maize Beer and Andean Social Transformations: Drunken Indians, Bread Babies and Chosen Women. *Modern Language Notes* 106(4): 861–879.

2001 *Cholas and Pishtacos: Stories of Race and Sex in the Andes*. Chicago: University of Chicago Press.

3

Working through Daughters

Strategies for Gaining and Maintaining Social Power among the *Chicheras* of Highland Bolivia

Diane C. Perlov

Since the 1970s, the study of women's roles in society has received considerable attention in anthropology. The increase of ethnographic case studies emphasizing the female perspective dramatically expanded our knowledge of women's goals, activities, and impact in society. Among other things, these early studies helped us to reassess and refine many standard assumptions about women's status, power, and economic influence, and allowed us to challenge our theoretical propositions from a greater variety of perspectives (see, e.g., Blumberg 1978; Boulding 1977; Buvinic 1976; Huntington 1975; Knaster 1976; McAlpin 1977; Tinker 1976; Ware 1975). My previously unpublished study, focusing specifically on the women beer makers of highland Bolivia, was undertaken in the late 1970s to add to the growing corpus of ethnographic literature on women's economy and to address some of the standard assumptions regarding women's work, power, and educational mobility.

Since the populist revolution of 1952, the rural communities of Bolivia have undergone drastic changes, and none more dramatic than those experienced in the Department of Cochabamba, the agricultural center of Bolivia. In this department, local peasant unions instigated events that brought about the Agrarian Reform Act of 1953, which resulted in the overthrow of the hacienda (estate) system and a massive redistribution of agricultural lands (Clark 1969; García 1969; Heath et al. 1969; Malloy 1970, 1971; Marschall 1970; Mitchell 1977; Patch 1961; Sotomayor 1971). As a result of this redistribution, the cities, villages, and countryside have undergone radical demographic changes.

Accompanying the geographic mobility in the rural areas was the commitment of the new revolutionary government to educational development. Adherence to this policy has continued through numerous governments to the present regime, which still considers education to be a means to success. No one in the rural arena is more committed to this ideology of education than the mestizo women of the pueblo.

From January to July 1978, I conducted anthropological fieldwork in such a Bolivian mestizo pueblo—the village of Pocona, which lies in the highland valley of Cochabamba. I chose Pocona because it was a village of Quechua speakers, where the men were agriculturalists and the women were predominately beer makers, with a nationwide reputation as shrewd and aggressive businesswomen. Throughout Bolivia the production and distribution of corn beer, or chicha, was considered women's work, and in Pocona it was exclusively a woman's activity. Surprisingly little attention at the time had focused on these beer makers, the chicheras, even though the beer-making industry and drinking habits of campesinos had been discussed in the literature for many years (Bejarano 1950; Gillin 1945; Heath 1971; Holmberg 1971). Chicheras have continued to escape scholarly attention.

One of the major results of my investigation is the indication of an educational preference given to sons over daughters. The study suggests that the educational preference given to males was not so much a result of the power structure as it was of the mode of production. Female control of economic resources constituted a substantial power base in its own right—and the goal of most women was to send both sons and daughters to school as a means to success and social mobility. However, because the production of chicha was dominated exclusively by women, and as the basic unit of production was the household, a chichera's economic power relied on keeping her daughter(s) in the family chicha business. Since the mode of chicha production restrained most daughters of chicheras in the rural community, the chichera's son(s) would always be given preferential access to education. By "working through daughters," chicheras gained power and autonomy in the rural community and the ability to finance the higher education of their children. At the same time, due to the mode of production, chicheras were deeply invested in reaffirming the existing gender roles, which hindered the educational mobility of their daughters. Only those chicheras who made enough money to replace their daughters' labor were able to overcome this constraint.

In the first section of this chapter, I review the theoretical issues relevant to the study. The second section discusses the village setting, while the third and fourth sections focus specifically on the chichera, her activity as beer maker, and her goals, which emphasize the educational mobility of her children. The concluding two sections of the chapter discuss this phenomenon as related to a woman's strategy for gaining and maintaining social power.

Theoretical Issues

The statement that educational preference is given to male children is not a novel one. For the most part, the literature presents the tendency of women to promote their sons over their daughters as a strategy women employ to increase their power or influence (Chodorow 1974; Collier 1974; Friedl 1967; Lamphere 1974; Parsons 1963; Paul 1974; Rosaldo 1974). This strategy is described in the landmark work of Lamphere (1974: 103) as "working through men," and has been seen as a "response to the distribution of power and authority"(1974: 99). Lamphere adds that a woman may not have access to an authoritative leadership position; however, by enabling her son to acquire political power or a ritual title, she is able to shorten the distance between herself and a position of power.

For a woman to exert influence over her husband, sons, or brothers, she may utilize her control over economic resources, or her special accessibility to "mystic powers." Paul, for example, describes the influential powers that women in a Guatemalan village hold, based on their special knowledge of childbirth (1974: 298): "Women's lives are more restricted than men's and men dominate women in sexual relations, but the cultural assignment of mystic powers to female sexuality gives women a symbolic weapon with which to counter the power of males." In other words, in a society where decision making in the domestic and political domains is differentiated, women attempt to influence the men who hold the authority. Parsons states, "Since women are often not in positions of authority, a key concept in understanding their strategies is that of influence, one of the most important forms of persuasion" (1963: 45).

The underlying assumption of this approach is that what social power women have in the society is tied to the power of men and is achieved through relations with men. These economic or mystic resources which women control are not conceived of as substantial power bases. Women who are involved in maintaining their control over these resources are generally seen as being trapped in an inferior social position, denied access to social mobility and the benefits of economic development (Boserup 1970; Leacock 1977; Safa 1977). This approach tends to neglect the fact that female control of economic or mystic resources does constitute social power. As my study indicates, the social power wielded by the chicheras of Pocona is not tied to the power of men, nor is it achieved through relations with men, nor is it a tool for "persuading" men. Based on their control of the chicha business, the chicheras' autonomy and social power are established and maintained through the achievements of women and, specifically, the mother/daughter unit. Chicheras achieve their success by working though their daughters.

While my fieldwork was conceived through a theoretical engagement with women's power in the 1970s, the issues that I examined remain relevant today. Women's roles in the political process in the Andes have continued to be neglected, because women are usually not vocal, passionate participants in public meetings. Instead, women often work in more subtle ways through nuances in how food and drink are served and in private conversations with family members and other women (Allen 2002: 96–98; Butler 2006: 99; Colloredo-Mansfeld 1999: 150–159). Chicheras, as described below, were powerful players in the 1970s. Since then, commercial beer varieties have replaced chicha as the beer of choice, unlike in the Amazon, where beer is still routinely made in the home (Bowser 2004; Weismantel, this volume). This decline in home-brewed chicha production in Bolivia has significantly eroded the chicheras' power base. While working through daughters in this way is no longer a tenable strategy for women in many parts of the Bolivian sierra, the study remains relevant to current debate as it illuminates the mechanisms of the relationship between food production and women's power in South America (Allen 2002 and this volume; Bowser 2000, 2004; Colloredo-Mansfeld 1999; Jennings and Chatfield, this volume; Mayer 2002; Weismantel 1988 and this volume).

Ethnographic Background

The focus of my study is the pueblo of Pocona, situated in a small highland valley of the Department of Cochabamba, 145 kilometers east of the principal city of Cochabamba. The valley extends approximately 26 square kilometers at 2,700 meters elevation (Fig. 3.1). The ethnographic present in

Figure 3.1. The fields around Pocona, in the highland valley of Cochabamba, Bolivia. Photo by the author.

my description of Pocona and the people who lived there is 1978—my field notes captured this moment in time.

In 1978, the pueblo consists of two streets of homes, with a few scattered houses beyond these. There is a central plaza, an infirmary, a church, a four-room primary school, eight *tiendas* (general stores), and twenty-two chicherías (beer halls) (Fig. 3.2). Pocona itself has a population of 248, con-

Figure 3.2. Local *chichería* in Pocona, Bolivia. Photo by the author.

sisting of 73 households, and serves as the political, socioeconomic, and religious center for the surrounding region, where approximately 1,000 campesinos reside in scattered homesteads (Pocona Educational Census 1976).

The people of the valley are almost exclusively agriculturalists, specializing in the cash crop of potatoes. The Pocona Valley is among the nation's most significant producers. Women of the *campo* (countryside) are generally agriculturalists along with their husbands, while twenty-six out of sixty-seven of the pueblo women are specialized chicheras.

Although women tend to specialize in one economic activity, they rarely follow one economic activity exclusively. It is common to find a woman who specializes in chicha production as well as operates a tienda, sells pork, and manages a number of agricultural fields. Regarding agricultural work, pueblo women are mainly concerned with the task of overseeing the labor of *peones* (hired labor), as agricultural labor is generally considered demeaning for a woman of the pueblo.

Chicha and the Chichera

Ethnographic studies have stressed the significant social role of Andean Bolivian women (Buechler and Buechler 1970; Knaster 1976; Nash 1977; Núñez del Prado Béjar 1975; Rohrlich-Leavitt 1975). This has generally been

Figure 3.3. A *chichera* pouring *chicha* into a *jara*. Photo by the author.

seen as a function of women's political and economic contributions to both urban and rural communities. The chichera of the Cochabamba Valley in 1978 is one such Bolivian woman. More precisely, due to the chichera's exclusive control over the production and distribution of the beverage chicha, she possesses considerable economic advantage in her rural community, creating for herself a position of social power and autonomy (Fig. 3.3). By "autonomy," I am referring to the extent to which one has control over one's own life.

Chicha is the name given to indigenous beverages that is most often used to refer to corn beer brewed throughout the Andean regions of Bolivia, Peru, Ecuador, and Colombia (Quechua terms for chicha are *acca, aka, asua, kusa, acha*) (Goldstein, Coleman Goldstein, and Williams, this volume). Along with coca, chicha has been important to Andean populations from pre-Inca times, when it was served at all festivals and funerals as well as carried into the fields for farmworkers (Gillin 1945). The social and religious importance of chicha has continued to the present day, and the beverage is served at all festivals, funerals, and afternoon meals. Moreover, a landowner will find it difficult to contract good agricultural labor unless he has access to good chicha.

A chief advantage of chicha making for women, according to Pocona informants, is that it affords the chichera the greatest, most reliable, income. Table 3.1 lists the estimated costs of ingredients for chicha production, assembled in order to assess the economic benefits of the chicha business.

There are various chicha recipes among the Pocona chicheras. The listed ingredients are from the standard recipe collected in the field. In addition to the cost of these ingredients, the equipment cost for chicha production includes a 225-liter metal vat, three 450-liter pottery vats, three 170-liter pottery *puñus* (large ceramic pots used for storing and fermenting chicha),

Table 3.1. Cost of *Chicha* Ingredients, 1978

Ingredient	Estimated cost per unit[a]	Total cost (Bolivian pesos)
Corn	7 arrobas,[b] 40 pesos per arroba	280
Sugar	½ arroba, 80 pesos per arroba	40
Wood	10 *cargas*,[c] 10 pesos per *carga*	100
Grinding fee	7 arrobas of corn	100
Tax	3 *puñus* of *chicha*	70
Total		590

[a] 1 unit = 3 *puñus*, approximately 510 liters.
[b] 1 arroba = 25 pounds.
[c] 1 *carga* = 60 pounds of wood.

two or three 17-liter pots, and a number of drinking glasses. Except for the large metal vat, which costs 600 Bolivian pesos (US$30), these costs are minimal, and neither they nor the cost of the chichería structure are incorporated into my tabulations.

In terms of revenue, one production cycle of chicha yields three puñus, or 512 liters (Fig. 3.4), which is sold by the *jarra* (pitcher). Each jarra holds one liter, and sells at 2.50 pesos. If all the chicha were sold, the chichera would bring in 1,280 pesos, or a net income of 690 pesos. However, not all of the chicha is sold. Of the three puñus of chicha, a half puñu is regularly used as part payment to laborers, and another half puñu is given away in the form of *galletas* (gifts). It is customary to give each person who enters the chichería a free glass of chicha, after which he or she may decide to buy

Figure 3.4. Three batches of *chicha* at different stages. The two vats on the left are *chicha* that was made a week earlier. The vat in the right rear (termed *kita*) is still fermenting and was put up a day earlier. Photo by the author.

Figure 3.5. Three *puñus* of *chicha* ready for sale. Photo by the author.

more chicha or not. This free glass is referred to as a galleta. Galletas are also given to people passing by the chichería to entice them inside. Also, depending on the chichera, up to a half puñu may be traded for material goods with campesinos not able to pay cash for their chicha. The net income from 512 liters of chicha is consequently reduced to 150–364 pesos. This coincides with informant estimates of 200–400 pesos' net income from three puñus of chicha (Fig. 3.5).

It is possible for a chichera to lose money if she is unable to sell her chicha before it spoils (in one to two weeks); yet such occurrences are said to be rare. As a chichera is well aware of fluctuations in the market, she curtails her production according to variations in the rural consumption level. When necessary, a chichera will activate other outlets for chicha, such as selling at the weekly market, or door-to-door to pueblo neighbors who use chicha to supplement pig feed.

The irregular nature of chicha revenues is looked upon as contributing to the chichera's economic independence from men. Chicha revenues can vary greatly, according to the amount that is consumed by workers, given away, traded, or drunk on credit. Therefore, the husband of the chichera is never certain of the profits his wife has gained during any one week, since both claim that the revenues from chicha are unknowable.

For the chichera, the "unknowable" nature of her revenues is a particular advantage not shared by campesinas or urban working women. One chichera's daughter delighted in telling me how economically independent a chichera is from her husband: "In the city, a husband won't let a wife work outside the home. If he does allow her to work, she will earn a salary, which he will take away from her. Then in the campo women don't have any work at all, except to work with their husbands in the field. Here in Pocona we keep the money we make because the husbands don't even know exactly how much we make. Women here are very independent!" This autonomy from men is reflected in the fact that chicheras are able to maintain a secret account of money that is separate from the household budget and hidden from their husbands.

Beyond gaining a financial profit, or keeping her income secret, the chichera is able to realize considerable social power. Social power, according to Weber (1947: 152), "is the probability that one actor within a social relationship will be in a position to carry out his will despite resistance, regardless of the basis on which this probability rests." The social power of the chichera is seen in the trading practices involving chicha. A campesino is likely to be short of cash at various times of the year, yet rarely short of the occasion to drink chicha. During these times, when a customer cannot pay for his chicha, he can negotiate to trade material goods or labor with the chichera, an exchange in which the chichera is inevitably in a strategic bargaining position. In the negotiations, a chichera will name her price in terms of the material goods she most needs at the time, such as potatoes, corn, wood, milk, textiles, or agricultural labor.

This ability to contract agricultural labor is particularly significant. Since the revolution, relations between the *vecinos* (people of the pueblo) and the campesinos have been decidedly strained. The campesino union leaders openly discourage campesinos from laboring for the mestizos, warning them of the exploitative nature of the relationship.

Ironically, the very vecinos who are most successful at contracting campesino labor are the most notoriously dishonest. Accounts of the exploitative practices of the chicheras are innumerable. Chicheras are accused of regularly overcharging drunken customers, then coercing the client to pay the bill with an exorbitant amount of agricultural labor. There are social pressures that limit such practices, for if a chichera has a reputation for being particularly dishonest, she will lose her clientele. The following excerpt from my field notes is one account of such dishonest practices.

> I spent the morning visiting with padre R. On the topic of chicheras he told me of this event: T. came to see him the other day, crying that A. (a local chichera) had cheated her husband. He had been drinking in her chichería, and when it came time to pay the account A. charged him for two more bottles of beer than he drank. Moreover, she told him to give her a day and a half of agricultural labor for the 30 pesos of beer and chicha he drank. (This is a standard rate of pay for hired labor.) T. was extremely bitter. She said that her husband has his own work to do, that he should not drink so much, and that he should have known A. would cheat him.
>
> I asked padre R. how T. could be so certain that her husband was overcharged. "There are always other customers who witness these things," he explained to me. "But they are afraid of the chichera, and never like to say anything. If a customer were to accuse the chichera of cheating, he believes that the chichera would then throw him out of her chichería. Not only that, but all of the other chicheras would hear of this trouble-maker, and he might find all of the chichería doors closed to him."

The threat of being barred from a chichería is not to be taken lightly. Far more than a place to drink, a chichería is of social importance to the members of the rural community. As the proprietor of the chichería, the chichera serves an important function in the daily life of the villagers and campesinos. Chicheras are familiar with the most current news and gossip and are an important source of short-term credit. They also act as arbitrators of arguments and advisors on legal problems. The following account from my field notes describes both a common tale of woe heard in a chichería and the appropriate reaction by the chichera. The deference given to the chichera in this account is not uncommon. As chicheras are generally more fluent in Spanish and more familiar with urban business practices than their campesino clientele, they can be an important resource for the campesino.

> As I entered Doña L.'s chichería there were only two customers there.

They were a campesino couple, both seated on one of the rickety wooden benches against the wall, drunk. The woman was crying. Doña L. told me that she was crying "just to cry." The woman told me she was crying because her uncle had never given her anything in her life, "not even so much as a blanket." Now he wants something from her, so that she refuses to speak with him. Her husband, V., was extremely sympathetic. He cuddled her and soothed her, coaxing her to drink some more chicha. Seated beside his wife, V. soon began to cry himself. He explained to Doña L. and myself that he had borrowed a large sum of money from the bank in order to buy some land. Yet before he could make the purchase, his friend and neighbor, S., had asked to borrow 5,000 pesos of the sum for a short while. "This is no small amount!" V. reminded me. V. told us that he has tried repeatedly to collect his money from his friend, yet each time he asks for the money, S. beats him.

The farther into his story, the more upset he became. "It is borrowed money!" V. kept lamenting. Doña L. was understanding, and suggested that he go to town T. to file a claim with Don M. As she gave him advice, the client nodded attentively, referring to her as "mamitay" (an endearing term used for addressing a Godmother). I asked V. if Doña L. was his comadre or madrina (Godmother). He said that she was only a good friend who helps him out a great deal, and that he uses the compadre term out of respect and appreciation. After a time, they both stopped crying. Then V. and his wife bowed their heads slightly, excusing themselves from "mamitay" and myself, and left the chichería.

A final note on the significant roles of chicha and the chichera considers the possibilities of land management. Bolivian women may own and manage land in their own names, as well as deal in the marketing of the potato cash crop. As one-fourth of the adult female population of Pocona are heads of household (either widowed or single), women manage a great deal of agricultural land. Of those women landowners and potato merchants, the chicheras are some of the wealthiest. They buy up the potato produce of the surrounding farmers to resell to the larger intermediaries. Particular chicheras purportedly bring chicha out into the potato fields when negotiating a sale. Once the owner of the potatoes is drunk, the chichera pushes through a lower price, readjusts the quantity, or otherwise is said to cheat the farmer.

In summary, there are various indications that chicheras, by control of the chicha resource, are able to amass considerable power and autonomy in the rural domain. First, chicha revenues allow a woman considerable economic independence from her husband. Second, chicha revenues allow investment in agricultural lands. Third, chicha production permits access to a variety of scarce resources and the ability to assemble them (i.e., labor, wood, potatoes, subsistence crops). Fourth, by means of her chichería, a chichera has access to pueblo gossip and market news. Fifth, a chichera can enable or deny a patron access to her chichería, an important social realm. Finally, the chichera plays an authoritative role in the daily life of the pueblo, as legal advisor, arbitrator, and creditor.

Social Status and Goal Orientation

Although chicheras maintain considerable social power and autonomy within the rural domain, their social status is ambivalent, as the vecino, identifying with the Hispano-Bolivian national culture, perceives the chichera as occupying a low status. In terms of defining the term, I refer to Sanday's treatment of social status as "a) the degree to which females have power and/or authority in the domestic and/or public domains, and b) the degree to which females are accorded deferential treatment and are respected and revered in the domestic and/or public domains" (1974: 191). From an urban perspective, the rural areas represent considerable igno-rance and poverty. By the very fact that chicha production constitutes a rural institution so central to rural society, the chichera profession derives a low status. Chicheras are identified with beer, drunks, and promiscuous sexual behavior. Every Cochabambino (resident of Cochabamba, the near-est large town) has heard at least a few stories of drunken men who have violated young girls in a chichería. Chicheras are also regarded as having low status attributed to their frequent interactions with campesinos; many vecinos believe that if their children associate too freely with campesinos they will in turn behave like them. According to one local schoolteacher who is educating her children in Cochabamba, "Life is horrible without my children. Yet I will not educate them here. I don't want them to speak Quechua and pick up dirty campesino habits."

One evening I overheard an old woman (not a chichera) berating two drunken vecino visitors for treating her home as if it were a chichería: "D. and N. stopped by Doña G's house, drunk, after spending the afternoon in a chichería. As they slumped comfortably on the old woman's floor, the irate Doña G. began to kick D. in the legs. 'Get up! Get out of here!' she cried. 'And take your drunken friend with you. What do you think this is, a chichería?!'"

As much as there is ambivalence regarding the chichera's status, there is certainty regarding the importance of education in advancing one's social status, as the vecino, in accordance with his urban orientation, embraces the ideology of formal education as a means to success and social mobility. When I asked my sample (forty-six women, representing 63 percent of households) of Pocona women what their priorities were for their children, they emphasized education for both sons and daughters. Since the school in Pocona teaches only through the primary grades, a higher education can be obtained only by leaving the pueblo for an urban secondary school. As residents lament, "Who will care for the parents when they're old if the children do not go to school and obtain good work?" Others state, "There is no future for children here."

Of the children taking advantage of this opportunity, most are sent to secondary schools in Cochabamba, where they live with relatives or compadres. Even when room and board are provided, the expense of supporting one child in a public secondary school in Cochabamba is estimated to cost $1,000 pesos a month (US$50). Due to the household division of the budget, this financial burden falls on the woman.

The importance of educational mobility is reflected in the numbers of pueblo children who migrate for educational purposes. As Table 3.2 illustrates, forty-seven of the sixty-three children who have migrated out of Pocona have left to pursue educational opportunities in the city.

Through interviews and census data, I examined the educational mobility of the children of chicheras and non-chicheras. My sample population is divided into three categories: (a) Level I chicheras—women who produce chicha every 1–2 weeks and represent 31 percent (eight out of twenty-six) of the chichera population; (b) Level II chicheras— women who produce

Table 3.2. Migration of Pocona Children

Household type	Total children over age 7	Number, percentage, and reason for migration		
		Higher education (%)	Manual labor/ domestic service (%)	Other (%)
Level I *chicheras*	17	16 (94)	1 (6)	0 (0)
Level II *chicheras*	22	14 (64)	6 (27)	2 (9)
Non-*chicheras*	24	17 (71)	4 (17)	3 (12)
Total	63	47 (75)	11 (17)	5 (21)

chicha every 2–4 weeks and represent 69 percent (eighteen of twenty-six) of the chichera population; (c) non-chicheras—women who do not now produce chicha, or who do so less often than once a month.

Tables 3.3 and 3.4 indicate a relationship between the extent of chicha produced in a household and the educational mobility of the household's children. As we see in Table 3.3, Pocona chicheras send a slightly higher percentage of their children to urban schools than do non-chicheras. Breaking down the category of chichera into Level I and Level II chicha producers, Table 3.4 illustrates that it is the children of Level I producers who have the greatest educational mobility. These tabulations support the expressed belief of the majority of chicheras that one of the chief advantages of increasing chicha production levels is an increased ability to finance the education of one's children.

Table 3.3. Pocona Children Educated in Urban Schools

Household type	Total number of women	Total number of children over age 7	Number of children over age 7 in urban schools	Percentage of total children in urban schools
Chicheras	26	60	30	50
Non-*chicheras*	20	47	17	36
Total	46	107	47	43

Table 3.4. Education of Pocona *Chicheras'* Children

Household type	Total number of women	Total number of children over age 7	Number of children over age 7 in urban schools	Percentage of total children in urban schools
Level I *chicheras*	8	24	16	67
Level II *chicheras*	18	36	14	39
Total	26	60	30	50

The Chichera's Strategy for Power and Social Mobility

The primary advantages of being a chichera are twofold: Chicheras attain power and autonomy in the rural community; and they have the ability to finance the higher education of their children. The benefits of chicha making, therefore, give the chichera the means to promote her interests in both the rural and the urban domains. In the rural domain, the chichera is concerned with maintaining her power base and autonomy from men, while in the urban domain she is concerned with promoting the upward mobility of her children. It is the particular labor requirements of chicha making that dictate that her daughters are especially useful in her strategy for strengthening her rural power and her sons are useful in her strategy for access to upward mobility and prestige.

The first priority of the chichera is to strengthen her chicha-making business, as this is the basis of her social power and enables her to accomplish her urban-oriented goals. Perhaps one of the most demanding features of chicha production, other than the unpleasantness of the task, is the requirement for labor. One woman alone cannot produce chicha. There is too much heavy work involved, too many continual hours of labor, and too many awkward tasks. As chicha making is exclusively a woman's economic activity and a household product, the daughters of the household satisfy the chichera's need for labor. The following is a case history of a chichera's daughter, from her entry into the chicha business as an assistant to her mother to her becoming a chichera.

Doña R. is a Level II chichera and pig seller, married to an agriculturalist. She has one son, whom she is supporting in the city's secondary school, and two daughters residing with her in Pocona. The two daughters are M. and L., sixteen and eight years old, respectively.

Since the age of ten, M. has helped her mother with her chicha and pig-selling businesses. After four years at the local primary school, she dropped out and concentrated her efforts on the household chicha business. When asked why her daughter didn't stay in school or go on to school in Cochabamba like her son, Doña R. replied that it was mainly due to lack of funds. M. began assisting her mother with the production process, and when she was thirteen began to work in the chichería regularly, taking on more of the daily business. A chichera's daughter is said to be a great asset in attracting customers to the chichería.

Shortly after M. turned sixteen, she ran off with a local campesino, S., only to return a week later with an announcement of marriage plans. Doña R. was furious, and there was a great deal of arbitration among compadres before Doña R. gave her consent. Within a week, the couple had established residence in a house that Doña R. owned a few houses down the street from her own.

It was only a month after the move that M. opened her own chichería in the main room of her new home. Her initial production was minimal, selling chicha only twice in the last two months that I was there. If her production was small, it must have been due in part to the great amount of time she continued to devote to her mother's business. One could often see M. literally running from her chichería to her mother's throughout the day.

This example illustrates two important features in the mode of chicha production. First, the mother's anxiety over her daughter's marriage was due not only to the fact that S. was a campesino and, as such, regarded as socially inferior, but to the fact that Doña R. was losing exclusive control over her daughter's labor. Second, the cooperation that remained between mother and daughter after the marriage indicates the importance of female solidarity in chicha making. Even though there were logistical problems in maintaining the mother/daughter work unit outside of the household, Doña R. continued to draw on her daughter's labor for chicha production rather than call on the assistance of her husband or that of a hired laborer.

It is primarily from this female solidarity that the chichera derives her social power. For in keeping all aspects of chicha production the exclusive activity of women, women gain autonomy from men and the control over the chicha resource. This "strength in unity" argument has been proposed by Sacks (1974) and others. "Female cooperative work patterns are an essential means by which women isolate themselves from male supervision and control" (Murphy and Murphy 1974: 211).

In this way, a chichera's strategy for maintaining the power and autonomy gained through her chicha resource actively excludes her sons from chicha making while actively socializing her daughters into this economic institution. This strategy functions to perpetuate the mode of production of chicha as (1) a household production process, and (2) an exclusively female activity.

Another advantage of chicha making is that it enables the chichera to accrue enough capital to be able to finance the higher education of her children in the urban domain. Educational mobility is perceived as a means by which the chichera's children may gain upward social mobility, from which the chichera benefits economically as well as socially.

Chicheras retain close ties with their children in the urban areas through frequent visits as well as exchanges of material goods. The chichera sends potatoes and other crops along with woven blankets, eggs, and bread to her children on the weekly truck into the city. For their part, these urban children send their pueblo households money, sugar, canned goods, and various prestige items such as radios, hats, jewelry, and Western clothing. Along with providing access to imports, manufactured goods, and prestige items, the upward mobility of the chichera's children reflects on her increased prestige in the pueblo.

A chichera may express educational ambitions for all of her children; however, not all of her children are given equal access to this avenue of social mobility. Table 3.5 indicates the number of chicheras' sons and daughters who have gained access to higher education, as opposed to the number of non-chicheras' sons and daughters. As this table illustrates, males receive preference over females, so that two to three times as many chicheras' sons as daughters are supported in city schools. The data assembled in Table 3.5 also suggest that the sons of non-chicheras are not given as strong educational preference as are the sons of chicheras. Among the chichera group, 71 percent of the total number of sons over seven years of age receive an urban education, while only 32 percent of the chicheras' daughters are given such opportunities. This contrasts sharply with the non-chichera group, where 41 percent of all sons and 30 percent of all daughters over seven receive an urban education.

Table 3.6 compares male and female educational mobility within the chichera population. We see that of the four possible categories of children, it is the daughters of Level II chicheras who have the least access to avenues of educational mobility. Of the total number of daughters over seven (nineteen), only 15 percent receive an urban education; this compares with

Table 3.5. Education of Pocona Children, by Gender

Household type	Total no. of daughters over age 7	No. of daughters over age 7 in urban schools	Percentage of total in urban schools	Total no. of sons over age 7	No. of sons over age 7 in urban schools	Percentage of total in urban schools
Chicheras	32	10	32	28	20	71
Non-*chicheras*	20	6	30	27	11	41
Total/percentage	52	16	31	55	31	56

Table 3.6. Education of Pocona *Chicheras'* Children, by Gender

Household type	Total number of daughters over age 7	Number in urban schools	Percentage of total in urban schools	Total number of sons over age 7	Number in urban schools	Percentage of total in urban schools
Level I *chicheras*	13	7	54	11	9	82
Level II *chicheras*	19	3	15	17	11	65
Total/percentage	32	10	32	28	20	71

54 percent mobility for the daughters of Level I chicheras, 65 percent for the sons of Level II chicheras, and 82 percent for the sons of Level I chicheras.

"Working through Men" and the Question of Power

As demonstrated in tables 3.4 and 3.5, the majority of chicheras gave preference to the educational mobility of their sons over their daughters. The literature at the time of this study referred to this tendency as "working through men" and presented it as a strategy women employed in order to influence men, who held the power and authority in society. What I am suggesting is that the educational preference given to males is not a result of the power structure, but of the mode of production.

This perspective serves to explain the difference in educational mobility between the three categories of my sample, which represent three levels of production. Access to an urban education appeared to be most limited for the non–chicha producing households (see Table 3.5). However, of the non-chicheras' children who were supported in urban schools, there was no indication of a strong preference for sending sons over daughters. If the strategy of giving male children educational preference were a function of a quest for indirect power, then one would expect that the non-chichera sector would concentrate its efforts on advancing sons over daughters, because this sector had the most limited access to social mobility. This does not appear to be the case. An explanation for the equitable access to educational opportunities can be found in the lack of constraints (from chicha production) on the daughters of the household.

Conversely, while the sons of Level I chicheras were given educational preference over daughters, the discrepancy was not as great as among the children of Level II chicheras. This was because Level I chicheras were able to financially support more of their children in urban schools. Therefore, they were able to provide a higher education for some of their daughters as well as for their sons. These women were able to maintain their level of chicha production while easing the mobility constraints on their daughters through the policy of hiring campesina labor. In fact, seven (all but one) of the top-level chicheras hired campesina girls to assist them with chicha production. This is opposed to the Level II chicheras, of whom only two out of the eighteen utilized campesina labor. These assistants were young girls who came from the surrounding countryside to live in the chichera's household and perform domestic tasks as well as chicha-related work.

Many of these young girls were informally adopted by chichera patrons. This was especially true among those chicheras who were single and had no children of their own. The chichera was then responsible for the primary school education, welfare, and upbringing of these girls until they married. The fact that these assistants were female and tended to be adopted into the chichera's household further indicates the importance of the existing mode of chicha production in maintaining the chichera's power base.

It is interesting to note that there is only one example of a chichera who hired a male from the countryside to assist her with chicha production. In this case, the man was described as a "half-crazed" hunchback who was about to be hanged when the chichera intervened and offered to take him into her custody.

Summary

The study describes how chicheras gained social and economic power through the production and distribution of chicha in Pocona in 1978. Moreover, it describes how they sought to use these resources to send both sons and daughters to school as a means to advance the family's economic and social status.

While chicha production provided the greatest and most reliable income needed to achieve these goals, it was also a major hindrance. Because the production of chicha was controlled exclusively by women, and as the basic unit of production was the household, a chichera's economic power relied on keeping her daughter(s) in the family chicha business. In this way, chicheras were deeply invested in reaffirming the existing gender roles, which hindered the educational and social mobility of their daughters. Only those chicheras who made enough money to replace their daughters' labor were able to overcome this constraint.

This study found five features concerning the educational mobility of Pocona children at the time of my fieldwork. First, education was the chief purpose of children's out-migration. Second, chicheras, particularly the greater producers, sent more of their children to urban schools than did non-chicheras. Third, sons were given educational preference over daughters. Fourth, the sons and daughters of non-chicheras had more equitable access to higher education than did the children of chicheras. Finally, the daughters of the lesser chicha producers had the least access to avenues of educational mobility.

In this chapter, I have focused my attention on the notion that male children receive educational preference as a strategy by which women seek indirect power. My ethnographic case study of the chicheras of Pocona indicates that the control of the chicha resource in 1978 constituted a power base for the female beer makers that was not tied to the power of men, achieved through relations with men, or justified as a tool of "persuading" men. Because the production of chicha was dominated exclusively by women in 1978, the power and autonomy of chicheras were established and maintained through the achievements of women. Moreover, as the basic unit of production was the household, a chichera's power base relied specifically on the achievements of the mother/daughter unit. Just as the mode of chicha production thus restrained the chichera's daughter in the pueblo by tying her to the family chicha business, it also dictated that her son would always be given preferential access to higher education.[1]

While I have not returned to Pocona since the time of my research, chicha drinking, and thus the role of the chichera, has almost certainly declined in the region over the last three decades. How this decline has affected women's power and educational mobility is a topic that warrants further research.

Notes

1. It is noteworthy that, to the extent that a chichera depended on her husband for the corn utilized in chicha production, her independence was limited. This is a limitation that the chicheras in my sample were well aware of at the time, as they expressed the importance of a woman's owning agricultural lands in her own name. In fact, a chief criticism of campesinas was that they allowed themselves to be "landless" individuals, at the mercy of "drunken husbands." A chichera told me of a specific campesina whose husband had squandered all of his money. When it came time for the wife to pay off debts owed in the village, she was unable to do so. I was told that if the unfortunate woman had had her own lands, she would have been able to sell some to repay the household debts. "Poor woman," lamented the chichera, "as it is, she can do nothing to help herself." Consequently, as pueblo women commonly inherited land, they tended to retain those lands in their own name. Beyond this measure, the wealthier chicheras invested some of their chicha profits in agricultural lands. It is important to realize that, although corn was consumed, it was first and foremost grown for the production of chicha. It was questionable whether there was any acceptable way a farmer could dispose of the bulk of his corn crop other than giving it to his chichera wife.

References Cited

Allen, Catherine J.
2002 *The Hold Life Has: Coca and Cultural Identity in an Andean Community.* 2nd edition. Washington, D.C.: Smithsonian Institution Press.

Bejarano, Jorge
1950 *La derrota de un vicio: Origen e historia de la chicha.* Bogotá: Editorial Iqueima.

Blumberg, Rae Lesser
1978 *Stratification: Socioeconomic and Sexual Inequality.* Dubuque: Wm. C. Brown.

Boserup, Ester
1970 *Women's Role in Economic Development.* London: George Allen and Unwin.

Boulding, Elsie
1977 *Women in the Twentieth Century World.* Beverly Hills: Sage.

Bowser, Brenda
2000 From Pottery to Politics: An Ethnoarchaeological Study of Political Factionalism, Ethnicity, and Domestic Pottery Style in the Ecuadorian Amazon. *Journal of Anthropological Method and Theory* 7(3): 219–248.

2004 The Amazonian House: A Place of Women's Politics, Pottery, and Prestige. *Expedition* 46(2): 18–23.

Buechler, Judith, and Hans Buechler
1970 *Bolivian Aymara.* New York: Holt, Rinehart and Winston.

Butler, Barbara
2006 *Holy Intoxication to Drunken Dissipation: Alcohol among Quichua Speakers in Otavalo, Ecuador.* Albuquerque: University of New Mexico Press.

Buvinic, Mayra
1976 A Critical Review of Some Research Concepts and Concerns. In *Women and World Development,* Irene Tinker and Michele Bramson, eds., pp. 224–243. Washington, D.C.: Overseas Development Council, American Association for the Advancement of Science.

Chodorow, Nancy
1974 Family Structure and Feminine Personality. In *Women, Culture and Society,* Michele Rosaldo and Louise Lamphere, eds., pp. 43–66. Stanford: Stanford University Press.

Clark, Ronald James
1969 *Problems and Conflicts over Land Ownership in Bolivia.* Reprint no. 54. Madison: Land Tenure Center, University of Wisconsin.

Collier, Jane
1974 Women in Politics. In *Women, Culture and Society,* Michele Rosaldo and Louise Lamphere, eds., pp. 89–96. Stanford: Stanford University Press.

Colloredo-Mansfeld, Rudi
1999 *The Native Leisure Class: Consumption and Cultural Creativity in the Andes.* Chicago: University of Chicago Press.

Friedl, Ernestine

1967 The Position of Women: Appearance and Reality. *Anthropological Quarterly* 40: 97–108.

García, Jaime Ponce

1969 El sindicalismo boliviano: Resumen histórico y perspectivas actuales. *Estudios Andinos* 1(1): 28–67.

Gillin, John

1945 *Moche: A Peruvian Coastal Community.* Institute of Social Anthropology Publication no. 3. Washington, D.C.: Smithsonian Institution.

Heath, Dwight B.

1971 Peasants, Revolution and Drinking: Inter-Ethnic Drinking Patterns. *Human Organization* 30: 179–186.

Heath, Dwight, Charles Erasmus, and Hans Buechler

1969 *Land Reform and Social Revolution in Bolivia.* New York: Praeger.

Holmberg, Alan

1971 The Rhythms of Drinking in a Peruvian Coastal Mestizo Community. *Human Organization* 30(2): 198–202.

Huntington, Sue Ellen

1975 Issues in Women's Role in Economic Development: Critique and Alternatives. *Journal of Marriage and the Family* 37: 1001–1012.

Knaster, Meri

1976 Women in Latin America: The State of Research. *Latin American Research Review* 11: 3–74.

Lamphere, Louise

1974 Strategies, Cooperation, and Conflict among Women in Domestic Groups. In *Women, Culture and Society*, Michele Rosaldo and Louise Lamphere, eds., pp. 97–112. Stanford: Stanford University Press.

Leacock, Eleanor

1977 Women, Development and Anthropological Facts and Fictions. *Latin American Perspectives* 4: 5–8.

Malloy, James

1970 *Bolivia: The Uncompleted Revolution.* Pittsburgh: University of Pittsburgh Press.

1971 Bolivia's MNR: A Study of a National Popular Movement in Latin America. Buffalo: Council on International Studies, State University of New York at Buffalo.

Marschall, Katherine Barnes

1970 Cabildos, corregimientos y sindicatos en Bolivia después 1952. *Estudios Andinos* 1(2): 61–79.

Mayer, Enrique

2002 *The Articulated Peasant: Household Economies in the Andes.* Boulder: Westview.

McAlpin, Michelle

1977 *Women and National Development: The Complexities of Change.* Chicago: University of Chicago Press.

Mitchell, Christopher

1977 *The Legacy of Populism in Bolivia*. New York: Praeger.

Murphy, Yolanda, and Robert Murphy

1974 *Women of the Forest*. New York: Columbia University Press.

Nash, June

1977 Myth and Ideology in the Andean Highlands. In *Ideology and Social Change in Latin America*, June Nash and Juan Corradi, eds., pp. 116–141. New York: Gordon and Breach Science.

Núñez del Prado Béjar, Daisy Irene

1975 El poder de decisión de la mujer quechua andina. *América Indígena* 35(3): 391–401.

Parsons, Talcott

1963 On the Concept of Influence. *Public Opinion Quarterly* 27: 37–62.

Patch, Richard

1961 *Bolivia: The Restrained Revolution*. Reprint no. 54. Madison: Land Tenure Center, University of Wisconsin.

Paul, Lois

1974 The Mastery of Work and the Mystery of Sex in a Guatemalan Village. In *Women, Culture and Society*, Michele Rosaldo and Louise Lamphere, eds., pp. 281–299. Stanford: Stanford University Press.

Rohrlich-Leavitt, Ruby (ed.)

1975 *Women Cross-Culturally: Change and Challenge*. The Hague: Mouton.

Rosaldo, Michelle Zimbalist

1974 Women, Culture and Society: A Theoretical Overview. In *Women, Culture and Society*, Michele Rosaldo and Louise Lamphere, eds., pp. 17–42. Stanford: Stanford University Press.

Sacks, Karen

1974 Engels Revisited: Women, the Organization of Production, and Private Property. In *Women, Culture and Society*, Michele Rosaldo and Louise Lamphere, eds., pp. 207–222. Stanford: Stanford University Press.

Safa, Helen

1977 The Changing Class Composition of the Female Labor Force in Latin America. *Latin American Perspectives* 4(4): 126–136.

Sanday, Peggy Reeves

1974 Female Status in the Public Domain. In *Women, Culture and Society*, Michele Rosaldo and Louise Lamphere, eds., pp. 189–206. Stanford: Stanford University Press.

Sotomayor, Marcelo

1971 *Land Reform in Three Communities of Cochabamba, Bolivia*. Reprint no. 44. Madison: Land Tenure Center, University of Wisconsin.

Tinker, Irene

1976 The Adverse Impact of Development on Women. In *Women and World Development*, Irene Tinker and Michele Bramson, eds., pp. 22–34. Washington,

D.C.: Overseas Development Council, American Association for the Advancement of Science.

Ware, Helen
1975 Relevance of Changes in Women's Roles to Fertility Behavior: The African Evidence. Paper presented at the Annual Meeting of the Population Association of America, Seattle.

Weber, Max
1947 *Theory of Social and Economic Organization.* Oxford: Oxford University Press.

Weismantel, Mary J.
1988 *Food, Gender, and Poverty in the Ecuadorian Andes.* Philadelphia: University of Pennsylvania Press.

4

Places to Partake

Chicha in the Andean Landscape

Melissa Goodman-Elgar

This chapter considers evidence that agricultural landscapes formed important loci for the consumption of chicha during the reign of the Inca and addresses the implications of this association for the study of terrace systems.[1] Maize had an elevated status under the Inca, and the chicha prepared from it played a significant role in their religious practices. The Inca promoted maize agriculture through terrace construction and in annual agricultural rituals conducted by the highest echelons of Inca society. By viewing Inca agricultural terraces as monumental landscapes, this chapter explores how certain terraces featured prominently in important state activities and reinforced Inca social hierarchies, gender roles, and state territorial expansion. This suggests an elevated status for agriculture under the Inca that can be further explored through field investigations and interpretative strategies that address the potential social significance of agricultural landscapes.

Research on chicha has tended to concentrate on its manufacture and consumption within ceremonial public spaces, domestic contexts, and institutions such as the Inca *acllawasi*, where *acllas*, women dedicated to the Sun cult prepared chicha and other goods for the state (Goldstein 2003; Jennings 2005; Moore 1989; Silverblatt 1987). However, historical documents also make frequent reference to the use of maize chicha in agricultural terraces, both as an offering in ritual activities and as a beverage during group cultivation.

Maize was sacred to the Inca and central to ceremonial practices, but it was also a crucial commodity used to extract labor and generate state wealth (see, e.g., Cobo 1961, bk. 14, 8: 188–189; Murra 1960). These varied uses made the control of maize production a central activity during Inca territorial expansion (D'Altroy 2002: 268–276). The Inca drew upon the symbolic associations of maize and chicha in agricultural ceremonies to provide a basis for legitimating the expanding Inca state (Bauer 1996). This discussion suggests that the locus of chicha consumption in ceremonies held in fields is central to the expression of chicha's social and symbolic uses. The terrace systems discussed here may be considered sacred landscapes with roles in myth, ritual, and power negotiations.

Our understanding of chicha is largely derived from contemporary ethnography and the experience of researchers working in regions where chicha is still made (e.g., Allen 1988; Bastien 1978; Bolin 1998; Gose 1994; Isbell 1978). In these communities, chicha and other alcoholic beverages are essential for acquiring labor and for use in rituals, especially those honoring the earth deity Pachamama. Andean ethnography has the benefit of "direct historical analogy" (see Lyman and O'Brien 2001), because many contemporary Andeans are direct descendants of pre-Columbian peoples. Traditional practices are therefore considered indigenous in origin and analogous to those of pre-Columbian farmers. However, we may question the accuracy of contemporary ethnography in recovering pre-Columbian religious meaning and power relationships. The Spanish radically restructured religious and political practices, frequently by force (see, e.g., Arriaga 1968). Many contemporary activities appear to be longstanding traditions, but they are conducted under very different social and ideological conditions from those found in pre-Columbian times.

Historical documents are also controversial and have been widely critiqued for obvious misrepresentations of truth, manipulation of indigenous traditions and historical facts, the foreigners' imperfect understanding of the Andean world, as well as the nature of historical recording during the sixteenth and seventeenth centuries (see, e.g., Adorno 2000; Jákfalvi-Leiva 1984; Julien 2000; Porras-Barrenechea 1962; Zapata 1989). These concerns may be partly addressed by cross-referencing sources, considering the biases of individual authors (see Julien 2000: 2–22), and incorporating relevant archaeological investigations (e.g., Bauer 1998; Zuidema 1964). Despite the limitations of historical sources, this literature can provide a closer approximation of Inca power relations and religious ideology than can contemporary ethnography for the aims of this chapter. An expanded consideration would draw more heavily on Andean ethnography and include a critical evaluation of its application to archaeological interpretation, as Hayashida (this volume) effectively illustrates.

Historical records document two parallel uses of chicha in agricultural fields: it was used as an offering in annual Inca ceremonies carried out in sacred terraces dedicated to this purpose; it was also expected that chicha would be generously distributed for consumption at agricultural work parties. There are many references to chicha in descriptions of the Inca calendar of agricultural work and associated agrarian festivals (see, e.g., Cieza de León 2001, bk. 2, chaps. 38–39: 436–441; Cobo 1964, bk. 13, chaps. 25–30: 207–222; Garcilaso de la Vega 1966, bk. 5, chap. 2: 243–245, bk. 6, chap. 20: 356–360, bk. 7, chap. 5–7: 412–417; Molina (de Cuzco) 1964: 16–58; Murúa 2001, bk. 3, chap. 38: 436–441; Polo 1987: 7–8, 21–34; Guaman Poma 1987, chap. 11: 235–260 [237–262], chap. 37, 1130–1168 [1140–1178]). These sources indicate that chicha consumption was deeply embedded in Inca ceremonial observances as a drink and as an offering. The most relevant accounts refer to the use of chicha in named ceremonial fields, as will be considered below. The use of chicha for pre-Columbian agricultural work parties is less well documented but is described by Bernabé Cobo (1961).

The contrast between elite ceremonies and farmers' communal work parties in these depictions reveals the complexity of chicha use and its role in the maintenance of class status. In this discussion, I will suggest that chicha provides a fundamental link between the earthly process of food production, the Inca sociopolitical order, and the requirements of divine beings as conceptualized in Inca telluric cosmology.

Situating Events: Landscape, Place, and Agency

Both elite Inca agricultural ceremonies and work-party celebrations shift chicha consumption off-site into agrarian landscapes. In archaeology, *landscape* has come to mean not only visible topography but also the cultural associations of places. Specific landscapes are increasingly investigated for their role in religion and sociopolitical negotiations (see, e.g., Ashmore and Knapp 1999; Barratt 1994; Koontz et al. 2001; Mitchell 1994; Moore 2005; Smith 2003). Culturally important locales may enable or substantiate power relations between people but require agency for their symbolic power to be actualized. The significance of such places is temporally limited through the social practices by which meaning is made and remade, interpreted and reinterpreted, memorialized, and, often, later forgotten.

The many discussions surrounding cultural landscapes may be simplified by contrasting approaches to natural landscapes with approaches to architectural landscapes. At one extreme, the enculturation of natural landscape features is common cross-culturally in hunter-gatherer societies, where offerings and special observances are often made to notable features such as caves, rock outcrops, and springs (see, e.g., Bradley 2000; Carmichael et al. 1994). These places are revered and used for their inherent qualities. In contrast, architectural landscapes are anthropogenic and have been designed to contain symbolically potent designs which may reflect such features as ethnic identity, religious ideology, and territoriality (see, e.g., Bender 1993, 1998; Bradley 1998; Carrasco 1991; Earle 2000; Edmonds 1999; Goldstein 2005; Koontz et al. 2001; Mitchell 1994; Moore 1996; Smith 2003; Thomas 1996). The significance of anthropogenic monuments has been the focus of intense debate, particularly in Britain (see, e.g., Barratt 1994; Bender 1998; Bradley 1998; Edmonds 1999; Pollard and Reynolds 2002; Thomas 1993). Monuments are generally seen as durable structures assumed to have been built to perpetuate the memory of people or events. Frequently, they required substantial labor investment and indicate that labor was coordinated at a community scale under centralized leadership. Monumental architecture may be on a landscape scale and contain related monuments (e.g., the pyramids at Giza) or a configuration of edifices across a large geographic area that appears to define a conceptual unit at the time they were constructed (e.g., Avebury). These monumental landscapes have characteristics of both their natural features and anthropogenic configurations (see, e.g., Koontz et al. 2001).

In the Andes, there is evidence of both the honoring of natural features as *huacas*, or shrines (see, e.g., Bauer 1998; Hyslop 1990), and the creation of monumental landscapes, such as Pachacamac (Silverman 1994). Andean approaches to landscape archaeology have concentrated largely on natural landscapes such as mountaintops, the Inca system of shrines (*ceques*), and the development of monumental landscapes (see, e.g., Aveni 2000; Bauer 1998; Bauer and Stanish 2001; Farrington 1992; McEwan and van de Guchte 1992; Moore 1996, 2004, 2005; Niles 1987, 1992; Silverman 1994; van de Guchte 1999; Zuidema 1964, 1986). Agricultural lands rarely figure in these discussions, as their primary role is crop production, and the social potency of this role is usually seen as residing in the crops, not the fields. This division may not accurately reflect pre-Columbian worldviews.

The exclusion of field systems from Andean discussions of cultural landscapes reflects a common ideological separation between a culturally construed residential built environment, or *domus*, which is imbued with symbolic features, and a "wild" agricultural *agrios* with limited anthropogenic associations (Hodder 1991). The domus:agrios conceptual duality is a common feature of European settlement planning, and Hodder illustrates its origin in the early Neolithic at sites such as Çatalhöyük.

Terraced fields figure prominently within the plans of many pre-Columbian Andean settlements. This may indicate that these settlements did not reflect a notion of separate conceptual spheres for domus and agrios. Many Inca settlements have terraced fields of high-quality masonry incorporated within their residential areas or built along the site perimeter (Fig. 4.1). In these cases, terraces appear to be conceptually integrated into Inca settlement planning, as seen in the Inca sites of Machu Picchu, Ollantaytambo, Pisac, Patallaqta, Puyupatamarka, Wiñay Wayna, and others (see Kendall 1985). This suggests that, in an Andean context, fields do not form a distinct conceptual sphere set apart from a domestic sphere. In the Andes, we may better follow the Spanish chronicler Fray Martín de Murúa (2001, bk. 2, chap. 28: 410) in distinguishing between cultivated and uncultivated landscapes to understand how Andean landscapes were used and perceived.

Cultivated landscapes arise from demands for crops, which are themselves culturally constrained. Archaeologists are increasingly addressing the associations between food choices and cuisine in group cultural iden-

Figure 4.1. Terracing below the Inca site of Pisac, Urubamba Valley, Peru. Photo by the author.

tity and the agricultural production of specific products (e.g., Bray 2003c; Dietler 1996; Dietler and Hayden 2001; Fuller 2005; Gumerman 1997). Food-consumption patterns are often important social markers of group membership, and changes in consumption may reflect changes in cultural affiliation and necessitate changes in cultivation (see, e.g., Goldstein 2003; Hastorf 1990, 1993; Hastorf and Johannessen 1993).

Stone-walled terraces are a predominant feature of Andean highland landscapes. Donkin (1979) points out that the scale of pre-Columbian terracing in the Andes eclipses even the largest traditional monuments in terms of both area and labor investment. The motivation for the construction of terraced fields is generally assumed to have been to support intensive agriculture. Terracing levels steep lands, facilitates cultivation and irrigation, and may also check soil erosion. The energy requirements of terracing are considerable and include labor and materials, design and planning, the negotiation of land-tenure relations, reshaping the slope, leveling the field surface, reorienting the field's aspect, and changing hydrology, and may even include replacing the natural soil (Guillet 1987; Keeley 1985; Treacy 1994; Treacy and Denevan 1994). Terrace construction requires planning, coordinated labor, acquisition of materials, and technical knowledge similar to that needed for the construction of settlements and monuments (see Treacy 1994: 141–155). Once in place, terraces permanently alter the natural landscape, and their impact on the land remains even if fields are subsequently abandoned (Denevan 2001: 172–173; Dick et al. 1994).

The prevalence and extent of Andean terrace systems suggest that they form an important corporate endeavor. Many contemporary Andean communities have an ayllu organization that includes bonds of kinship, reciprocal exchange, and corporate landholding (see, e.g., Alberti and Mayer 1974; Allen 1988; Bastien 1978; Castro Pozo 1946; Gose 1994; Isbell 1978; Mayer 1981; Murra 1980). The Spanish found that a version of ayllu organization was used by the Inca for administration and taxation (see Moore 1958), and the ayllu may be a long-standing Andean tradition (see, e.g., Isbell 1997; Salomon 1995). The development of common lands into terraced fields represents valuable long-term investments for ayllu-based communities. These projects provide opportunities for community solidarity and strengthening land-tenure claims. Earle addresses the relationships between landscape development and tenure (2000: 40–41): "Land is improved by social labor. . . . Property rights in land are secured primarily through original possession, improvement, inheritance, and conquest. Ownership is often based on claims of first possession and of improvements, such as clearing and fencing a field, that change future returns." Access to these group holdings is institutionalized through community leadership structures, especially in chiefdoms (Earle 1991b, 2000). The construction of field systems may therefore be implicated in establishing a territorial basis for communities (Renfrew 2001).

In his study of Irish agricultural landscapes, Cooney further relates land enclosure with community identity (1994: 34–35): "The creation of larger field systems . . . is indicative of both social cohesion and the organization of dispersed families together to create a communal landscape which may itself have been seen as symbolizing and articulating this community." In some instances, field systems can be constructed and maintained at the family level incrementally over time (see, e.g., Doolittle 1984; Erickson 1985, 1993), but the development of large field systems provides an opportunity to reinforce community identity through communal activities while the resultant constructions serve to materialize group unity and land tenure (Demarrais et al. 1996).

The relative permanence of Andean stone-walled field systems lends them to long-term multigenerational use. Fields are therefore used through phases of technological and cultural changes (e.g., the Colca Canyon; see Treacy 1994) and become substrates for the preservation of cultural memories. In profoundly altering the land, the establishment of terraces structures human behavior by limiting movement through terraced landscapes and formalizes territorial boundaries. Over time, field systems also become inscribed with myth and memory, as documented in the stories contemporary farmers often relate about their fields. These qualities all suggest a variety of roles for walled terracing in addition to the mundane functions of cultivation.

Terrace masonry is usually made with uncut fieldstones piled into walls without mortar, called *pirka* masonry, that angle back into the slope for stability (see Denevan 2001; Donkin 1979). This vernacular masonry style is also commonly used for residential construction, but terrace walls are more porous than building walls, because drainage is needed to keep the walls from becoming waterlogged and collapsing. More elaborate pirka terraces are sometimes made by sandwiching two layers of pirka walling around a core of pebbles to allow for greater stability and drainage.

Andean terraces are often overbuilt for the functional requirements of agriculture. This is particularly the case for Inca "staircase" terraces (*andenes*), which have architectural features that far exceed the needs of cultivation. In her study of Callachaca, Niles (1987) found that terraces near this elite Inca estate employed masonry techniques and aesthetic principles similar to those of elite Inca residential architecture. The highly planned geometric designs, specialist cut-stone masonry, niches, and other embedded features are all distinctive in elite Inca architecture and serve to identify specific places with Inca hegemony (see, e.g., Farrington 1992; Gasparini and Margolies 1980; Moore 2004; Niles 1987; Protzen 1993). The use of these elite features in certain Inca terrace systems indicates that they may have had roles beyond crop production. These terraces may be considered monumental landscapes in terms of their aesthetic and highly planned designs as well as their considerable labor requirements. It remains to consider what they may have been designed to commemorate.

Terraces, Maize, and the Inca Sacred Landscapes

The Ritual Elaboration of Inca Maize Production

> Harawayu, harawayu
> Create me, magic maize
> If you will not, I will uproot you
> Magic mother! Queen!

> —Guaman Poma[2]

Early historical documents from Peru present a convincing case for the use of terraced fields as cultural substrates through practices related to maize agriculture and associated rituals. The *harawayu* song to Mamasara, or Maize Mother, cited above, illustrates an important religious association of maize with creation and nobility, both of which underpin the ritual significance of chicha. The expression "Create me, magic maize" emphasizes the essential life-giving qualities cultivators associated with their maize crops. Hastorf and Johannessen (1993: 121) claim that chicha was made even more socially potent than maize because it was transformed from a raw product to a cooked one.

The documents produced by Garcilaso de la Vega and Guaman Poma, first-generation mestizo writers, are the most revealing in their accounts of the Inca calendar and maize festivals. Living between the worlds of the indigenous Andean and Spanish cultures, both writers attempted to negotiate their mixed heritage in their writing. In his chronicle, Garcilaso strove to defend his Andean heritage, sometimes to the point of obscuring the truth (see, e.g., Adorno 2000; Zapata 1989). Guaman Poma's lengthy letter to the king of Spain represents the Inca within their own cultural system. In addition, the Jesuit priest Bernabé Cobo made detailed observations as he traversed the Andean landscape (Cobo 1964) observing everyday agricultural practices (see, e.g., Cobo 1961, bk. 14, chap. 8: 193) and the Inca elite (Cobo 1979, 1990). His accounts of ceremonial events in the cycle of maize agriculture include plowing, sowing, and harvesting.

Garcilaso claims to have observed the Inca plowing festival as a child in a specific sacred terrace. He indicates that this Inca ritual was not conducted solely in Cuzco, but rather, that it was imitated across the Inca territories. It is therefore worthwhile exploring his account in detail:

> Inside the city of Cuzco, on the skirts of the hill where the fortress is, there used to be a large terrace of many fanegas of soil . . . called Collcampata. The quarter takes its name from the name of the terrace, which was the special and chief jewel of the Sun, for it was the first to be dedicated to him in the whole empire. This terrace was tilled and cared for by those of the royal blood, and none but the Inca and Palla could work in it. The work was done amid the greatest celebrations, especially at ploughing time, when the Inca came dressed in all their insignia and finery. The songs they recited in praise of the Sun and their kings were all based on the meaning of the word *hailli*, which means triumph over the soil, which they ploughed and disemboweled so that it should give fruit. The songs included elegant phrases by noble lovers and brave soldiers on the subject of their triumph over the earth they were ploughing. The refrain of each verse was the word, "hailli" repeated as often as was necessary to mark the beats of a certain rhythm, corresponding to the movements made by the Indians in raising their implements and dropping them, the more easily to break the soil. . . . They work in bands of seven or eight, more or less, according to family or neighborhood groups. By all lowering their ploughs at once they can raise clods of earth so large that anyone who has not seen it could hardly credit it. . . . The women work opposite the men and help lift the clods with their hands, turning the grass roots upwards so that they dry and die, and the harrowing requires less effort. They join with their husbands in the singing, especially the hailli chorus. (Garcilaso de la Vega 1966, bk. 5 chap. 2: 244–245)[3]

This passage illustrates several salient themes. Garcilaso indicates that Col-lcampata was dedicated to the Sun cult. The Sun was a principal Inca de-ity, and their most sacred monument, the Coricancha, was devoted to the Sun (see Bauer 2004: 139–157). The Inca claimed a mythical descent from the sun, which provided the Inca ruler with semidivine status. Only Inca and Palla elites participated in the Collcampata plowing and harvest festi-vals (Garcilaso de la Vega 1966, bk. 2, chap. 21: 117), but the Inca forced their subjugated populations to participate in their state religion, including the Sun cult (see, e.g., Silverblatt 1988). The Quechua term *hailli* (and its spelling variants) may be understood as "songs of triumph," which have been associ-ated with victory over enemies in warfare (Bauer 1996). This account also speaks generally of the organization of agricultural work in gendered rows.

Cobo describes another annual cycle of agricultural ceremonies in a maize field called Sausero. He emphasizes the sacrificial use of the maize from this field and the use of aclla chicha and animal sacrifices:

> In the ninth month . . . they performed a festival called *guayara*, ask-ing for a good and abundant year . . . they sowed the field of Sausero, they did this sowing with great solemnity because this field was the sun's, and the harvest from it was for ordinary sacrifices . . . and while it was sown, in the middle there was a white ram [llama] with gold earspools, and with it many Indians and *mamacuna* of the sun, spill-ing a lot of chicha in the name of this ram [llama]. And when the sow-ing came to an end, they brought from all the provinces a thousand guinea pigs, as fitted to each one in agreement with the allocation that was done, and with great solemnity they beheaded them and they burned them all in this field, except for a certain number that were distributed for the *huacas* and shrines of the city in the name of the sun. They directed this sacrifice to hail, air, water and sun, to all that seemed to them to have the power to raise or to offend the crop. (Cobo 1964, bk. 13, chap. 28: 216; all translations are mine unless otherwise noted)[4]

Cobo indicates that Sausero was also dedicated to the sun and that its harvests were for ritual sacrifices, but he does not refer to the Inca ar-istocracy as seen in the Collcampata ceremonies. *Mamacona* is another term for *acllacuna*, and this depiction has the Inca pouring their chicha directly onto the terrace field. The acllacuna were often from elite families and had a sacred status. The chicha they produced was for consumption at state events and also had sacred connotations. This passage suggests a strong association between maize production, the Sun cult, and chicha designated for religious purposes. The profuse animal sacrifices were also clearly situated within the field itself. These ritual observances and their mythical significance indicate that this field has many of the qualities commonly associated with temples and ritual centers. The field has a dual role in providing sacrificial maize and serving as a sacred site for placating deities.

Elsewhere, Cobo emphasizes that participation in Sausero rituals enables rites of passage for Inca boys to become warriors (Cobo 1964, bk. 13, chap. 27: 215). Bauer (1996) considers this association between warfare and agriculture as indispensable to the legitimization of Inca power and the semidivine status of their leaders.

The mythical associations of Sausero are further elaborated in the chronicle of Cristóbal Molina de Cuzco (1964: 52), who reports that the harvest from Sausero was used for making chicha for the cult of Mama Wako (Huaco, Waqo, Waqu), the first Inca queen. Fink (2001: 39) further suggests that there is linguistic evidence that Mama Wako assumed the role of Mamasara, the maize mother (see also Bauer 1998: 100–101). As Mama Wako was considered the daughter of the solar deity (Garcilaso de la Vega 1966, bk. 1, chap. 17: 46), these associations may not conflict with Cobo's assertion that Sausero was dedicated to the Sun. The Dominican missionary Fray Martín de Murúa (2001, bk. 1, chap. 4: 47–49) directly associates Mama Wako with maize, chicha, and power. Murúa states that the cultivation of Sausero and other sacred fields was for the ritual production of maize for use as chicha. Thus, several chroniclers provide evidence that the fields of Collcampata and Sausero were monumental landscapes and the loci for ritual activities associated with Inka elites, maize, and chicha.

Researchers have identified the physical locations of both Collcampata (Squier 1877: chap. 22) and Sausero (Bauer 1998: map 7.2). Bauer (1998: 26; see also app. 1), identifies several other named fields, including Anaypampa (Exquisite Plain) and Mancochuqui (Gold Band), from which the maize harvests were dedicated to ancestors and deities.

Agricultural Practice and the Social Order

In his chapter on land division, Cobo provides a detailed account of the social context of the start of agricultural work in Inca state fields that can be summarized as follows:

The towns responded to [Inca labor demands] and cultivated them this way: if by chance the Inca himself was found present or his governor, or any other principal lord, he was the first one to put his hand to work with a gold *taclla*, or plow, which was carried for the Inca, and with this example all the gentlemen and warriors who accompanied him did the same; soon the Inca stopped, and after him the other gentlemen and principals stopped; and they sat down with their king to have their banquets and festivals, which in this instance were very solemn. The common people remained working with only the *curacas-pachacas* [lower administrators], who worked a while longer than the nobles; and later they helped oversee the work by giving any necessary orders. (Cobo 1964, vol. 2, bk. 12, chap. 28: 120)[5]

Cobo's depiction shows that the commencement of plowing perpetuated a strict political hierarchy, with the highest-ranking male present initiating both cultivation and feasting. A ranking of governors, lords, petty officials, and commoner workers was followed in terms of how much they worked and their leadership roles. Elements of Cobo's account are corroborated by a rare witness account attributed to Cristóbal de Molina (el Almagrista, 1968: 81–82) from April 1535 of harvesting rituals in Cuzco. El Almagrista describes an elegant festival where the Sapa, or ruling Inca, turns the soil with a gold-tipped plow amid tremendous sacrifices and celebrations.

Agricultural ceremonies allowed elites to demonstrate their powerful status, which serves to illustrate that participation in maize agriculture was itself an important elite activity. The Inca ruler's leadership in agricultural rituals is a demonstration of his ability to negotiate with deities and upholds the legitimacy of his reign (Bauer 1996). These demonstrations of his authority distinguished the *capac* status that defined his ability to rule (see Julien 2000: 22–48). The Inca and Palla elites, and indeed elites in general, followed the Sapa Inca in performing agricultural work, however symbolically, in the regalia that designated their privileged rank. The hailli songs remind us of the warrior connotations implicit in these agricultural festivals. The inclusion of warriors reinforces the association between agrarian rituals and Inca dominion over productive lands and, by association, conquered territories.

Elements of this stratified social order are depicted in Poma's drawing of the plowing festival Travaxa Haillichacraiapuic. He depicts an elite Inca male, identified by earspools and dress, holding a *chaquitaclla* and possibly a *quipu* (knotted-string recording device), while three shoeless men in more simple attire actually plow (see Fig. 4.2). Three attendant

women sing hailli and assist on their knees while a woman with an elaborate headdress, shawl with *tupu* pin, and a long skirt with a decorated
belt stands above them with a kero (drinking vessel) in her hand. The
standing woman's attire and the kero indicate that she is an aclla. These
representations are mirrored in the illustration for Agusto Chacraiapui,
although the standing woman's head there is uncovered and she wears
less elaborate clothing.

In his illustration for the June harvest festival, Guaman Poma demonstrates a relationship between Inca festivities and chicha (Fig. 4.3). Both the

Figure 4.2. Guaman Poma's illustration of Inca agricultural activities in August,
called Travaxa: Haillichacraiapuic (work: triumphant songs, opening the fields)
(Guaman Poma 1987: 1163).

vessels held by the aclla are associated with chicha, the serving aríbalo or urpu vessels from which she is serving, and the kero she holds in her hand. The Inca ruler is drinking from a kero, and a fantastical flying creature offers another cup to the anthropomorphic sun, another reference to the solar deity. The text does not explain this scene, instead noting that it was a time of harvest and abundance, when the Inca played and the storehouses were filled (Guaman Poma 1987, chap. 11: 245 [247]).

As with Garcilaso's account of Collcampata, cited above, Guaman Poma's depiction illustrates not only class structure but also formal gender

Figure 4.3. Guaman Poma's depiction of the Inca harvest festival in June, Huacaicusqui (Guaman Poma 1987: 246 [248]). Contrast this elite drinking scene to the humble potato harvesting depicted for June, Travaxos: Papaallaimitanpacha (work: occasion of digging potatoes) (Guaman Poma 1987: 1147 [1157]).

roles. In Figures 4.2 and 4.3, we are presented with two different female roles: women working the soil as men plow; and women associated with drinking vessels and, presumably, chicha (for discussions, see Bray 2003a, 2003b; Moore 1989; Silverblatt 1987). Men are shown using the chaquita-clla, and the standing male figure in elite dress appears to be overseeing the work. If these are accurate depictions of the social order, the rituals served to reinforce gender roles as well as the Inca class structure.

The foregoing has considered the representation of elite activities, but these offer little direct consideration of the rest of the populace. There are rare references to the practices of commoners, such in the writing of Lic. Juan Polo de Ondegardo, who was a colonial magistrate. His work appears to have been an important source for Cobo but is now largely lost to us (Rowe 1990). In the documents that survive, Polo describes Andean agricultural practices as follows:

> It is a common thing among the Indians to worship fertile soil, the soil which they call Pachamama, or Cámac Páchac, by spilling chicha upon it, or coca, or other things, that it may be good to them. . . . To the same end, when the time comes to plow, prepare, and plant the land, and to harvest maize or potatoes or quinoa, yuca, sweet potatoes, and other vegetables and fruits of the earth, they offer to it burned tallow, coca, cavies, lambs, and other things, while drinking and dancing. (Polo 1987, app. A, chap. 2: 198)[6]

Polo's reference to nonelite foods such as tubers and quinoa suggest that this is a depiction of the common farmers rather than Inca elites (see Murra 1960). This depiction mirrors the elite Inca festivals in the dual use of chicha as an offering and as a drink for participants and suggests that both of these uses were commonly practiced. Offerings including chicha were made to the fertile earth, here conflated as Pachamama, the Earth Mother, and Pachacamac (Cámac Páchac), who is generally male and sometimes seen as a creator deity.

The second ceque of Collasuyo contained Sausero and another field or plaza, Limapampa, where important maize festivals were held (Bauer 1998: 98-100). Molina associates Limapampa with another field, Aucaypacta, or Terrace of Tranquillity, where commoners held maize-sowing festivals with drinking and dancing while priests made offerings (Bauer 1998: 181).

Thus, within this ceque there may have been a spatial representation of class structure with a practical division between the ritual space allocated to commoners at Limapampa/Aucaypacta and ritual space allocated to the elites at Sausero. Given that these sites are located in the imperial center,

Cuzco, even the commoners in these depictions may be considered relatively elite in comparison to the status of non-Inca and provincial populations.

Guaman Poma further alludes to class with reference to ritual sacrifice
during plowing festivals in August: "In this month they sacrifice to the
idols, huacas, the poor of this kingdom with what they can, with guinea
pigs and spondylus shell, and bread prepared with blood [*zanco*] and chicha and sheep" (Guaman Poma 1987, bk. 1, chap. 11: 251 [253]).[7] In this passage chicha is a common offering among many others.

These ritual practices appear to reflect a split in Late Horizon society
where the Inca elites operated exclusive rituals construed within the Inca
solar cult, while the commoners and non-Inca population maintained related, but distinct, traditions. State rituals had to be fluid enough to accom-
modate an expanding empire and could be manipulated to legitimate the
claims of various political factions in the scramble for power. The imposition of myths of the Inca state, such as the cult of the Sun god, would be
unlikely to have effectively replaced indigenous religious practices outside
Cuzco, particularly in highland communities that were conquered by force.
Maxwell (1956) contends that the cult of Pachamama was deeply rooted in
the rural, non-Inca population, an assertion that is supported by its persistence.

The Role of Agricultural Rituals in Inca Cultural and Territorial Authority

Under a succession of rulers, the Inca state expanded its territorial control
rapidly in the thirteenth through the fifteenth centuries, often by force (see
Rostworowski de Diez Canseco 1999). Inca expansion was aggressive in agriculturally productive regions, where the Inca took control of existing field
systems and often augmented these with new agricultural projects, such
as terraces. Stone-masonry terrace systems with Inca features are found
across Peru in the Cajamarca Valley (Fig. 4.4), the Colca Valley (Treacy
1994), Huánuco Viejo (Morris and Thompson 1985), the Mantaro Valley
(Goodman-Elgar 2003), and the Urubamba Valley (Niles 1987), as well as
in Saraguro, Ecuador (Ogburn 2006). Although there is considerable evidence that the state's maize fields were set aside for various deities (see,
e.g., D'Altroy 2002; Moore 1958; Murra 1980), the Inca staple economy
relied on basic foodstuffs to underwrite its basic functions, including military action, making agriculture and food storage a central part of the state's
activities (D'Altroy and Earle 1985; LeVine 1992).

Figure 4.4. Curvilinear terraces above the city of Cajamarca. The lower terrace is under wheat, maize is growing at the top left. Photo by the author.

Garcilaso (1966, bk. 5, chap. 1: 242) refers to an Inca mandate to expand maize agriculture in conquered territories by selecting sites with irrigable, fertile soil for terrace construction. He continues that terraces were taken by the state, which implies that the Inca claimed the best maize lands. Hastorf (1990) has documented how the Inca substantially increased maize production in the Mantaro Valley by constructing new fields and reoccupying existing terraces where maize could be grown. D'Altroy (2002: 268–278) traces the expansion of maize in Inca plantations at Cochabamba and elsewhere. Investigations in the Colca Canyon (Treacy 1994) found evidence for substantial Inca reconstruction of existing terracing.

This expansion into conquered territories made it necessary to create a ritual framework that sanctioned Inca dominion. Through agricultural rituals, the Inca made the production of maize redolent with symbolic and mythical associations that naturalized their control. The extravagant ceremonies performed in the imperial heartland were intended to serve for all the agricultural lands that the Inca held through their sacred royal status and the actions of elites performing within them. Representatives from conquered territories were sent to Cuzco to witness or participate in Inca state culture, including these rituals.

Nevertheless, we must explain how such exceptional, localized events are used to justify control in toto. One means of addressing this is to consider the significance of the Inca calendar and how temporal manipulation may be linked to control of the landscape (Bender 2002).

In contrast to notions of progressive or historical time, in many agrarian societies time is seen as cyclical and is attributed to the sun (Eliade 1957). The cyclical nature of time is formulated in calendrical systems that take on an essential or eternal quality. In societies such as the Inca, the sequence of events does not emerge from a historical marker, the year, but time unfolds in the repeating cycle of months. In these contexts, time is given meaning through "codified calendric knowledge" rather than historical knowledge, and calendrical understandings provide a basis for situating everyday activities into a meaningful temporal framework (Bender 2002: 104, quoting Gell 1992: 299, 308). Individuals or groups who possess this calendrical knowledge have a source of power that extends into everyday activities and sanctions their control.

The ritual observances performed at Sausero, Collcampata, and related loci provided the opportunity for Inca elites to demonstrate a specialized calendrical knowledge that linked the divinity of the sun and the sacred characteristics of offerings to their production of maize. The historical descriptions of these events indicate that such knowledge was specialized, elite controlled, and publicly flaunted. These ceremonies offered opportunities for ostentatious display to further reinforce social ranking and power (see, e.g., Moore 1996; Ramírez 2005: 179–211). If we attempt to re-create the scene shown in Figure 4.2, the arrival of the participants in their finery would make an impressive display.

Rural communities likely had calendrical knowledge based on astronomical observations, as they do today (see, e.g., Orlove 1979; Orlove et al. 2000, 2002; Urton 1981, 1982; Zuidema 1982). However, the grandiose nature of elite Inca ceremonies, with their heavy ritual elaboration and material display, indicates that Inca elites were attempting to undermine such knowledge through major state-sponsored events. Conquered communities could not hope to match the scale of these ceremonies and were forced to concede ritual control of production along with territory. The ritual cycle provided a mechanism for the creation and maintenance of the symbolic power that enabled the Inca to support the costs of state expansion by extracting agricultural land and its products from conquered peoples (D'Altroy and Earle 1985; Earle 1991a).

The imposition of Inca religious customs may have obscured the indigenous religious behavior of conquered peoples (see Silverblatt 1988). Jennings (2003a, 2003b) has shown that the Inca conquest of Cotahuasi led to the cessation of a local ritual wherein painted tablets were deposited near agricultural fields. This long-standing local tradition was stopped after the Inca took control of the region, although other local ritual activities were permitted to continue. This suggests that the Inca found it necessary to control activities that conflicted with their control, such as those associated with legitimating land tenure. Given the extent of terracing in the Andes, we may expect to identify other culturally distinct ritual observances in fields elsewhere.

Identifying Chicha in the Landscape

The high-status Inca agricultural fields considered above serve to illustrate a more general trend, which is that Andean field systems have long played an important role as the focal point for significant political and religious events. In the accounts detailed above, agricultural rituals linked the production of maize to the liquid transfer of power in society with chicha. It is precisely because of the important social role of maize that these fields were singled out for extraordinary treatment. Sites appropriate to ritual elaboration would have been subject to careful selection, as would designs and materials. The reports of the chroniclers indicate that myths about such locales could be deliberately evoked to help provide authority both to the rituals and to the larger enterprise that they represented.

If we are to address the potential roles of field systems beyond production, they must be given a more prominent role in field investigations and interpretation. The heavy emphasis in archaeology on identifying occupation sites, dwellings, and monuments has long been challenged (see, e.g., Dunnell 1992; Dunnell and Dancey 1983; Ebert 1992; Foley 1981; see Brück and Goodman [Elgar] 1999 for discussion). Field survey is often conducted at wide intervals (e.g., 100-meter transects), which is successful in identifying settlements and monuments but largely precludes recognizing variation in artifact density across landscape features. In contrast, dense stratified archaeological surveys in the Andes have revealed distinctive patterns of land-use off-site (see, e.g., Goldstein 2003, 2005).

If terraces are considered built environments, their architectural features and any artifacts they contain may be employed to detect variations in their use, including ceremonial uses. Here I will summarize a method I found effective for the study of terraced field systems in the Mantaro Valley (Goodman-Elgar 2003). The size and extent of field systems relate to their development and use. The boundaries of field systems are often visible on aerial photographs, and agricultural property maps help to generate survey areas. As elevation is a limiting factor for Andean agriculture, the elevation of field systems has interpretative relevance. Pre-Columbian crop limits may not reflect modern cropping patterns, but can be reconstructed to identify likely crop limits from different times in the past (Seltzer and Hastorf 1990). Physical inspection of standing field walls for masonry style, evidence of reconstruction, and associations with features such as paths or roads, rock outcrops, springs, and irrigation canals all provide evidence of cultural affiliation. Inca features, including geometric design, cut-stone masonry, and niches, may be readily identified during survey. Fields that possess these and other aesthetic characteristics indicate candidates for special-use fields. Absolute dating of agricultural features is notoriously difficult to achieve because of bioturbation, but datable material may be recovered from under standing walls to provide basal dates.

Surveys of terraces can help determine the range of activities conducted within them. However, surface surveys of fields may not accurately recover artifact distribution, because plowing and erosion can obscure surface artifacts. This is particularly the case for the lower terraces, where maize grows, which receive the bulk of transported sediment. Therefore, scrape survey and excavation should also be considered, particularly for lower terraces.

Activities we may expect in pre-Columbian fields include cultivation in all cases and, commonly, domestic settlement and midden accumulation with household refuse, as well as the exceptional ceremonies considered above. These possible uses require an interpretative framework that differentiates these activities. Evidence of cultivation is generally seen in stone hoe fragments, whereas both domestic occupation and midden areas should include artifacts such as cooking pots and other plain wares that represent a wide range of everyday activities. Feasting and chicha consumption have distinct ceramic serving assemblages that reflect local consumption patterns. Contemporary studies have defined different ceramic assemblages for chicha manufacture, transport, and consumption (e.g., Arnold 1993; Cutler and Cárdenas 1947; Jennings 2005; Jennings et al. 2005; Sillar 2000). Pre-Columbian material culture for chicha has long been recognized, and distinctive ceramic assemblages have been defined for many cultures from the Middle Horizon, including Tiwanaku (Goldstein 2003), Wari (Cook and Glowacki 2003), Chimú (Moore 1989), and the Inca (e.g., Bray 2003a, 2003b; D'Altroy 1992; Rowe 1946).

Local artifact assemblages for chicha consumption and feasting may be distinguishable from other activities through the definition of pottery used to transport and consume liquids and serve food (see, e.g., Anderson, this volume; Bray, this volume; Jennings 2005; and Jennings and Chatfield, this volume). Feasting-scale production of chicha is unlikely to occur in fields because the heavy weight of large chicha-manufacturing pots and the required fuel to heat them would make manufacture in walled fields cumbersome. We would therefore expect that the more mobile transport and serving pots, such as medium and small urpus and keros, would be brought to fields. Sillar (2000: fig. 6.12) includes a photograph of medium-transport vessels holding chicha being used in fields after a work party.

Transport vessels have several characteristics that would limit their encounter rates within agricultural fields. The larger forms are expensive to make and have thick walls of coarse paste, which are sturdy and resistant to breakage (Sillar 2000: 69; Jennings and Chatfield, this volume). When they do break, large pot fragments are inconvenient for cultivation and would probably be cleared. Many large sherds may also be reused for other purposes. We may therefore expect to find only the most breakable parts of transport vessels, such as lugs and necks, in fields.

In contrast, drinking vessels are generally made of finer paste with thinner walls that are more delicate and subject to breakage (see, e.g., Anderson, this volume; D'Altroy 1992; Goldstein 2005) and may even be ritually consumed by breaking them. Fragments of serving vessels do not generally hinder cultivation and serve little useful purpose and so are generally left in situ. The recovery of assemblages of kero and urpus vessels would suggest chicha consumption in fields that could be differentiated from other assemblages and further analyzed for insight into context.

In addition to mapping field systems and surface collection, more intensive study through excavation can recover buried artifacts or, as this researcher once found in Marcacocha, Peru, buried terraces covered intentionally or by erosion. Excavation also provides an opportunity to collect samples for paleoethnobotany, which may be used to identify crops associated with specific fields, and geoarchaeology to reconstruct the sediment history of the field (see Goodman-Elgar 2003, 2008).

Conclusion

In this chapter, I have suggested that roles for terraced fields lie beyond simple food production. Particular fields may be designated loci for ceremonial events involving the consumption of ritual chicha that are used to demonstrate power with significance equal to the activities recovered from materials found in public spaces or elite residences. This discussion provides a framework for the identification of fields as loci for social relations, which may demonstrate political hegemony, religious ideology, class, and gender relations. The Inca did not leave to chance the symbolic power associated with the control of productive land and its socially potent products, such as maize. They created places where such power could be dramatized, manipulated, and controlled under their own authority. This outlook presents an opportunity for the further development of landscape approaches in the Andes through focused fieldwork in field systems, which will provide a more nuanced appreciation of pre-Columbian behavior. In the Andean region, agricultural terraces are built environments that not only support cultivation but may also represent the power to placate deities, control land and labor, and reinforce a stratified social order.

Notes

1. Many thanks to Brenda Bowser and Justin Jennings for inviting me to participate in this volume and for their editorial guidance. I am also grateful to Emily Dean and Todd Butler for comments on a now-distant version and to Richard Elgar and Kathy Bork for their editorial improvements. Remaining errors are mine

2. Harawayu, harawayu,/Créame, maíz mágico./Si no lo haces, te arrancaré/Madre mágica, ¡Reina! (Guaman Poma 1987 chap. 11: 246 [244]; all translations are mine unless otherwise noted).

3. From Garcilaso de la Vega 1963, vol. 2, bk. 5, chap. 2: 151,

Dentro en la ciudad del Cozco, a las faldas del cerro donde está la fortaleza, había un andén grande de muchas hanegas de tierra . . . llámase *Collcampata*. El barrio donde está tomó el nombre propio del andén, el cual era particular y principal del sol, porque fué la primera que en todo el imperio de los Incas le dedicaron. Este andén labraban y beneficiaban los de la sangre real, y no podían trabajar otros en él sino los Incas y Pallas. Hacíase con grandísima fiesta, principalmente el barbechar; iban los Incas con todas sus mayores galas y arreos. Los cantares que decían en loor del sol y sus reyes, todos eran compuestos sobre la significación de esta palabra *haylli* que en la lengua general del Perú quiere decir triunfo, como que triunfaban de la tierra barbechándola y desentrañándola, para que diese fruto. En estos cantares entremetían dichos graciosos de enamorados discretos y de soldados valientes, todo a propósito de triunfar de la tierra que labraban; y así el retruécano de todas sus coplas era la palabra *haylli*, repetida muchas veces cuantas eran menester parar cumplir el compás que los indios traen en cierto contrapaso que hacen barbechando la tierra, con entradas y salidas que hacen para tomar vuelo y romperla mejor. . . . Andan en cuadrillas de siete en siete y de ocho en ocho, más o menos como es la parentela o camarada, y apalancando todos juntos a una levantan grandísimos céspedes, increíbles a quien no los ha visto. . . . Las mujeres andan contrapuestas a los varones, para ayudar con las manos a levantar los céspedes y volcar las raíces de las yerbas arriba, para que se sequen y mueran y haya menos que escardar. Ayudan también a cantar a sus maridos, particularmente con el retruécano *haylli*.

4. En el noveno mes . . . hacían una fiesta llamada guayara, pidiendo en ella bueno y abundante año . . . se sembraban la *chácara* de *Sausero* la cual sementera hacían con mucha solemnidad; porque esta *chácara* era del sol, y lo que se cogía della era para los sacrificios ordinarios . . . y en tanto que se sembraba, estaba en medio della un carnero blanco con sus orejeras de oro, y con él cantidad de indios y *mamacuna* del sol, derramando mucha *chicha* en el nombre de dicho carnero. Ya que se iba acabando la sementera, traían de todas las provincias mil *cuíes*, como cabía a cada una, conforme el repartimiento que estaba hecho, y con gran solemnidad los degollaban y quemaban todos en esta *chácara*, excepto cierto número dellos, que en nombre del sol se repartían por las *guacas* y adoratorios de la ciudad. Dirigían este sacrificio al hielo, al aire, al agua y al sol a todo aquello que les parecía a ellos que tenía poder de criar y ofender los sembrados.

5.
Acudían los pueblos y cultivarlas desta manera: que si acaso el mismo Inca se hallaba presente o su gobernador, o otro cualquiera señor principal, era el primero que ponía mano en labor con una *tacla*, o arado, de oro, que para ello llevaban al Inca, y por ejemplo hacían lo mismo todos los señores y caballeros que le acompañaban; mas, dejábalo luego el Inca, y tras él lo iban dejando otros señores y principales; y se asentaban con el rey a hacer sus banquetes y fiestas, que en aquellos eran muy solemnes. Quedaba en el trabajo la gente común, y con ella solos los *curacas-pachacas*, que trabajaban un rato más que los nobles; y después entendían en asistir al trabajo, mandando lo que convenía.

6. A transcript of Polo's original text is not available.

7. Agosto, Chacra Yapuy Quilla [mes de romper tierras]: En este mes sacrificauan en los ýdolos, *uacas*, pobres deste rreyno con lo que podían, con *cuuies* y *mullo* y *zanco* y chicha y carneros.

References Cited

Adorno, Rolena

2000 [1988] *Guaman Poma: Writing and Resistance in Colonial Peru*. 2nd edition. Austin: University of Texas Press.

Alberti, Giorgio, and Enrique Mayer (eds.)

1974 *Reciprocidad e intercambio en los Andes peruanos*. Lima: Instituto de Estudios Peruanos.

Allen, Catherine J.

1988 *The Hold Life Has: Coca and Cultural Identity in an Andean Community*. Washington, D.C.: Smithsonian Institution Press.

Arnold, Dean E.

1993 *Ecology and Ceramic Production in an Andean Community*. New York: Cambridge University Press.

Arriaga, Fray Pablo José

1968 [1621] *Extirpación de la idolatría del Perú*. Biblioteca de Autores Españoles. Madrid: Ediciones Atlas.

Ashmore, Wendy, and A. Bernard Knapp (eds.)

1999 *Archaeologies of Landscape: Contemporary Perspectives*. Malden: Blackwell.

Aveni, Anthony

2000 *Between the Lines: The Mystery of the Giant Ground Drawings of Ancient Nasca, Peru*. Austin: University of Texas Press.

Barratt, John

1994 *Fragments from Antiquity*. New York: Routledge.

2001 Agency, the Duality of Structure, and the Problem of the Archaeological Record. In *Archaeological Theory Today*, Ian Hodder, ed., pp. 141–164. Malden: Polity.

Bastien, Joseph W.

1978 *Mountain of the Condor: Metaphor and Ritual in an Andean Ayllu*. Monograph 64. Washington, D.C.: American Ethnological Society.

Bauer, Brian S.

1996 Legitimization of the State in Inca Myth and Ritual. *American Anthropologist* 98(2): 327–337.

1998 *The Sacred Landscape of the Inca: The Cusco Ceque System*. Austin: University of Texas Press.

Bauer, Brian S., and Charles Stanish

2001 *Ritual and Pilgrimage in the Ancient Andes: The Islands of the Sun and the Moon*. Austin: University of Texas Press.

2004 *Ancient Cuzco: Heartland of the Inca*. Austin: University of Texas Press.

Bender, Barbara (ed.)

1993 *Landscape: Politics and Perspectives*. New York: Berg.

1998 *Stonehenge: Making Space*. Oxford: Berg.

2002 Time and Landscape. *Current Anthropology* 43: 103–112.

Bolin, Inge

1998 *Rituals of Respect: The Secret of Survival in the High Peruvian Andes.* Austin: University of Texas Press.

Bradley, Richard

1998 *The Significance of Monuments.* London: Routledge.

2000 *An Archaeology of Natural Places.* New York: Routledge.

Bray, Tamara L.

2003a Inka Pottery as Culinary Equipment: Food, Feasting, and Gender in Imperial State Design. *Latin American Antiquity* 14: 3–28.

2003b To Dine Splendidly: Imperial Pottery, Commensal Politics, and the Inca State. In *The Archaeology and Politics of Food and Feasting in Early States and Empires*, Tamara L. Bray, ed., pp. 93–142. New York: Kluwer Academic/Plenum.

Bray, Tamara L. (ed.)

2003c *The Archaeology and Politics of Food and Feasting in Early States and Empires.* New York: Kluwer Academic/Plenum.

Brück, Joanna, and Melissa Goodman (Elgar)

1999 Introduction: Themes for a Critical Archaeology of Prehistoric Settlement. In *Making Places in the Prehistoric World*, J. Brück and M. Goodman (Elgar), eds., pp. 1–19. New York: Routledge.

Carmichael, David L., Jane Hubert, Brian Reeves, Audhild Schanche (eds.)

1994 *Sacred Sites, Sacred Places.* New York: Routledge.

Carrasco, David (ed.)

1991 *Aztec Ceremonial Landscapes.* Niwot: University Press of Colorado.

Castro Pozo, H.

1946 Social and Economico-political Evolution of the Communities of Central Peru. In *Handbook of South American Indians*, vol. 2: *Andean Civilizations.* Julian H. Steward, ed., pp. 483–500. Washington, D.C.: Smithsonian Institution Bureau of American Ethnology Bulletin 143.

Cerrón-Palomino, Rodolfo

2004 Las etimologías toponímicas del Inca Garcilaso. *Revista Andina* 38: 9–64.

Cieza de Léon, Pedro de

2001 [1553] *Descubrimiento y conquista del Perú.* Translated by Carmelo Sáenz de Santa María. Crónicas de América 18. Madrid: Dastin.

Cobo, Bernabé

1961 [1653] *History of the New World.* Vol. 4. Edited by Marcos Jiménez de la Espada. Translated by Ariane Brunel. Seville: Sociedad de Bibiófilos Andaluces.

1964 [1653] *Obras.* Vols. 1 and 2. Edited by P. Francisco Mateos. Madrid: Ediciones Atlas.

1979 [1653] *History of the Inca Empire: An Account of the Indians' Customs and Their Origin Together with a Treatise on Inca Legends, History, and Social Institutions.* Edited and translated by Roland Hamilton. Austin: University of Texas Press.

1990 *Inca Religion and Customs.* Edited and translated by Roland Hamilton. Austin: University of Texas Press.

Cook, Anita, and Mark Glowacki
2003 Pots, Politics and Power: Huari Ceramic Assemblages and Imperial Administration. In *The Archaeology and Politics of Food and Feasting in Early States
and Empires*, Tamara L. Bray, ed., pp. 173–202. New York: Kluwer Academic/
Plenum.
Cooney, Gabriel
1994 Sacred and Secular Neolithic Landscapes in Ireland. In *Sacred Sites, Sacred
Places*, David L. Carmichael, Jane Hubert, Brian Reeves, and Audhild Schanche,
eds., pp. 32–43. New York: Routledge.
Cutler, Hugh, and Martín Cárdenas
1947 Chicha, a Native South American Beer. *Botanical Museum Leaflets* (Harvard
University) 13(3): 33–60.
D'Altroy, Terence N.
1992 *Provincial Power in the Inka Empire*. Washington, D.C.: Smithsonian Institution Press.
2002 *The Incas*. Oxford: Blackwell.
D'Altroy, Terence N., and Timothy K. Earle
1985 Staple Finance, Wealth Finance, and Storage in the Inka Political Economy. *Current Anthropology* 26(2): 187–206.
Demarrais, Elizabeth, Luis Jaime Castillo, and Timothy Earle
1996 Ideology, Materialization, and Power Strategies. *Current Anthropology* 37:
15–31.
Denevan, William H.
2001 *Cultivated Landscapes of Native Amazonia and the Andes*. New York: Oxford
University Press.
Dick, Richard P., Jonathan A. Sandor, and Neil S. Eash
1994 Soil Enzyme Activities after 1500 Years of Terrace Agriculture in the Colca Val-
ley, Peru. *Agriculture, Ecosystems and Environment* 50: 123–131.
Dietler, Michael
1996 Feasts and Commensal Politics in the Political Economy: Food, Status, and
Power in Prehistoric Europe. In *Food and the Status Quest*, Polly Wiessner and
Wulf Shiefenhovel, eds., pp. 87–126. Providence: Berghahn Books.
Dietler, Michael, and Brian Hayden (eds.)
2001 *Feasts: Archaeological and Ethnographic Perspectives on Food, Politics, and
Power*. Washington, D.C.: Smithsonian Institution Press.
Donkin, Rubin A.
1979 *Agricultural Terracing in the Aboriginal New World*. Tucson: University of Ari-
zona Press for the Wenner-Gren Foundation for Anthropological Research.
Doolittle, William E.
1984 Agricultural Change as an Incremental Process. *Annals of the Association of
American Geographers* 74(1): 124–137.
Dunnell, Robert C.
1992 The Notion Site. In *Space, Time, and Archaeological Landscapes*, Jacqueline
Rossignol and LuAnn Wandsnider, eds., pp. 21–41. New York: Plenum.

Dunnell, Robert C., and William S. Dancey
1983 The Siteless Survey: A Regional Scale Data Collection Survey. *Advances in Ar-chaeological Method and Theory* 6: 267–287.

Earle, Timothy
1991a The Evolution of Chiefdoms. In *Chiefdoms: Power, Economy, and Ideology*, Timothy Earle, ed., pp. 1–15. New York: Cambridge University Press.
1991b Property Rights and the Evolution of Chiefdoms. In *Chiefdoms: Power, Econ-omy, and Ideology*, Timothy Earle, ed., pp. 71–99. New York: Cambridge Uni-versity Press.
2000 Archaeology, Property, and Prehistory. *Annual Review of Anthropology* 29: 39–60.

Ebert, James I.
1992 *Distributional Archaeology*. Albuquerque: University of New Mexico Press.

Edmonds, Mark
1999 *Ancestral Geographies of the Neolithic: Landscapes, Monuments and Memories*. London: Routledge.

Eliade, Mircea
1957 *The Sacred and the Profane: The Nature of Religion*. London: Harcourt, Brace, Jovanovich.

Erickson, Clark L.
1985 Application of Prehistoric Andean Technology: Experiments in Raised Field Agriculture, Huatta, Lake Titicaca 1981–82. In *Prehistoric Intensive Agriculture in the Tropics*, Ian Farrington, ed., pp. 209–232. BAR International Series 232. Oxford: British Archaeological Reports.
1993 The Social Organization of Prehispanic Raised Field Agriculture in the Lake Titicaca Basin. *Research in Economic Anthropology*, Supplement 7: 369–426.

Farrington, Ian S.
1992 Ritual Geography, Settlement Patterns and the Characterization of the Prov-inces of the Inka Heartland. *World Archaeology* 23(3): 368–385.

Fink, Rita
2001 La cosmología en el dibujo del Altar del Quri Kancha según don Joan de Santa Cruz Pachacuti Yamqui Salca Maygua. *Histórica* (Revista del Departamento de Humanidades, Pontifica Universidad Católica del Perú) 25(1): 9–75.

Foley, Robert A.
1981 Off-Site Archaeology: An Alternative Approach for the Short-Sited. In *Pat-tern of the Past: Essays in Honour of David Clarke*, Ian Hodder, Glynn Isaac, and Norman Hammond, eds., pp. 152–184. New York: Cambridge University Press.

Fuller, Dorian Q.
2005 Ceramics, Seeds and Culinary Change in Prehistoric India. *Antiquity* 79(306): 761–777.

Garcilaso de la Vega, El Inca
1963 [1609] *Obras completas del Inca Garcilaso de la Vega*. Vols. 1–3. Edited by P. Carmelo Sáenz de Santa Marica. Madrid: Ediciones Atlas.

1966 [1609] *Royal Commentaries of the Incas*, Part I. Translated by H. V. Livermore. Austin: University of Texas Press.

Gasparini, Graziano, and Luise Margolies

1980 *Inca Architecture*. Translated by Patricia L. Lyon. Bloomington: Indiana University Press.

Gell, Alfred

1992 *The Anthropology of Time: Cultural Construction of Temporal Maps and Images*. Providence: Berg.

Goldstein, Paul

2003 From Stew-Eaters to Maize-Drinkers: The Chicha Economy and the Tiwanaku Expansion. In *The Archaeology and Politics of Food and Feasting in Early States and Empires*, Tamara L. Bray, ed., pp. 143–172. New York: Kluwer Academic/Plenum.

2005 *Andean Diaspora: The Tiwanaku Colonies and the Origins of South American Empire*. Gainesville: University Press of Florida.

Goodman-Elgar, Melissa

2003 Anthropogenic Landscapes in the Andes: A Multidisciplinary Approach to Pre-Columbian Agricultural Terraces and Their Sustainable Use. Doctoral dissertation, Cambridge University.

2008 Evaluating Pre-Columbian Terraces as a Salient Strategy for Long-term Cultivation. *Journal of Archaeological Science* 35: 3072–3086.

Gose, Peter

1994 *Deathly Waters and Hungry Mountains: Agrarian Ritual and Class Formation in an Andean Town*. London: University of Toronto Press.

Guaman Poma de Ayala, Felipe

1987 [1584–1615] *El primer nueva crónica y buen gobierno*. Vols. A, B, C. Edited by John V. Murra, Rolena Adorno, and Jorge Urioste. Crónicas de América no. 29. Madrid: Historia 16.

Guillet, David

1987 Terracing and Irrigation in the Peruvian Highlands. *Current Anthropology* 28(4): 409–430.

Gumerman, George, IV

1997 Food and Complex Societies. *Journal of Archaeological Method and Theory* 4(2): 105–139.

Hastorf, Christine A.

1990 The Effect of the Inka State on Sausa Agricultural Production and Crop Consumption. *American Antiquity* 55(2): 262–290.

1993 *Agriculture and the Onset of Political Inequality before the Inka*. New York: Cambridge University Press.

Hastorf, Christine A., and Sissel Johannessen

1993 Pre-Hispanic Political Change and the Role of Maize in the Central Andes of Peru. *American Anthropologist* 95(1): 115–138.

Hodder, Ian

1991 *The Domestication of Europe: Structure and Contingency in Neolithic Societies.* Cambridge: Basil Blackwell.

Hyslop, John

1990 *Inca Settlement Planning.* Austin: University of Texas Press.

Isbell, Billie Jean

1978 *To Defend Ourselves: Ecology and Ritual in an Andean Village.* Prospect Heights: Waveland Press.

Isbell, William H.

1997 *Mummies and Mortuary Monuments: A Postprocessual Prehistory of Central Andean Social Organization.* Austin: University of Texas Press.

Jákfalvi-Leiva, Susana

1984 *Traducción, escritura y violencia colonizadora: Un estudio de la obra del Inca Garcilaso.* Foreign and Comparative Studies/Latin American Series no. 7. Syracuse: Maxwell School of Citizenship and Public Affairs.

Jennings, Justin

2003a Inca Imperialism, Ritual Change, and Cosmological Continuity in the Cotahuasi Valley of Peru. *Journal of Anthropological Research* 59(4): 433–462.

2003b The Fragility of Imperialist Ideology and the End of Local Traditions, an Inca Example. *Cambridge Archaeological Journal* 13(1): 107–120.

2005 La Chichera y el Patrón: Chicha and the Energetics of Feasting in the Prehistoric Andes. In *Foundations of Power in the Prehispanic Andes*, Christina A. Conlee, Dennis Ogburn, and Kevin Vaughn, eds., pp. 241–260. Archaeological Publications of the American Anthropological Association, vol. 14. Washington, D.C.: American Anthropological Association.

Jennings, Justin, Kathy L. Antrobus, Sam J. Atencio, Erin Glavich, Rebecca Johnson, German Loffler, and Christine Luu

2005 "Drinking Beer in a Blissful Mood": Alcohol Production, Operational Chains and Feasting in the Ancient World. *Current Anthropology* 46(2): 275–303.

Julien, Catherine

2000 *Reading Inca History.* Iowa City: University of Iowa Press.

Keeley, Helen C. M.

1985 Soils of Prehispanic Terrace Systems in the Cusichaca Valley, Peru. In *Prehistoric Intensive Agriculture in the Tropics*, Ian A. Farrington, ed., pp. 547–568. British Archaeological Reports International Series 232, vol. 2. Oxford: British Archaeological Reports.

Kendall, Ann

1985 *Aspects of Inca Architecture: Description, Function, and Chronology.* 2 vols. BAR International Series 242. Oxford: British Archaeological Reports.

Koontz, Rex, Kathryn Reese-Taylor, and Annabeth Headrick

2001 *Landscape and Power in Ancient Mesoamerica.* Boulder: Westview.

LeVine, Terry (ed.)

1992 *Inka Storage Systems*. Norman: University of Oklahoma Press.

Lyman, R. Lee, and Michael J. O'Brien

2001 The Direct Historical Approach, Analogical Reasoning, and Theory in Americanist Archaeology. *Journal of Archaeological Method and Theory* 8(4): 303–342.

Maxwell, Thomas J., Jr.

1956 Agricultural Ceremonies of the Central Andes during Four Hundred Years of Spanish Contact. *Ethnohistory* 3(1): 46–71.

Mayer, Enrique

1981 *A Tribute to the Household: Domestic Economy and the Encomienda in Colonial Peru*. Austin: Institute of Latin American Studies, University of Texas at Austin.

McEwan, Colin, and Maarten van de Guchte

1992 Ancestral Time and Sacred Space in Inca State Religion. In *The Ancient Americas: Art from Sacred Landscapes*, Richard F. Townsend, ed., pp. 358–371. Chicago: Art Institute of Chicago.

Mitchell, W. J. Thomas (ed.)

1994 *Landscape and Power*. Chicago: University of Chicago Press.

Molina, Cristoval (Cristóbal) de (Molina de Cuzco)

1964 [c. 1570–1584] An Account of the Fables and Rites of the Inkas. In *Narratives of the Rites and Laws of the Yncas*, Clements R. Markham, ed. and trans., pp. 4–65. Hakluyt Society, First Series, no. 48. New York: B. Franklin.

Molina, Cristóbal de (El Almagrista)

1968 [1553] Relación de muchas cosas acaecidas en el Perú. In *Crónicas peruanas de interés indígena*, Francisco Esteve Barba, ed., pp. 56–95. Madrid: Ediciones Atlas.

Moore, Jerry D.

1989 Pre-Hispanic Beer in Coastal Peru: Technology and Social Context of Prehistoric Production. *American Anthropologist* 91: 682–695.

1996 *Architecture and Power in the Ancient Andes*. New York: Cambridge University Press.

2004 The Social Basis of Sacred Spaces in the Prehispanic Andes: Ritual Landscapes of the Dead in Chimú and Inka Societies. *Journal of Archaeological Method and Theory* 11(1): 83–124.

2005 *Cultural Landscapes in the Ancient Andes: Archaeologies of Place*. Gainesville: University Press of Florida.

Moore, Sally F.

1958 *Power and Property in Inca Peru*. Morningside Heights: Columbia University Press.

Morris, Craig, and Donald E. Thompson

1985 *Huánuco Pampa: An Inca City and Its Hinterland*. New York: Thames and Hudson.

Murra, John V.

1960 Rite and Crop in the Inca State. In *Culture in History: Essays in Honor of Paul Radin*, Stanley Diamond, ed., pp. 393–407. New York: Columbia University Press.

1980 [1956] *The Economic Organization of the Inka State*. Greenwich: JAI Press.

Murúa, Fray Martín de

2001 [1611] *Historia general del Perú*. Edited by Manuel Ballesteros Gaibrois. Madrid: Dastein.

Niles, Susan

1987 *Style and Status in an Inca Community*. Iowa City: University of Iowa Press.

1992 Inca Architecture and the Sacred Landscape. In *The Ancient Americas: Art from Sacred Landscapes*, Richard F. Townsend, ed., pp. 346–357. Chicago: Art Institute of Chicago.

Ogburn, Dennis

2006 Assessing the Level of Visibility of Cultural Objects in Past Landscapes. *Journal of Archaeological Science* 33(3): 405–413.

Orlove, Benjamin

1979 Two Rituals and Three Hypotheses: An Examination of Solstice Divination in Southern Highland Peru. *Anthropological Quarterly* 52(2): 86–98.

Orlove, Benjamin, John Chiang, and Mark Cane

2000 Forecasting Andean Rainfall and Crop Yield from the Influence of El Niño on Pleiades Visibility. *Nature* 403: 68–71.

2002 Ethnoclimatology in the Andes: A Cross-disciplinary Study Uncovers a Scientific Basis for the Scheme Andean Potato Farmers Traditionally Use to Predict the Coming Rains. *American Scientist* 90(5): 428–435.

Pollard, Josh, and Andrew Reynolds

2002 *Avebury: The Biography of a Landscape*. Charleston: Tempus.

Polo de Ondegardo, Juan

1987 [1575] *Information Concerning the Religion and Government of the Incas*. Edited and translated by Horacio Carlos Romero, Alberto Hoyo, Juan Josef del Ariane Brunel, and John Murra. Sydney: Muerden.

Porras Barrenechea, Raúl

1962 *Cronistas del Perú*. Lima: Sanmartí.

Protzen, Jean-Pierre

1993 *Inca Architecture and Construction at Ollantaytambo*. New York: Oxford University Press.

Ramírez, Susan Elizabeth

2005 *To Feed and Be Fed: The Cosmological Bases of Authority and Identity in the Andes*. Stanford: Stanford University Press.

Renfrew, Colin

2001 Symbol before Concept: Material Engagement and the Early Development of Society. In *Archaeological Theory Today*, Ian Hodder, ed., pp. 122–140. Malden: Blackwell.

Rostworowski de Diez Canseco, María

1999 *History of the Inca Realm.* New York: Cambridge University Press.

Rowe, John H.

1946 Inca Culture at the Time of the Spanish Conquest. In *Handbook of South American Indians*, vol. 2: *Andean Civilizations*, Julian H. Steward, ed., pp. 183–330. Washington, D.C.: Smithsonian Institution Bureau of American Ethnology Bulletin 143.

1990 Foreword. In *Inca Religion and Customs*, by Bernabé Cobo, pp. vii–ix. Austin: University of Texas Press.

Salomon, Frank

1995 "The Beautiful Grandparents": Andean Ancestor Shrines and Mortuary Ritual as Seen through Colonial Records. In *Tombs for the Living: Andean Mortuary Practices*, Tom D. Dillehay, ed., pp. 315–354. Washington, D.C.: Dumbarton Oaks.

Seltzer, Geoffrey O., and Christine A. Hastorf

1990 Climatic Change and Its Effects on Prehispanic Agriculture in the Central Peruvian Andes. *Journal of Field Archaeology* 17: 397–414.

Sillar, Bill

2000 *Shaping Culture: Making Pots and Constructing Households: An Ethnoarchaeological Study of Pottery Production, Trade and Use in the Andes.* BAR International Series 883. Oxford: British Archaeological Reports.

Silverblatt, Irene M.

1987 *Moon, Sun, and Witches: Gender Ideologies and Class in Inca and Colonial Peru.* Princeton: Princeton University Press.

1988 Imperial Dilemmas, the Politics of Kinship, and Inca Reconstructions of History. *Comparative Studies in Society and History* 30(1): 83–102.

Silverman, Helaine

1994 The Archaeological Identification of an Ancient Peruvian Pilgrimage Center. *World Archaeology* 26(1): 1–18.

Smith, Adam T.

2003 *The Political Landscape: Constellations of Authority in Early Complex Polities.* Berkeley & Los Angeles: University of California Press.

Squier, Ephraim George

1877 *Peru: Incidents of Travel and Exploration in the Land of the Incas.* New York: Harper Brothers.

Thomas, Julian

1993 The Hermeneutics of Megalithic Space. In *Interpretive Archaeology*, Christopher Tilley, ed., pp. 73–97. Oxford: Berg.

1996 *Time, Culture and Identity: An Interpretive Archaeology.* New York: Routledge.

Treacy, John

1994 *Las chacras de Coporaque: Andenería y riego en el valle del Colca.* Lima: Instituto de Estudios Peruanos.

Treacy, John, and William Denevan
1994 The Creation of Cultivable Land through Terracing. In *The Archaeology of Garden and Field*, Naomi F. Miller and Kathryn L. Gleason, eds., pp. 91–110. Philadelphia: University of Pennsylvania Press.

Urton, Gary
1981 *At the Crossroads of the Earth and the Sky: An Andean Cosmology*. Austin: University of Texas Press.
1982 Astronomy and Calendrics on the Coast of Peru. In *Ethnoastronomy and Archaeoastronomy in the American Tropics*, Anthony F. Aveni and Gary Urton, eds., pp. 231–247. New York: New York Academy of Sciences.

van de Guchte, Maartin
1999 The Inca Cognition of Landscape: Archaeology, Ethnohistory, and the Aesthetic of Alterity. In *Archaeologies of Landscape: Contemporary Perspectives*, Wendy Ashmore and A. Bernard Knapp, eds., pp. 149–68. Malden: Blackwell.

Zapata, Roger A.
1989 *Guaman Poma, indigenismo y estética de la dependencia en la cultura peruana*. Minneapolis: Institute for the Study of Ideologies and Literatures.

Zuidema, R. Tom
1964 *The Ceque System of Cusco: The Social Organization of the Capital of the Inca*. Leiden: Brill.
1982 Catachillay: The Role of the Pleiades and of the Southern Cross and "d" and ß Centauri in the Calendar of the Incas. In *Ethnoastronomy and Archaeoastronomy in the American Tropics*, Anthony F. Aveni and Gary Urton, eds., pp. 203–229. New York: New York Academy of Sciences.
1986 The Place of Chamay Wariqsa in the Rituals of Cuzco. *Amerindia* 11: 58–67.

5

The Role of *Chicha* in Inca State Expansion

A Distributional Study of Inca *Aríbalos*

Tamara L. Bray

The Inca were the architects of the largest empire ever created in the Americas. During the fifteenth century AD, through a skillful combination of force and inducement, they became the unrivalled masters of the Andean world. At the height of their power, the long arm of Inca control stretched 2,600 miles along the mountainous spine of South America, from northern Ecuador to central Chile, encompassing at least eighty distinct ethnic provinces. Throughout this realm, one finds the broken bits of richly decorated polychrome vessels that mark the influence, if not the presence, of the imperial masters. The degree of standardization and the ubiquity of these state-produced wares hint at their importance to the imperial project.

A basic premise of this study is that imperial Inca pottery, the "fine china" of the Inca state, as well as the foodstuffs served from it, played a key role in the negotiation of political authority and the territorial expansion of the state. In this chapter, I focus on the functional, contextual, and iconographic significance of one vessel in particular: the classic Inca jar commonly known as the aríbalo. The most widely recognized and characteristic of Inca vessel forms, the aríbalo is a tall-necked jar with a high, pronounced shoulder and a conical base (Fig. 5.1). Scholars are in general agreement that this vessel served as a container for chicha de maíz, the ubiquitous corn beer of the Andes (e.g., Bray 2000, 2003a; D'Altroy 2001; Morris 1982). This interpretation is supported by various morphological characteristics, including the tall neck and restricted vessel orifice, which emphasize containment of contents, and the flared rim and conical base, which would facilitate the pouring of liquids. Recent residue analyses offer further confirmation of the posited association of this vessel with chicha de maíz (Gibaja 2004: 178; R. Thompson, personal communication, 2002).

Figure 5.1. Classic Inca *aríbalo* (from Pachacamac; in collection of the University of Pennsylvania Museum of Archaeology and Anthropology, cat. no. 34431). Photo by the author.

This chapter offers a comparative study of the distribution of aríbalos from different sectors of Tawantinsuyu. In it, I focus on vessel size, frequencies, and contexts of finds for the purpose of exploring how chicha figured in the imperial agenda through time and across space. The frequency data presented here are assembled primarily from archaeological reports, while the metric data derive from a long-term study of complete Inca vessels housed in repositories across North and South America (Bray n.d.). These two data sets complement one another insofar as archaeological specimens are rarely found whole and hence do not afford the possibility of detailed metric analysis, while the complete museum specimens often, though not always, lack precise provenience information. The metric data presented here indicate that the Inca aríbalo exhibits an extreme degree of standardization in terms of both morphology and proportionality, a finding that allows for the calculation of effective vessel volume from rim diameter. The data on the distribution of aríbalos, discussed here in terms of both context and geography, provide new insights into the political strategies of the imperial Inca state.[1]

Chicha and the Inca State

In the Andean context, the importance of reciprocity and hospitality as key components of Inca statecraft was first discussed by John Murra (1980 [1956]). The labor services owed the state by local communities, which could range from cultivating fields to massive public-works projects, were typically couched in terms of the reciprocal obligations created through chiefly generosity. An important aspect of reciprocal labor obligations in the Andes was the understanding that the work party would be fully provisioned by the sponsor with the necessary raw materials, tools, food, and drink (Murra 1980: 97, 121–134).

Within this framework, chicha played a key role in the workings of the Inca state (Murra 1960). As various sixteenth-century chroniclers attest, though food was important at state-sponsored feasting events, the main concern centered on the serving and drinking of large amounts of corn beer. The early written accounts seem to be borne out archaeologically at Inca state administrative centers like Huánuco Pampa where immense quantities of imperial Inca jar and plate fragments, suggesting large-scale chicha and food serving activities, have been found in structures associated with the main plaza (Morris 1979; Morris and Thompson 1985: 83–91).

Corn was, by far, the most highly esteemed crop in the pre-Columbian Andes, and one of its most important uses was for the production of chicha (Murra 1960). Besides being the daily beverage of the local populace, chicha was also an indispensable element in social and ceremonial gatherings, where ritual drunkenness was often obligatory (see Allen, this volume; Jennings and Chatfield, this volume). The manufacture of chicha was one of the most elaborated culinary tasks in Andean cuisine (Bray 2003b: 143–144). The production process required several weeks and involved numerous steps, including the grinding of dried maize kernels, chewing of the maize flour, soaking the mash, separating the constituent elements, boiling, fermentation, and subsequent decanting.

Native peoples reportedly had more accoutrements for making and storing chicha than for any other purpose. According to Cobo (1964: bk. 14, chap. 4: 242), Andean peoples used "clay jars, the largest being four and six arrobas,[2] as well as other smaller ones; . . . a large quantity of large and small jugs, and three or four types of cups and glasses" in the process (my translation). Chicha production was one of the fundamental culinary tasks of Andean women and was typically associated with the female domain (Gómez Huamán 1966: 35; Sachún Cedeño 2001; Silverblatt 1987: 39; Vokral 1991: 202).

Imperial Inca Ceramic Assemblage

The Inca state ceramic assemblage comprised a limited number of distinctive and highly standardized vessel forms. Through a collections-based study of Inca pottery from both archaeological contexts and museum repositories, I have developed a database that now contains over 3,000 records of individual vessels from throughout the empire. As part of the documentation process, I registered a variety of measurements on each vessel; made observations on manufacturing technique, paste, surface finish, decorative treatment, use wear; and recorded information on provenience, context, and collector. While the number of vessels documented is large and the sample, I believe, representative of the range of variation found within the imperial ceramic corpus, it cannot be considered random. As such, the use of significance tests is not technically justified, though I do make limited reference to the results of such tests to demonstrate that the perceived differences would be considered robust if the sample were random. Given the size of the data set, it offers an important basis for new observations and proposals for further investigation.

In categorizing the vessels included in the study, I follow the morphological classification system devised by Albert Meyers (1975), who divided the Inca corpus into seven formal classes comprising fourteen different vessel forms. The seven classes include (a) elongated, tall-necked jars (Form 1, the aríbalo); (b) flat-bottomed, narrow-necked vessels (Forms 2–5); (c) wide-necked vessels (Forms 6 and 7); (d) wide-mouthed pots (Forms 8 and 9); (e) pots with or without feet (Forms 10 and 11); (f) shallow plates and bowls (Forms 12 and 13); and (g) cups (Form 14) (see Bray 2003a). Sixty-three percent of the vessels in the above-mentioned database have site-level provenience information, while a good many more (94 percent) could at least be assigned to the sector (or *suyu*) of the empire from which they were recovered. Insofar as my primary interest in this study concerns the contexts of vessel use (rather than where they were produced), having a general idea of where the vessel was recovered is adequate for preliminary comparative purposes.[3] Table 5.1 provides a list of the better-known

Table 5.1. Archaeological Sites Included in Study

Suyu	Site name	Site type	Total vessels	Total *aríbalos*	Data source
Heartland	Cuzco	Capital	549	189	AMNH; INC-CM; Lehmann and Doering 1924; Matos 1999; Miller 2004; MI; Montez Coll., FMNH; NMNH; Pardo 1938, 1939, 1957; Uhle Coll., LM-UCB
Heartland	Sacsaywaman	Capital	125	34	Julien 2004; MI; Valencia 1975
Heartland	Tipón	Ceremonial center	6	0	MI
Heartland	Raqchi	Settlement	3	0	Pardo 1957
Heartland	Pisac	Royal estate	4	3	MI
Heartland	Ollantaytambo	Royal estate	89	15	Gibaja 2004; Llanos 1936
Heartland	Machu Picchu	Royal estate	242	68	Bingham 1915, 1979; Eaton 1916; Salazar & Burger 2004
Heartland	Chincheros	Royal estate	19	3	INC-C; Rivera Dorado 1976
Heartland	Choquepukio	Settlement	32	5	G. McEwan Coll., MI
Colla	Hatunqolla	Admin. center	3	2	Julien 1983; Tschopik 1946
Colla	Tiwanaku	Ceremonial center	12	2	Museo Tiwanaku, Bol.; NMAI
Colla	Isla del Sol	Ceremonial center	75	20	Bandelier Coll., AMNH
Colla	Copacabana	Ceremonial center	14	2	Casanova 1942; Reyniers 1966
Colla	Chucuito	Cemetery	7	3	Tschopik 1946
Colla	Incaray	Admin. center	4	4	Gyarmati & Vargas 1999
Colla	Sipe Sipe	Village	4	2	Gyarmati & Vargas 1999
Colla	Lerma	Pucara	3	1	Boman 1991
Colla	Tilcara	Pucara	2	1	Debenedetti 1917
Colla	Río Frío	Tambo	2	1	Lynch 1993
Colla	La Paya	Village	14	5	Ambrosetti 1907; Boman 1991
Colla	AZ-15	Village	4	1	Santoro and Muñoz Ovalle 1981
Colla	Chena	Pucara	19	5	Stehberg 1976
Colla	Nos	Cemetery	12	7	Stehberg 1976
Colla	La Reina	Cemetery	18	3	Mostny 1955
Colla	Catarpe	Admin. Center	2	1	Tarragó 1968
Colla	Llullaillaco	Capacocha	19	3	Catholic Univ., Salta, Arg.
Colla	Cerro Esmeraldas	Capacocha	18	2	Checura 1977
Chincha	Quito	Admin. center	17	12	Jijón y Caamaño & Larrea 1918; MJJC
Chincha	Caranqui	Admin. center	14	5	MBC-I
Chincha	El Quinche	Ceremonial center	4	2	MJJC
Chincha	Cochasquí	Village	2	2	Wentscher 1989
Chincha	Cumbayá	Cemetery	6	4	INPC-Q
Chincha	Rumicucho	Pucara	64	25	Almeida 1999; Almeida & Jara 1984; MBC-Q
Chincha	Latacunga	Settlement	11	7	MBC-Q; MJJC
Chincha	La Plata	Capacocha	9	2	Dorsey Coll., FMNH
Chincha	Guano	Village	28	6	JJC 1927; Saville Coll., NMAI
Chincha	Alacao	Cemetery	11	3	Miranda; Coll., MBC-Q; Jijón y Caamaño 1927
Chincha	Salinas-Tomevela	Settlement	19	14	Museo El Refugio Hotel, Salinas
Chincha	Pucara	Pucara	6	5	MBC-C
Chincha	Puyugata	Cemetery	11	3	Davies 1996

Suyu	Site name	Site type	Total vessels	Total *aríbalos*	Data source
Chincha	Mullubamba	Pucara	21	0	MBC-C
Chincha	Cerro Narrío	Cemetery	5	1	Collier & Murra 1943
Chincha	Hatún Cañar	Admin. center	18	9	MBC-C; MBC-Q; Verneau & Rivet 1912
Chincha	Tomebamba	Admin. center	119	11	MBC-C; Idrovo 2000
Chincha	Huánaco Pampa	Admin. center	2	2	Morris & Thompson 1985; Thompson 1968
Chincha	Huamachuco	Admin. center	2	2	LM-UCB
Chincha	Pachacamac	Ceremonial center	99	25	AMNH; FMNH; Uhle 1903; Uhle Coll., UPMAA
Conde	Tambo Viejo	Admin. center	9	1	Menzel & Riddell 1986
Conde	La Centinela	Admin. center	27	8	Uhle Coll., LM-UCB; Menzel 1966
Conde	Old Ica	Village	35	7	Uhle Coll., LM-UCB; Menzel 1971, 1976
Conde	Pichu Pichu	Capacocha	7	2	Linares Málaga 1966
Conde	Ampato Volcán	Capacocha	37	9	Reinhard Coll., MSA
Conde	Maucallacta	Settlement	26	6	Bauer 1990
Anti	Cochabamba	Admin. center	5	5	Schjellerup 1997

Notes: Museum repository abbreviations are as follows: AMNH, American Museum of Natural History, New York City; FMNH, Field Museum of Natural History, Chicago; INC-CM, Museo del Instituto Nacional de Cultura, Cuzco; INPC-Q, Instituto Nacional de Patrimonio Cultural, Quito; LM-UCB, Lowie Museum (now the Phoebe Hearst Museum), University of California, Berkeley; MBC-C, Museo del Banco Central, Cuenca; MBC-I, Museo del Banco Central, Ibarra; MBC-Q, Museo del Banco Central, Quito; MI, Museo Inka, Universidad de Cuzco; MJJC, Museo de Jijón y Caamaño, Quito; MSA, Museo Santuarios Andinos, Arequipa; NMAI, National Museum of the American Indian, Washington, D.C.; NMNH, National Museum of Natural History, Washington, D.C.; UPMAA, University of Pennsylvania Museum of Archaeology and Anthropology.

The data used in this study are based either on collections documentation research or taken from published reports. The sources used for each site are listed in the data source column. When a repository is listed, it indicates that I collected the data.

archaeological sites from which I have ceramic data, the total number of vessels from each, how I classified the site in terms of region and type, and the source of the information I used. Only items with secure provenience are included in the distributional analysis.

With regard to geographical organization, the Inca Empire was conceptualized by its originators as the Kingdom of the Four Quarters (Tawantinsuyu), with the capital city of Cuzco situated at the sacred and political center. The four quarters of the empire (the four suyus) were radically uneven from a geographic standpoint, and the Inca were well aware of this fact. The first zone to come under Inca control, and the sector that would eventually be extended the farthest, was Collasuyu. This sector, which lies

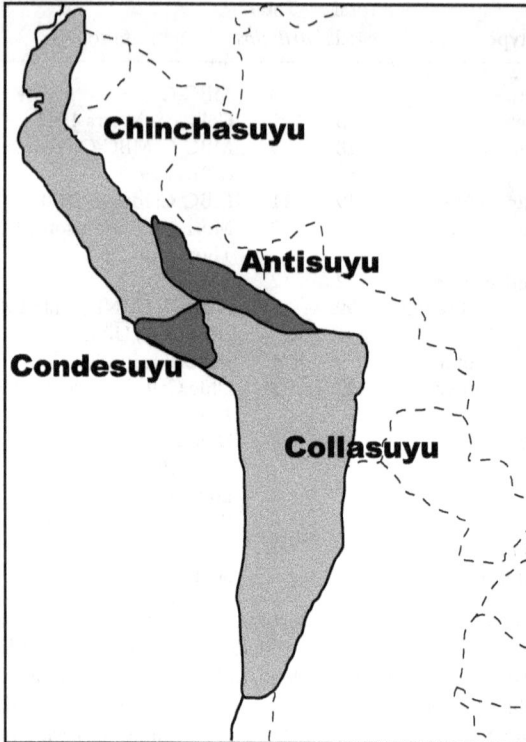

Figure 5.2. The four *suyus* of the Inca Empire. Drawing by Justin Jennings.

to the south of Cuzco, was centered on the Lake Titicaca basin. Its counter-weight to the north and west was Chinchasuyu, the most populous sector of the empire. To the north and east of Cuzco lay Antisuyu, the region comprising the tropical eastern flanks of the Andean massif. Its inclusion in the geography of the state was more a part of the imperial imaginary than a fact on the ground.[4] The smallest, and arguably least-prestigious quarter of the empire (see Zuidema 1964), was Condesuyu, comprising a wedge-shaped territory to the west of Cuzco that extended to the Pacific coast (Fig. 5.2).

The Inca Aríbalo

The hallmark vessel of the imperial assemblage, Meyers' Form 1, is the aríbalo. This vessel is readily recognizable on the basis of both formal and decorative attributes. The defining morphological features include the tall flared neck, the pierced "ears" on the underside of the rim, the zoomorphic lug on the upper front and center of the body, the vertical side-strap han-

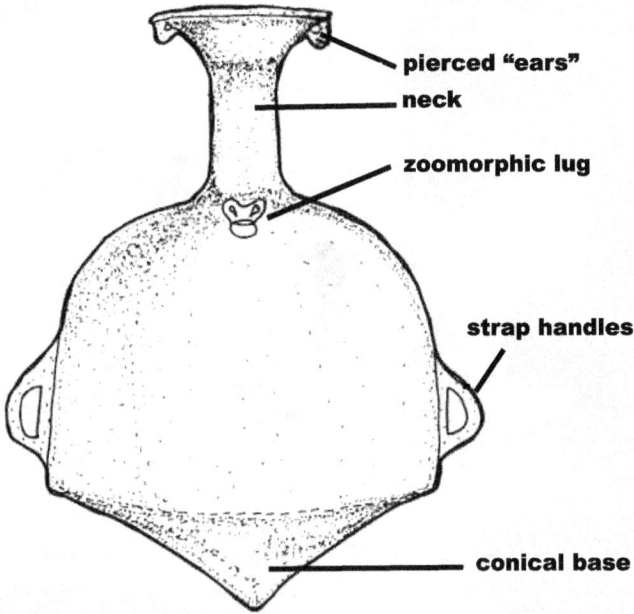

Figure 5.3. Diagnostic morphological elements of the *aríbalo*. Drawing by the author.

dles, and the conical base (Fig. 5.3). While these vessels vary considerably in terms of size and, to some extent, decorative treatment, these five morphological features seem to be necessarily present. Similarly, there appears to have been a fairly strict set of rules governing the type and placement of decorative embellishment on aríbalos. The primary design fields include the neck, the upper shoulder of the back side, and the front panel.

The disproportionate number of aríbalos found in the provinces vis-à-vis other Inca vessel forms suggests that state offerings of chicha may have been of greater importance in the outlying regions than in the core of the empire. Within the empirewide sample of Inca pottery included in this study (n = 3,063), aríbalos make up 39 percent of the total (n = 1,200), with the next most common vessel type, the shallow plate (Form 13), representing only half that number (n = 611). When the sample is divided into items from the imperial heartland versus the provincial districts (Fig. 5.4), aríbalos are notably less abundant as a percentage of the total assemblage in the heartland and more abundant in the provinces (37 percent and 44 percent, respectively, chi sq = 88.9, df = 12, p<0.01).

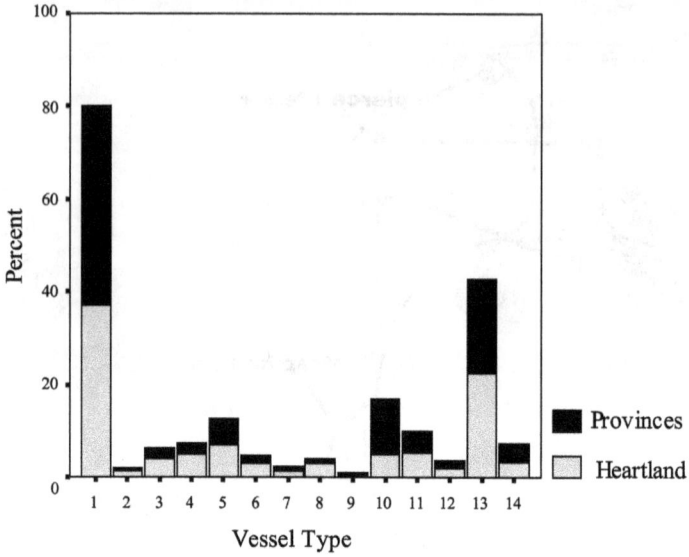

Figure 5.4. Distribution of Inca vessel forms in the composite assemblage, and the relative proportion of individual forms from heartland versus provincial districts.

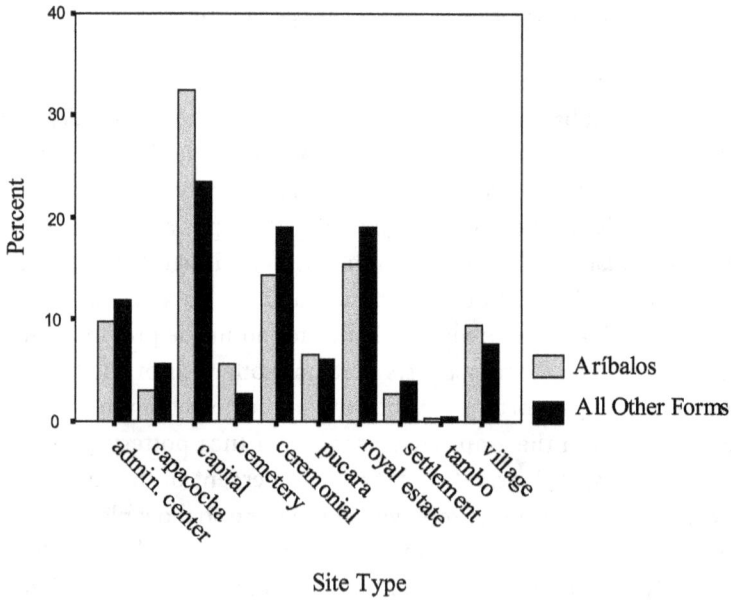

Figure 5.5. Relative percentages of *aríbalos* compared to all other Inca vessels by site type.

These data may reflect differences in the political exigencies of imperial statecraft in the heartland versus the provincial and frontier districts, as discussed further below.

It is also interesting to note that, at the imperial administrative centers, which in this study are best represented by Tomebamba, Hatun Cañar, Caranqui, Quito, Tambo Viejo, and La Centinela, aríbalos make up only about one-quarter of the total vessel assemblage at each site. This percentage is slightly below that found at other Inca site types (e.g., royal estates; hilltop fortresses, or *pucaras*; ceremonial centers; villages; and the capital) (Fig. 5.5). This finding would seem counterintuitive, given that the administrative centers were presumably the sites of state-sponsored feasting and drinking parties, where one would expect to find larger-than-normal quantities of chicha-serving vessels. Ideally, this observation would be checked against quantitative information on sherd assemblages from such well-investigated Inca administrative centers as Huánuco Pampa, Pumpu, and Hatún Xauxa, but such data are not currently available.

Vessel-size Classes

The Inca aríbalo exhibits a remarkable degree of standardization with regard to the proportional relations among the basic elements of vessel form, including diameter of the rim, neck height, total vessel height, and maximum vessel diameter. The relationship among these variables is illustrated in the graphs in Figure 5.6, which show the strong positive correlation between them. These findings demonstrate that rim diameter, a measurement typically available for archaeologically recovered sherd collections, is a highly accurate predictor of total vessel height and maximum vessel diameter for this vessel form. Given the basic shape of the Inca aríbalo, calculating the volume of a sphere on the basis of the maximum vessel diameter measurement provides a reliable approximation of effective vessel volume.[5] Using rim diameter to predict maximum vessel diameter, it is possible to estimate the effective volume of aríbalos recovered in archaeological contexts.[6] For sherd collections from thoughtfully sampled archaeological sites, this should prove a valuable tool for gaining insight into the quantities of drink being offered in different settings, approximate numbers of people involved in state events, state storage requirements and capacities, and so forth.

The size range of Inca aríbalos is extreme. In the current sample of 663 specimens for which either vessel height or rim diameter is available, the

A

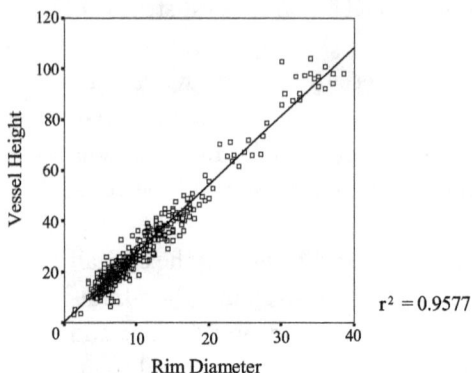

$r^2 = 0.9577$

B

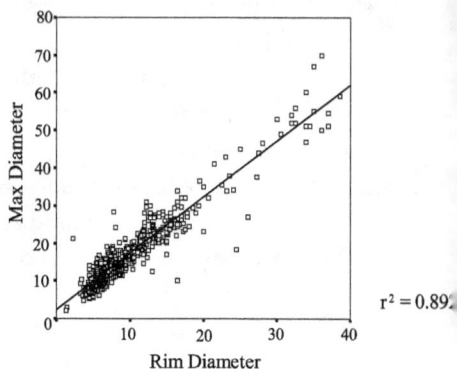

$r^2 = 0.89$

C

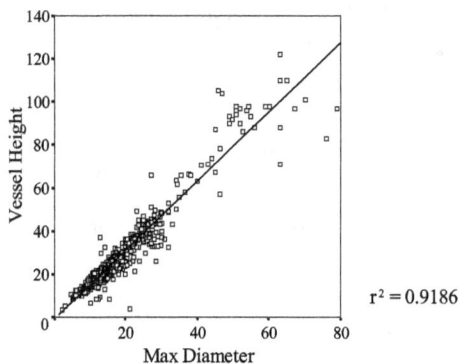

$r^2 = 0.9186$

D

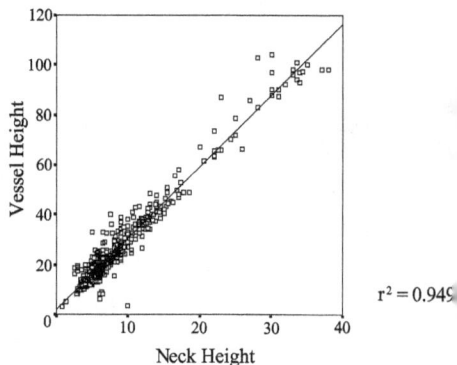

$r^2 = 0.949$

Figure 5.6. Bivariate scatterplots of *aríbalos* showing correlation between rim diameter and vessel height (A); rim diameter and maximum vessel diameter (B); vessel height and maximum vessel diameter (C); and vessel height and neck height (D).

vessels range from miniatures 5–10 centimeters tall to extraordinarily large vessels topping 120 centimeters in height. Looking at the vessel-size distribution in terms of both rim diameter and total vessel height (Fig. 5.7), it is clear that size variation is continuous, with a dominant mode between 5 and 9 centimeters, a mean rim diameter of 10 centimeters, and a long tail at the larger end of the spectrum. While the range of vessel sizes in my data set is similar to what Miller (2004: 128–129) found with a smaller sample of aríbalos from just Cuzco (n = 58), the larger data set indicates that size variation is in fact more complicated than a simple bimodal distribution, as suggested in his report. The shape of the normal

A

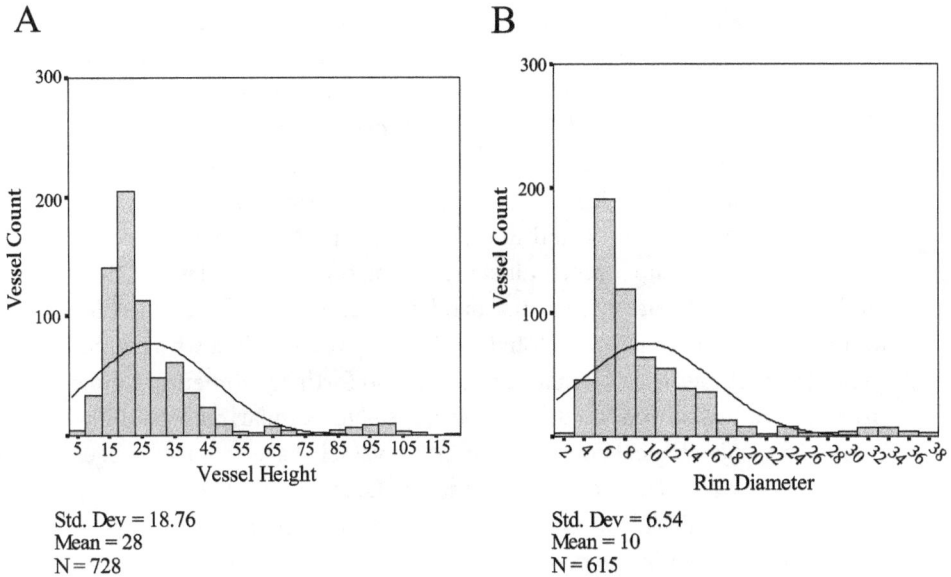

B

Figure 5.7. Size distribution of *aríbalos* in terms of total vessel height (A) and rim diameter (B).

curve actually suggests the presence of several secondary modes with overlapping distributions.

To explore the possibility that the Inca may have had different functional subclasses in mind relating to vessel size, the sample was divided into five classes based on variations in the size distribution of rim diameters. These classes were constituted for heuristic purposes only. The subgroups created are as follows: (1) miniature—rims less than 5 centimeters in diameter; (2) small—rims 5–9.9 centimeters in diameter; (3) medium—rims 10–17.9 centimeters in diameter; (4) large—rims 18–29.9 centimeters in diameter; and (5) extra-large—rims greater than 30 centimeters in diameter. These five size categories were cross-tabulated with site location (suyu), site type, and context information to ascertain whether any significant differences were discernible in terms of their distribution. While the sample size necessarily shrinks when restricted to vessels with measurable rims and valid provenience information, the findings permit several observations.

First, the smallest size class, which comprises miniature aríbalos (n = 49), appears to be generally more common in the heartland than in the provinces. These vessels comprise 11 percent of measurable aríbalos in the former region and 5 percent in the latter (chi sq = 61, df = 4). The miniature aríbalos are significantly more common in the capital city of Cuzco and notably less abundant in the northern Chinchasuyu sector of the empire. While the total number of measurable aríbalos with associated context information is small (n = 39), miniatures comprise 21 percent of such vessels found in burial contexts and 27 percent of those from temple contexts.

Ethnographic information indicates that miniature vessels are typically linked to ritual and religious practices and associated with material well-being, prosperity, fertility, and ancestor worship (Allen 1997; Meddens 1994). In Raqchi, near Cuzco, for instance, miniature pots filled with chicha and coca are still buried near llama corrals to ensure the health and fertility of the herd, while in parts of Bolivia, miniature vessels filled with chicha, trago (a spirituous liquor), maize, coca, and so forth are sometimes hung from the rafters of newly constructed houses for similar reasons (Sillar 1996). In archaeological contexts, miniature vessels have reportedly been found in both Late Horizon offering caches (Gibaja 2004; Meddens 1994) and human burials (Idrovo 2000: 242). The higher percentages of miniature aríbalos noted in the core of the empire suggest that the use of such vessels for making offerings may have been an ethnic Inca tradition not widely diffused among the subject population.

The distribution of small aríbalos (n = 273) that constitute the second subgroup is more strongly differentiated geographically, with a significantly higher proportion of such vessels coming from the imperial heartland, where they account for 61 percent of the 213 measurable aríbalos (compared to 41 percent of the 346 vessels from the provincial districts) (Fig. 5.8). Interestingly, while significantly larger percentages of aríbalos were recovered from Capacocha (12 of 15) and burial contexts (17 of 24), there were fewer than expected vessels of this size from habitation sites such as pucaras and villages. As Miller (2004: 129) notes, all 12 of the aríbalos from the burials excavated at Sacsaywaman above Cuzco fall within this size range. These data suggest that small aríbalos with rim diameters between 5 and 10 centimeters may have constituted the normative size for offerings to the dead.

The medium-sized subgroup (n = 185) of vessels, with rim diameters between 10 and 17.9 centimeters, exhibits the strongest degree of differential distribution, with significantly more vessels in this size class found in the provinces (n = 146), where they make up 42 percent of all aríbalos with measurable rim diameters. Conversely, this vessel size is significantly less common than would be expected in the imperial heartland, particularly in the capital city of Cuzco, where it constitutes only 18 percent (n = 23) of the 127 aríbalos with measurable rims.

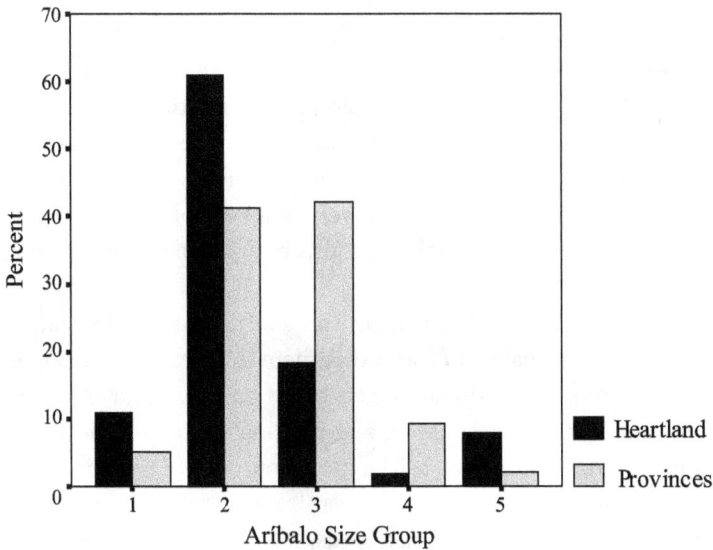

Figure 5.8. Percentages of *aríbalo* size groups found in the Inca heartland and provinces.

Vessels in this subgroup would have held anywhere from 3 to 11 liters of liquid. This suggests that a quantity in this range might have been the standard batch size for chicha brewed and consumed in the provincial districts. Pucara and village sites have high percentages of the mid-sized aríbalos (71 and 62 percent, respectively, of the total count of such jars at these sites), whereas medium-sized aríbalos constitute only 20 percent of the total count of such vessels at Inca administrative centers. Given that the number of vessels for which I have metric data from these site types is small, these observations cannot be taken too far at this point. It would, however, be particularly interesting to check these ideas against the ceramic data from previously investigated Inca administrative centers when such information becomes available.

While there were relatively few vessels in the large (n = 37) and extra-large size categories (n = 24), the former size group (with rims 18 to 29.9 centimeters in diameter) was significantly more common in the provinces, while the inverse is true of the extra-large vessels. Pucara sites have the highest combined percentage of large and extra-large aríbalos (18), while vessels in this size range constitute 13 percent of the total number of measurable aríbalos at both administrative centers and village sites. The fact that the large-sized aríbalos are more prevalent in the hinterlands suggests that the use of chicha may have figured more prominently in state politics in the outlying sectors of the empire. The extra-large variety of aríbalos (with rims greater than 30 centimeters in diameter) are found with greater frequency in the heartland of the empire, indicating that such enormous receptacles may have been intended principally for special state occasions, such as coronations and religious ceremonies which were conducted only in the imperial capital. Given the relatively small sample size for these two subcategories, however, these observations may be taken only as suggestive of possibly significant patterning.

This initial attempt at compressing and analyzing the information on metric variation in aríbalos indicates that there might have been some notion among potters of functional subsets based on size. Small aríbalos with rim diameters of 5–10 centimeters and ranging from 10 to 30 centimeters tall may have been viewed as the most appropriate size for offerings. Medium-sized aríbalos from 30 to 50 centimeters tall seem to have been the preferred size mode in the hinterlands, the upper end of this range being about the maximum size of ready portability when full. The extra-large size aríbalos, which would have stood anywhere from 75 to 120 centimeters tall, may have been reserved for grand affairs of state conducted exclusively in the capital of Cuzco or at the royal estates, where the majority of these vessels are found. These observations must be tested against sherd collections from archaeological excavations, but they offer a point of departure for further study of state deployment of chicha.

Aríbalo Design Formats

The design elements and design formats found on Inca aríbalos are as highly standardized as vessel form and proportionality. The primary zones of decoration include the neck, the upper shoulder of the back side, and the front panel. Three general design formats have been identified based on an analysis of the decorative treatments found on the front of such vessels (Fig. 5.9). This classification scheme builds on Rowe's (1944) pioneering study of Inca aríbalos from the Cuzco region in which he identifies two major formats that he labels Cuzco Polychrome A and B. The first style consists of two central vertical bands filled with alternating Xs and short horizontal bars. The central panel is flanked on either side by a vertically oriented phytomorphic motif that I have suggested elsewhere represents the mythical family tree of the Inca lineage (Bray 2000, 2004).[7]

The second and third styles differ principally with regard to the orienta-

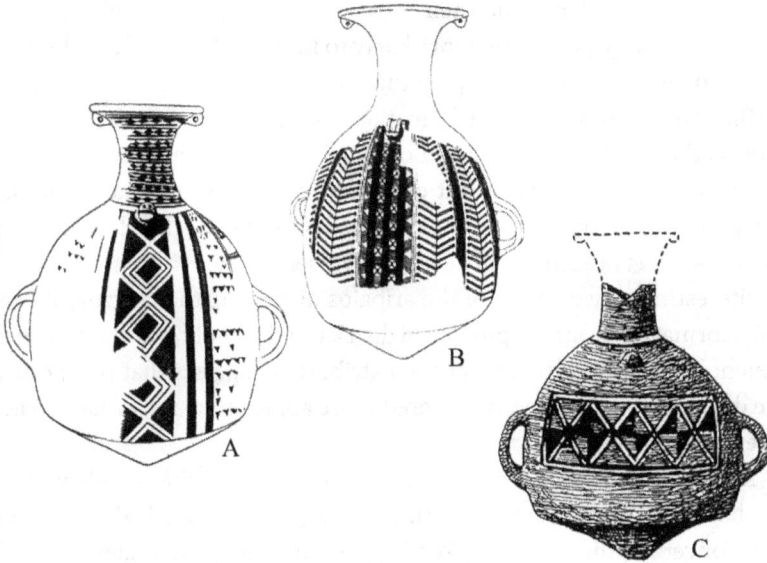

Figure 5.9. Principal design formats noted for Inca *aríbalos*: (a) vertical center panel with concentric diamonds; (b) vertical center panel with X and bar motif; (c) horizontal center panel with concentric diamonds. Redrawn by the author.

tion of the main design element, which consists of a central band containing a row of diamonds. This central band may be aligned either vertically or horizontally. The rhombus motif contained within the central band is typically filled with either concentric diamonds or a checkerboard pattern. When horizontally oriented, the band of rhombuses stands alone across the center of the vessel. When vertically oriented, the central band with rhombuses is flanked on either side by horizontal rows of pendent black triangles or,[8] less frequently, by the tree motif.

Of the total number of aríbalos in the database at present, approximately 1,025 vessels have been coded for design type (which includes the category "plain"). Perhaps not unexpectedly, 70 percent of the plain Inca aríbalos (which include unslipped, slipped with a single color, or simply divided into upper and lower halves through the use of slip) are from the provincial districts, where they constitute 30 percent (n = 194) of the 629 design-coded aríbalos from this zone. It is interesting to note, as well, that 90 percent (n = 31) of blackware aríbalos are from the provinces—specifically Chinchasuyu—while 87 percent of vessels coded as "Urcosuyu style" (13 of 15) are from Collasuyu. Though these observations are not unexpected, it is important that the sample bears out our commonplace assumptions regarding stylistic types and their presumed regional associations, as well as the idea that we would be more likely to find highly embellished vessels in Cuzco and the heartland region than in the provinces.

The most common design format among the aríbalos included in this study is the horizontal front band or panel (n = 184), which typically contains concentric rhombuses but occasionally exhibits alternative fill patterns such as zigzag lines or pendant tassels (Fig. 5.9C). This design format accounts for 25 percent of all decorated vessels.[9]

Interestingly, two-thirds of the aríbalos displaying the horizontal front panel format are from the provincial districts, while only one-third are provenienced to the heartland. Such a distribution suggests that this decorative device may have been considered more appropriate for, or had greater salience in, the hinterlands.

The other two main design formats, the vertical center bands with Xs and bars flanked by the tree motif (n = 150) and the vertical front panel with concentric diamonds flanked by rows of pendant triangles (n = 126), constitute the second and third most common types (Figs. 5.9A and 5.9B). Together, these three principal design formats account for 61 percent of decorated aríbalos in my sample.

Both of the latter two design layouts entail a tripartite division of the vessel front. While the distribution of these two formats is slightly more even between the heartland and the provinces than is the horizontal front panel, the majority are associated with the heartland zone. There is also a significant difference in the frequency of these two design formats with respect to the total number of decorated aríbalos in each of the two zones. In the imperial heartland, the tripartite formats account for 60 percent of decorated aríbalos, while in the provinces they constitute only 40 percent of all decorated vessels.

Elsewhere, I have offered more detailed analysis and discussion of the possible symbolic meanings and associations of the three design formats based on considerations of vessel form, function, context, the use of metaphor, and ethnographic analogy (Bray 2000, 2004, 2008). My interpretations center on metaphorical linkages between the aríbalo and the human body, and the idea of genealogical iconography. With regard to the tripartite structure of two of the design formats, I suggest that it represents a form of genealogical symbolism referencing both the significance of tripartite organization within Andean conceptual systems and the notion of the individual as composed of two halves deriving from the union of one's parents (Bray 2000, 2004).

In another study, I demonstrate the correspondence between ceramic design motifs and layouts and the clothing of the Inca elite, suggesting that state potters were drawing a conscious analogy between the clothing of the royal body and the clothing of the ceramic bodies of imperial pots (Bray 2008). This is evidenced in the close correspondence between the characteristic design formats of Inca men's tunics, or *unkus*, and the arábalo. Regardless of specific interpretations, it is clear that these design elements and formats held meaning for the state and its subjects.

The degree of standardization reflected in the imagery found on these serving vessels suggests that the Inca viewed the event of chicha consumption as an important context for the projection of what might be construed as state propaganda. The differential distribution of design formats suggests that the Inca may have intended different messages for the subject populations of the hinterlands versus their more immediate kinfolk in the heartland. The fact that the two design formats emphasizing tripartite division are found with much greater frequency in the imperial center suggests that the symbolic meaning of this imagery, perhaps linked to internal politics at the core of the state, had greater salience among the Inca themselves. Beyond the heartland, the imagery deployed on arábalos may have been intended to convey entirely different sets of meanings, like symbolizing the presence of the Inca himself in the capacity of benevolent host at chicha-drinking sessions.

Conclusion

In this broad-based study of the Inca state ceramic corpus, I view pottery, chicha, food, and politics as intimately linked. By focusing on the arábalo, the quintessential Inca vessel form, it is possible to quantitatively demonstrate the significance of chicha to the imperial agenda. The fact that this vessel constitutes a significantly larger percentage of the imperial ceramic assemblage in the provincial zones suggests that it was of particular importance to the process of imperial expansion. In general, the medium and large arábalos are more common in the provinces, while the small and miniature versions predominate in the imperial heartland. The former are most likely associated with public-consumption rituals, given the volumes of liquid involved, while the smaller varieties are more typically associated with offerings to the deities and the dead.

The differential distribution of various sizes and styles of Inca arábalos suggests that the state did not have a one-size-fits-all policy with regard to the circulation and presentation of chicha. Rather, the range of variation indicates that the quantity as well as, perhaps, the quality of this essential substance was differentially deployed in the context of Inca state expansion and consolidation.

In addition to the findings with respect to the distribution of different size classes and design formats, this chapter provides valuable new insights into the dimensional standardization of this vessel form. The consistency of proportionality demonstrated for Inca aríbalos across different size classes and from various parts of the empire is significant insofar as it establishes our ability to calculate vessel capacity from fragmentary remains. Volumetric data from archaeological sites and contexts has the potential to significantly enhance our understanding of the politics of food, ritual drinking, and feasting practice as these relate to Inca statecraft and within a broader comparative framework.

Notes

1. I wish to acknowledge the help of Eric Blinman and Wolky Toll of the Office of Archaeological Studies at the Museum of New Mexico for their generous assistance with the statistical analyses performed in this study and in thinking through issues of vessel-size classes and volumes. John Klein of the Math Department and Elaine Hockman of the Office of Computing and Technology at Wayne State University also deserve thanks for the assistance and expertise offered earlier in the life of this larger project on Inca pottery.

2. An arroba is a Spanish measure that equals approximately 25 pounds.

3. Though production data are limited, a growing number of technical studies suggest that Inca state pottery was being manufactured locally rather than being distributed from a single or centralized locale (see, e.g., Bray 1991; D'Altroy and Bishop 1990; Espinosa 1970; Hayashida 1999; Spurling 1992).

4. Due to the general lack of investigation in the Antisuyu sector of the Inca Empire, my database includes only a handful of Inca vessels from this zone.

5. I am not including the neck of the aríbalo in the calculation of effective volume in the present study.

6. Regression analysis indicates that the coefficients for predicting the maximum vessel diameter (MVD) of an Inca aríbalo from its rim diameter (RD) are as follows: MVD = 1.49 x RD + 2.36. This figure is divided in half to obtain the vessel radius (r). The formula for calculating the volume of a sphere is: $V_s = 4/3$ pi r^3 [pi = 3.14159].

7. This style corresponds to Rowe's (1944: 47) Cuzco Polychrome Type A.

8. This style corresponds to Rowe's (1944: 47) Cuzco Polychrome Type B.

9. Aríbalos coded as "plain" are not included in this count.

References Cited

Allen, Catherine J.
1997 When Pebbles Move Mountains: Iconicity and Symbolism in Quechua Ritual. In *Creating Context in Andean Cultures*, Rosaleen Howard-Malverde, ed., pp. 73–84. Oxford: Oxford University Press.

Almeida, Eduardo
1999 *Estudios arqueológicos en el pucara rumicucho*. Quito: Banco Central del Ecuador.

Almeida, Eduardo, and Holguer Jara
1984 *El pucara de Rumicucho*. Miscelánea Antropológica Ecuatoriana, Serie Monografía 1. Quito: Museo del Banco Central del Ecuador.

Ambrosetti, Juan
1907 Exploraciones arqueológicas en la ciudad prehistórica de La Paya (Valle Calchaqui, Provincia de Salta). *Revista de la Universidad de Buenos Aires* 8: 5–534.

Bauer, Brian S.
1990 State Development in the Cusco Region: Archaeological Research on the Incas in the province of Paruro. Doctoral dissertation, University of Chicago.

Bingham, Hiram
1915 Types of Machu Picchu Pottery. *American Anthropologist* 17: 257–271.
1979 [1930] *Machu Picchu: Citadel of the Incas*. New York: Hacker Art Books.

Boman, Eric
1991 [1908] *Antiquités de la région andine de la République Argentine et du Désert d'Atacama*. Paris: Imprimerie Nationale.

Bray, Tamara L.
1991 The Effects of Inca Imperialism on the Northern Frontier. Doctoral dissertation, State University of New York at Binghamton.
2000 Imperial Inca Iconography: The Art of Empire in the Andes. *RES Anthropology and Aesthetics* 38: 168–178.
2003a To Dine Splendidly: Imperial Pottery, Commensal Politics, and the Inca State. In *The Archaeology and Politics of Food and Feasting in Early States and Empires*, Tamara L. Bray, ed., pp. 93–142. New York: Kluwer Academic/ Plenum.
2003b *Los efectos del imperialismo incaico en la frontera norte*. Quito: Abya-Yala.
2004 La alfarcría imperial incaica: Una comparación entre la cerámica estatal del área del Cuzco y la cerámica de las provincias. *Chungara, Revista de la Arqueología Chilena* 36(2): 363–372.
2008 Exploring Inca State Religion through Material Metaphors: A Cross-Media Analysis of Inca Iconography. In *The Archaeology of Religion*, Lars Fogelin, ed., pp. 118–138. Carbondale: Southern Illinois University Press.
N.d. Materializing Ideology: Form, Function, and Style in the Service of the Imperial Inca State. Book manuscript in preparation.

Casanova, Eduardo

1942 *Dos yacimientos arqueológicos en la península de Copacabana (Bolivia).* Buenos Aires: Imprenta de la Universidad.

Checura Jeria, J.

1977 Funebria incaica en el Cerro Esmeraldas (Iquique, I Región). *Estudios Atacameños* 5: 1125–1141.

Cobo, Bernabé

1964 [1653] *Historia del Nuevo Mundo.* Biblioteca de Autores Españoles, vols. 91–92. Madrid: Ediciones Atlas.

Collier, Donald, and John Murra

1943 *Survey and Excavations in Southern Ecuador.* Anthropological Series, Field Museum of Natural History no. 35. Chicago: Field Museum of Natural History.

D'Altroy, Terence N.

2001 State Ceramic Assemblage. In *Empire and Domestic Economy,* Terence D'Altroy and Christine Hastorf, eds., pp. 242–264. Boston: Kluwer Academic/Plenum.

D'Altroy, Terence, and Ronald Bishop

1990 The Provincial Organization of Inka Ceramic Production. *American Antiquity* 55: 120–137.

Davies, Dennis

1996 Integration Period Chimbo Culture in Bolivar, Ecuador: The Ceramic Evidence. Master's thesis, Trent University.

Debenedetti, Salvador

1917 *Investigaciones arqueológicas en los valles preandinos de la Provincia de San Juan.* Facultad de Filosofía y Letras, Publicación de la Sección Antropológica no. 15. Buenos Aires: Universidad de Buenos Aires.

Eaton, George

1916 The Collection of Osteological Materials from Machu Picchu. *Memoirs of the Connecticut Academy of Arts and Sciences* 5: 3–96.

Espinosa Soriano, Waldemar

1970 Los mitmas yungas de Collique en Cajamarca, siglos XV, XVI y XVII. *Revista del Museo Nacional* (Lima) 36: 9–57.

Gibaja, Arminda

2004 Dos ofrendas al agua de Ollantaytambo. *Ñawpa Pacha* 25–27: 177–188.

Gómez Huamán, Nilo

1966 Importancia social de la chicha como bebida popular en Huamanga. *Wamani* 1(1): 33–57.

Gyarmati, János, and Andras Vargas

1999 *The Chacaras of War: An Inka Estate in the Cochabamba Valley, Bolivia.* Budapest: Museum of Ethnography.

Hayashida, Frances

1999 Style, Technology and State Production: Inka Pottery Manufacture in the Leche Valley, Peru. *Latin American Antiquity* 10(4): 337–352.

Idrovo, Jaime
2000 *Tomebamba: Arqueología e historia de una ciudad imperial.* Cuenca: Ediciones del Banco Central del Ecuador.
Jijón y Caamaño, Jacinto
1927 *Puruhá: Contribución al conocimiento de los aborígenes de la Provincia de Chimborazo.* Quito: Editorial Ecuatoriana.
Jijón y Caamaño, Jacinto, and Manuel Larrea
1918 *Un cementario incasico en Quito y notas acerca de los inca en el Ecuador.* Quito: Imprenta de la Universidad Central.
Julien, Catherine
1983 *Hatunqolla: A View of Inca Rule from the Lake Titicaca Region.* University of California Publications in Anthropology, vol. 15. Berkeley & Los Angeles: University of California Press.
2004 Las tumbas de Sacsahuaman y el estilo Cuzco-Inca. *Ñawpa Pacha* 25–27: 1–126.
Lehmann, Walter, and Heinrich Doering
1924 *The Art of Old Peru.* New York: Hacker Art Books.
Linares Málaga, Eloy
1966 Restos arqueológicos en el nevado Pichu Pichu. *Anales de Arqueología y Etnología* 21: 7–47.
Llanos, Luis
1936 Informe sobre Ollantaytambo. *Revista del Museo Nacional* (Lima) 5(2): 123–156.
Lynch, Tom
1993 The Identification of Inca Posts and Roads from Catarpe to Río Frío, Chile. In *Provincial Inca,* Michael Malpass, ed., pp. 117–144. Iowa City: University of Iowa Press.
Matos, Ramiro
1999 La cerámica inca. In *Los incas: Arte y símbolos,* Franklin Pease, ed., pp. 109–166. Lima: Banco de Crédito del Perú.
Meddens, Frank
1994 Mountains, Miniatures, Ancestors, and Fertility: The Meaning of a Late Horizon Offering in a Middle Horizon Structure in Peru. *Bulletin of the Institute of Archaeology* 31: 127–150.
Menzel, Dorothy
1966 Pottery of Chincha. *Ñawpa Pacha* 4: 77–153.
1971 Estudios arqueológicos en los valles de Ica, Pisco, Chincha y Cañete. *Arqueología y Sociedad* 6(1): 1–158.
1976 *Pottery Style and Society in Ancient Peru.* Berkeley & Los Angeles: University of California Press.
Menzel, Dorothy, and Francis Riddell
1986 *Archaeological Investigations at Tambo Viejo, Acari Valley, Peru, 1954.* Sacramento: California Institute for Peruvian Studies.

Meyers, Albert
1975 Algunos problemas en la clasificación del estilo incaico. *Pumapunku* 8: 7–25.
Miller, George
2004 An Investigation of Cuzco-Inca Ceramics: Canons of Form, Proportion, and Size. *Ñawpa Pacha* 25–27: 127–150.
Morris, Craig
1979 Maize Beer in the Economics, Politics, and Religion of the Inca Empire. In *Fermented Food Beverages in Nutrition*, Clifford F. Gastineau, William J. Darby, and Thomas B. Turner, eds., pp. 21–34. New York: Academic Press.
1982 The Infrastructure of Inka Control in the Peruvian Central Highlands. In *The Inca and Aztec States, 1400–1800*, George Collier, Renato Rosaldo, and John Wirth, eds., pp. 153–171. New York: Academic Press.
Morris, Craig, and Donald Thompson
1985 *Huánuco Pampa: An Inca City and Its Hinterland*. New York: Thames and Hudson.
Mostny, Grete
1955 Un cementario incasico en Chile central. *Boletín del Museo Nacional de Historia Natural* 23: 17–41.
Murra, John V.
1960 Rite and Crop in the Inca State. In *Culture in History: Essays in Honor of Paul Radin*, Stanley Diamond, ed., pp. 393–407. New York: Columbia University Press.
1980 [1956] *The Economic Organization of the Inka State*. Greenwich: JAI.
Pardo, Luis
1938 Hacia una nueva clasificación de la cerámica cuzqueña del antiguo imperio de los incas. *Revista del Instituto Arqueológico del Cuzco* 3(4–5): 1–22.
1939 Arte peruano: Clasificación de la cerámica cuzqueña (época incaica). *Revista del Instituto Arqueológico del Cuzco* 4(6–7): 3–27.
1957 *Historia y arqueología del Cuzco*. Vol. 2. Cuzco: Ediciones.
Reyniers, François
1966 *Céramiques américaines*. Paris: Ediciones des Musées Nationaux.
Rivera Dorado, Miguel
1976 La cerámica inca de Chincheros. In *Arqueología de Chincheros: Cerámica y otros materiales*, vol. 2, José Alcina Franch, ed., pp. 27–90. Madrid: Memorias de la Misión Científica Española en Hispanoamérica.
Rowe, John H.
1944 *An Introduction to the Archaeology of Cuzco*. Papers of the Peabody Museum of American Archaeology and Ethnology, Harvard University 27(2). Cambridge: Peabody Museum of American Archaeology and Ethnology.
Sachún Cedeño, María Teresa
2001 La chicha en Moche. *Boletín de Lima* 124: 8–11.
Salazar, Lucy, and Richard Burger
2004 Catalogue. In *Machu Picchu: Unveiling the Mystery of the Inca*, Richard Burger and Lucy Salazar, eds., pp. 125–217. New Haven: Yale University Press.

Santoro, Calogero, and Iván Muñoz Ovalle
1981 Patrón habitacional incaico en el área de Pampa Alto Ramírez (Arica, Chile). *Revista Chungará* 7: 144–171.

Schjellerup, Inge
1997 *Incas and Spaniards in the Conquest of the Chachapoyas.* Goteborg: Goteborg University Press.

Sillar, Bill
1996 Playing with God: Cultural Perception of Children, Play and Miniatures in the Andes. *Archaeological Review from Cambridge* 13(2): 47–63.

Silverblatt, Irene M.
1987 *Moon, Sun, and Witches: Gender Ideologies and Class in Inca and Colonial Peru.* Princeton: Princeton University Press.

Spurling, Geoff
1992 The Organization of Craft Production in the Inka State: The Potters and Weavers of Milliraya. Doctoral dissertation, Cornell University.

Stehberg, Rubén
1976 La cerámica inca de Chincheros. In *Arqueología de Chincheros: Cerámica y otros materiales*, vol. 2, José Alcina Franch, ed., pp. 27–90. Madrid: Memorias de la Misión Científica Española en Hispanoamérica.

Tarragó, Myriam
1968 Secuencias culturales de la etapa agro-alfarera de San Pedro de Atacama de Chile. *Actas y memorias del 37th Congreso Internacional de Americanistas* 2 (1966): 119–145.

Thompson, Donald
1968 Incaic Installations at Huánuco and Pumpu. *Actas y memorias del 37th Congreso Internacional de Americanistas* 1 (1966): 67–74.

Tschopik, Marion
1946 *Some Notes on the Archaeology of the Department of Puno.* Papers of the Peabody Museum of American Archaeology and Ethnology, Harvard University 27(3). Cambridge: Peabody Museum of American Archaeology and Ethnology.

Uhle, Max
1903 *Pachacamac: Report of the William Pepper Peruvian Expedition of 1896.* Philadelphia: University of Pennsylvania.

Valencia, Alfredo
1970 Dos tumbas de Saqsaywaman. *Saqsaywaman* 1: 173–177.
1975 Alfarería de Saqsaywaman. *Arte y Arqueología* (Academia Nacional del Ciencias de Bolivia) 3–4: 217–225.

Verneau, René, and Paul Rivet
1912 *Ethnographie ancienne de l'equateur.* Paris: Gauthier-Villares.

Vokral, Edita
1991 *Qoñi-Chiri: La organización de la cocina y estructuras simbólicas en el altiplano del Perú.* Quito: Abya-Yala.

Wentscher, Jürgen

1989 Montículos y otras áreas de excavación. In *Excavaciones en Cochasquí, Ecuador, 1964–1965*, Udo Oberem and Wolfgang Wurster, eds., pp. 70–103. Mainz: Philipp Von Zabern.

Zuidema, R. Tom

1964 *The Ceque System of Cusco: The Social Organization of the Capital of the Inca.* Leiden: Brill.

6

You Are What You Drink

A Sociocultural Reconstruction of Pre-Hispanic Fermented Beverage Use at Cerro Baúl, Moquegua, Peru

David J. Goldstein, Robin C. Coleman Goldstein, and Patrick R. Williams

> When you talk about chicha it is important to specify the kind as the word chicha was used by the Spaniards to describe both alcoholic and non-alcoholic beverages, many of which are made from a vast variety of plants prepared in distinct ways.
>
> —*Cutler and Cárdenas (1947: 33)*

The ethnobotanical and ethnohistorical record of the Andes is replete with examples of fermented beverages made from a large number of grains and fruits. As Cutler and Cárdenas observe, the Spaniards recognized that there were many different kinds of chicha. Andean anthropology and archaeology, however, often focus largely on beer made from *Zea mays* (maize, or corn). There is no doubt that maize beer was central to Inca culture and remains important today throughout portions of this region. This emphasis on maize beer nonetheless neglects beverages made from other grains, such as *Chenopodium quinoa* (quinoa), *Amaranthus caudatus* (kiwicha), and fruits that also have been essential to Andean society.

The production and consumption patterns of fermented beverages varied in space and time across a landscape that was far more multilingual, multiethnic, and multicultural before the Columbian encounter. Since fermented beverages continue to play a significant role in daily consumption, small-scale ritual, and scheduled religious and agricultural festivals in the Andes, we can look at differences in the use and production of these drinks as potentially distinct ethnic markers in the Andean past. The choice of a particular beverage was dependent in part on regional resource availability and gustatory preference, and these choices helped to shape the historical trajectories of Andean cultures.

We suggest that archaeologists have yet to offer a sufficiently nuanced interpretation of fermented beverages at an archaeological site. Spatial and temporal components of alcohol consumption and production, coupled with ethnohistorical and ethnographic evidence, may serve as keys for understanding cultural preference and, potentially, for deciphering issues of identity and ethnicity in the archaeological record. Like other authors in this book (see Hayashida, this volume), we examine chicha consumption within a single historical and spatial context. Instead of ascribing modern

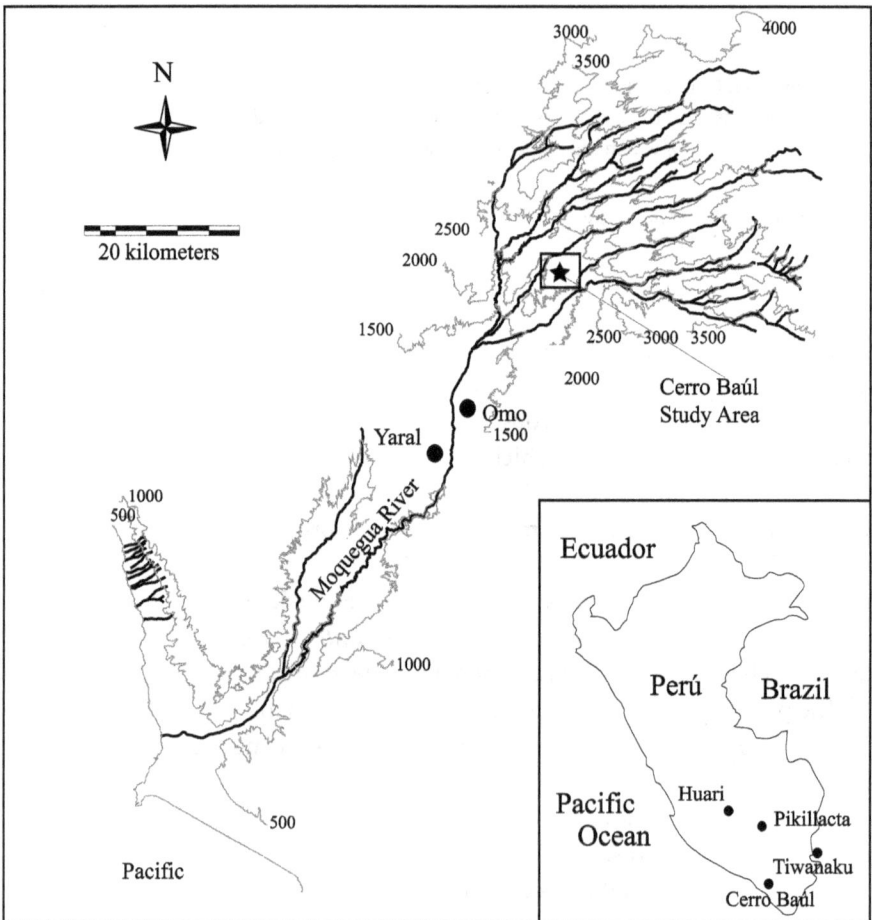

Figure 6.1. The Osmore Drainage, Peru. Map by Patrick R. Williams.

or colonial meanings associated with the production of similar beverages to our interpretations of a pre-Hispanic brewery context, we stress the significance of associating the consumption of a single beverage with a single place, time, and people. In this case study, we look at the use of fermented beverages in the Middle Horizon (AD 500–1000) Wari imperial state at Cerro Baúl, Peru (Fig. 6.1).

Over nine years of excavation in the Upper Moquegua River drainage, our research focused on the Middle Horizon settlements on Cerro Mejía and Cerro Baúl, as well as surrounding areas. The most recent seasons have recovered elite Wari contexts at Cerro Baúl with evidence of a variety of scales and kinds of fermented beverage production. Instead of fermented beverages made from corn, evidence indicates that the fruits from the *Schinus molle* L. (Anacardiaceae) tree were used to brew most of the beer consumed at the site. In this chapter, we trace the production and consumption of beverages made from molle and other fruits and grains through Middle Horizon excavation contexts in the Upper Moquegua Valley. Our approach teases out the complexities of the roles that fermented beverages played in this Middle Horizon society and interprets their use as more than aides for interpreting reciprocal labor arrangements and political power.

We begin our discussion by looking at the diversity of Andean fermented beverages in the colonial period and the present. After examining the relationship between food preferences and identity, we look at the centrality of fermented beverages produced from sources other than corn at Cerro Baúl. We explore the potential for the use of other kinds of grains—kiwicha and quinoa—for fermented beverage production within different settings at the site and then examine the use of molle drinks. In conclusion, we discuss the significance of the molle data with regard to how fermented beverage production is interpreted at other pre-Hispanic sites in the Andes.

Chicha: Defining Terms

Although anthropologists and archaeologists often use the term *chicha*, its genesis is rarely explored. As others have noted, the word *chicha* originates either in the Caribbean region from *chibcha* (Arawakan language family), a general word for fermented beverages (Cutler and Cárdenas 1947), or is derived from the contact-period languages spoken by the Cuna (in present-day Panama) (Pardo B. 2004). Regardless of its origin, when the Spanish arrived in the Americas they adopted the word *chicha* to describe a great variety of indigenous beverages, fermented and nonfermented. The term was used instead of other distinguishing terms common to European parlance at the time, for example, wine (fermented and aged fruit beverages) and beer (grain-based fermented beverages) to categorize all of these indigenous beverages in a single term.

Indigenous peoples today, as well as at the time of contact, used the term *chicha* for beers made from both grains and fruits. Thus, *chicha* glosses all indigenous fermented beverages. Since the primary beverage in the Inca Empire was maize beer, the term *chicha* became most commonly associated with this type of beverage in European discussions of indigenous fermented beverages. Five hundred years later, Andean archaeologists and anthropologists continue to use this term to refer to maize beer, as do many of the Spanish-speaking peoples in the region—despite the many varieties of fermented beverages consumed since the pre-Hispanic period.

There is increasing dissatisfaction with using direct historical analogies to interpret the role of fermented beverages in Andean prehistory. In this volume, for example, Hayashida constructs a persuasive argument for the importance of examining fermented beverages within their specific historical and economic contexts. We build on this approach in this chapter. Sidney Mintz argues that food use "implicates meaning" (1985: 6), and that the terms used within cuisines of distinct ethnic and cultural traditions are critical to the understanding of how food is used and symbolically interpreted by a given group. Even so, anthropologists have often conflated meaningful distinctions when it comes to Andean fermented beverages, and chicha de maíz (corn beer) is perhaps the most common example of this conflation (Guillet 1979; Hastorf and Johannessen 1993; Mayer 2002; Mitchell 1991; Weismantel 1998).

Maize drinks have a variety of linguistically distinct names that originated in the region's myriad languages. Table 6.1 demonstrates the diversity of modern indigenous concepts of fermented beverages made from corn. The list in Table 6.1 is not exhaustive but is representative in illustrating the diversity of terms used in different contexts of corn beer consumption in the region today.[1]

Overall, the Andean watershed is home to some 100 language groups, and each of these languages includes words, methods, and contexts of use for fermented beverages made from fruits or grains. Each particular fruit or grain requires different methods and technologies for the successful conversion of plant starches to sugars and, eventually, into alcohol. Table 6.2 illustrates that there are both significant gaps in our knowledge of names of the beverages (col. 1) and in our understanding of preparation techniques

Table 6.1. Fermented Beverages Produced from Maize in the Andes

Beverage	Language	Use	Sugar conversion technology	Fermentation level[a]	Date source
Tekkte	Quechua	Magic/ divination	--[b]	--	Antúñez de Mayolo (1981)
Huiñapo, Wiñapo, Guiñapo	Quechua	Drinking & cooking	Sprouted	Medium	Garcilaso de la Vega (1829)
Chicha de jora	Spanish	Drinking & cooking	Sprouted	Medium	Garcilaso de la Vega (1829)
Mocchi haca	Quechua	--	Masticated	High	Antúñez de Mayolo (1981)
Ñocña	Quechua	--	--	Low	Antúñez de Mayolo (1981)
Sekke, upi	Quechua	--	--	Not fermented	Antúñez de Mayolo (1981)
Cutitakuis	Quechua	--	Decanted/ refermented	Highest	Antúñez de Mayolo (1981)
Huarapo	Mochica	--	--	--	De Jaegher & Valverde (1991)
Aque, aksa, akka, asua, a'qa	Quechua	--	Milled	--	Cárdenas (1989); Garcilaso de la Vega (1829); Horkheimer (1973); La Barre (1938)
Wiñapo aque	Quechua	--	Germinated	--	Horkheimer (1973)
Upu aque	Quechua	--	Germinated	Not Fermented	Horkheimer (1973)
Verde	Spanish	--	--	Not Fermented	Camino (1987)
Sora, jora	Quechua	--	Germinated	--	Camino (1987); Garcilaso de la Vega (1829); Olivias W. (2001)
Atole	Nahuatl/ Spanish	--	Milled	--	La Barre (1938)
Guiñapo	Quechua	--	Toasted & milled	--	Nicholson (1960)
Huiroqqueqque	Quechua	--	Germinated	Tastes of mildew, bad quality	Nicholson (1960)
Caliente	Spanish	--	Germinated	Tastes of mildew, bad quality	Nicholson (1960)
Chiriguana	?/Spanish[c]	--	Masticated	Medium	Cárdenas (1989)
Kusa	Aymara	--	--	--	Cárdenas (1989)
Chicha	Arawak/ Spanish	Offerings to Spaniards	Toasted & milled	--	Cárdenas (1989)

[a] Some of the fermentation level information is subjective. In some cases, only the taste of the beverage is recorded, and we use taste to estimate the fermentation level of the beverage.

[b] Dashes indicate that there is no information available.

[c] Chiriguana was recorded in Spanish, but the original language is unknown.

Table 6.2. Fermented Beverages Produced from Plants Other than Maize in the Andes

Beverage	Language	Plant species	Botanical family	Part of plant used	Preparation	Source
Ttako, tusca	Quechua?	*Acacia* sp.	Fabaceae	Seed		Cárdenas (1989); La Barre (1938)
		Acrocomia sp.	Araceae	Fruit	Ground & chewed	Cárdenas (1989)
		Agave americana	Agavaceae	Stem/heart		Acosta 1954
		Anacardium occidentale	Anacardiaceae	Fruit	Ground & chewed	Cárdenas (1989)
		Ananas sp.	Bromeliaceae	Fruit	Ground & chewed	Cárdenas (1989)
Tekkti	Quechua	*Arachis hypogea*	Fabaceae	Seed	Malted & ground	Cárdenas (1989); Olivias W. (2001)
Chontar'uru	Quechua	*Arracacia xanthorrhiza*	Apiaceae	Tuber		Olivias W. (2001)
	Quechua	*Bactris* sp.	Araceae	Fruit		La Barre (1938)
Aloja	Quechua	*Chenopodium quinoa*	Chenopodiaceae	Seed	Ground	Sokup (1970)
		Chenopodium pallidicaule	Chenopodiaceae	Seed		Antúñez de Mayolo (1981); Cutler & Cárdenas (1947)
		Cucurbita ficifolia	Cucurbitaceae	Fruit		Cutler & Cárdenas (1947)
		Genipa americana	Rubiaceae	Fruit		Cárdenas (1989)
		Andira sp. (ex *Geoffroea*)	Fabaceae	Seed		Cutler & Cárdenas (1947)
Chañar	Spanish?	*Gourelia decorticans*	Fabaceae	Fruit		La Barre (1938)
Chontar'uru	Quechua	*Bactris* sp. (ex *Guilielma insignis*)	Araceae	Fruit		La Barre (1938)
Masato, cachiri	Spanish?	*Ipomoea batata*	Covulvulaceae	Tuber		Antúñez de Mayolo (1981)
		Manihot esculenta	Euphorbiaceae	Tuber	Chewed & boiled	La Barre (1938); Schultes & Raffauf (1990); Sokup (1970)
		Mauritia flexuosa	Araceae	Fruit	Ground	Cutler & Cárdenas (1947); Sokup (1970)
Colonche	Spanish?	*Opuntia* sp.	Cactaceae	Fruit		La Barre (1938)
		Oxalis tuberosa	Oxalidaceae	Tuber		Olivias W. (2001)
Atole, algarroba, ttako	Quechua, Nahuatl/ Spanish	*Prosopis* sp.	Fabaceae	Seed	Boiled	Cárdenas (1989); La Barre (1938)
Chicha de molle	Spanish	*Schinus molle*	Anacardiaceae	Fruit	Boiled or soaked	Garcilaso de la Vega (1829); Goldstein & Coleman (2004)
		Solanum tuberosum	Solanaceae	Tuber		Antúñez de Mayolo (1981); Camino (1987)
		Zizyphus mistol	Rhamnaceae	Fruit		Cárdenas (1989)

and local uses. Despite the inconsistent data gathered by regional ethnographers, it is clear that differences in indigenous terminology extend from basic ingredients to production steps, fermentation time, social contexts of consumption, and other factors.

Whereas a body of research about alcoholic beverage production exists for Central America from the colonial period to the present (see, e.g., Bruman 2000), this type of study is still lacking for the Andes. The umbrella term *chicha*, in the historical-colonial sense, is a legacy of the conquest of the Americas. The term (see Table 6.1), as researched by Cárdenas (1989), is particular to ritual offerings to foreigners—non-native speakers or relations who are seen as Spaniards. What we know in Peruvian Spanish as chicha de maíz, however, is known in Quechua and Aymara, the most extensive modern Andean languages, as *akka* and *kusa*, respectively (see Table 6.1). In these instances, the root meaning of these words is "fermented" or "fermented beverage" (Cárdenas 1989). The term *chicha* as currently used homogenizes the variety of indigenous fermented beverage production and consumption contexts that make each beverage and tradition distinct. In continuing this usage in archaeology, we unwittingly erase the social and cultural complexities that fermented beverages play in society today and create our own problematic within our archaeological reconstructions.

Chicha as an Ethnic Marker

Mary Douglas notes that "drinking is essentially a social act, performed in a recognized social context" (1987: 4). In choosing what you drink, what you do not drink, where you drink, with whom you drink, and how much you drink, you construct your identity and ethnicity. In North America, for example, it is almost obligatory to offer beer at major sporting events, whether you are at the stadium or participating virtually by watching television or listening to the radio; drunkenness is often seen as a rite of passage into adulthood, but is not generally accepted for other age groups. Just as alcohol can define "American" and "adolescence," the identity-constructing character of alcohol recognized by Douglas (1987) has long played an important role in the Andean world.

In the modern Andes, what one drinks serves as a marker of origins and ethnicity, both ascribed and self-determined. In Arequipa, for example, residents commonly drink a purple-colored chicha de maíz made from the short black corn that grows at the highest elevations in provincial Arequipa; this is not to be confused with the common nonalcoholic beverage *chicha morada*, found throughout Peru and made with a purple corn grown at a lower elevation. In the central Andean valley of Cuzco, the people make a white chicha de maíz, fermented from specific kinds of corn that grow only in certain parts of the Upper Urubamba River Valley, long known as the Sacred Valley of the Inca. In urban areas, indigenous fermented beverages have become markers of origins and affiliation to *tierra* (homeland), and chichas are often celebrated through *concursos de chicha*, fermented beverage taste-offs that feature a number of beverages made from a variety of fruits, grains, and animal parts (Cárdenas 1989).

The importance of drinking to identity in the Andes also leads to its imposition as an identity marker. In the Amazon, for example, many people drink a beverage fermented from manioc. People who live in the coastal city of Lima call the drink *masato* and describe the people who live in the eastern lowlands as masato drinkers. Returning tourists are asked if they drank it, and people from the Amazon region visiting Lima are quizzed about their consumption of the beverage. For people who live in the Amazon, however, the term *masato* can refer to fermented beverages made not only from manioc but also from a variety of fruits and tubers. The beverages of the region are sometimes called chicha and are sometimes made of corn. For the people of Lima, masato consumption nevertheless is used to categorize lowland indigenous peoples, marking them as distinct from other Andean peoples.

As is the case today (see, e.g., Goody 1982), gustatory preference likely played a significant role in ethnic distinctions during the Inca and colonial periods. While we do not have a full record of pre-Hispanic beverage preferences, we know that food preferences were used by the Inca authority to ascribe ethnicity. High-altitude peoples of the Lurín Valley are derogatorily referred to as "potato eaters" in the Huarochirí manuscript, and the nonagricultural Uros peoples of Lake Titicaca are referred to as "lazy raw meat eaters" ignorant of agriculture (Murra 2001: 146). Given the variety of names, fruits and grains, and fermentation technologies used in the Andes historically (Tables 6.1 and 6.2), we suggest that the fermented beverage likely played a similar role to that played by masato today in asserting identity and ethnic distinctions in antiquity.

Andean ethnography is full of references that describe the role that alcohol played throughout the colonial and modern periods (Allen 1988; Camino 1987; Cobo 1964; Guaman Poma 2005), and the role of alcoholic beverages in shaping identity and ethnicity is well known from the Inca chronicles. The Incas produced and consumed massive amounts of maize beer. The beverage held a dual political and religious status due to the role corn played in the cosmology of Inca legitimization and spiritual origins (Goodman-Elgar, this volume; Hastorf and Johannessen 1993: 121). The Spanish recounted that, among the Incas, corn was a divine gift to humanity, and its consumption as a fermented beverage in political meetings formed a communion between those who were drinking and the ancestors, the land, and the entirety of the Inca cosmology. To maintain the integrity and sanctity of this drink, only chosen sequestered women, mamacunas, produced maize beers from special types of corn for consumption at feasts and rituals attended by elites (Hastorf and Johannessen 1993; Staller 2006). Political pacts were always sealed with the Inca himself offering to drink a cup of akka with the leader of the defeated group, thereby incorporating the vanquished group into the customs and cosmology of the Incas (Garcilaso de la Vega 1829; Staller 2006).

Hastorf and Johannessen (1993) have applied Allen's (1988) notion of "transformation" to explain the importance of maize beer in the lives of the Incas: natural or raw materials, through cultural practices of transformation, become imbued with historical and social meaning (see, e.g., Mayer 2002; Mintz 1985).[2] In this sense, all fermented beverages are transformative, and other fermented drinks could have proved integral to forming ethnic identities by holding a place of prominence in ceremonies, political rituals, and daily life (also see Hayashida, this volume). We suggest that this occurred at Cerro Baúl.

Archaeological Fermented Beverage Consumption at Cerro Baúl

Located in the modern Department of Moquegua at the divergence of the Torata and Tambo river watersheds, Cerro Baúl (2,575 meters above sea level) is an impressive mesa that punctuates the local landscape (see Fig. 6.1). The mesa, still a sacred pilgrimage site in the modern period, is located at the juncture of modern and ancient routes of communication between the ecological zones of the highlands and the lowland coastal plain (Rice 1989). While the drainage shows almost continuous occupation by humans during the Holocene, the area was sparsely populated until the Wari at Cerro Baúl initiated a massive construction and canalization project after their arrival around AD 600 (Moseley et al. 2005; Williams 2001). Located at the southern frontier of the empire, the site's architecture ("D"-shaped structures and agglutinated buildings with central patios), ceramics (face neck jar motifs and ceramic drinking keros), and trade items (obsidian from specifically Wari highland sources) clearly demonstrate the presence of elites, the establishment of Wari ethnic affiliation, and the incorporation into Wari trade networks (Williams 2001; Williams and Nash 2002). Based on these data, Cerro Baúl is interpreted as the Wari elite settlement where either colonial officials from the Ayacucho highlands or very acculturated Wari elites of local origin lived (Moseley et al. 2005: fig. 2).

Excavations of the surrounding area indicate that elite Wari activity was restricted to the Baúl summit (Moseley et al. 2005), while local elites used local pottery to perform some elements of Wari-like ritual and feasting on the summit of adjacent Cerro Mejía and other sites (Moseley et al. 2005; Nash 2002; Williams and Nash 2002: fig. 2). Toward the end of the Middle Horizon (AD 800), the affirmation of Wari identity occurring at Cerro Baúl became particularly important as the rival imperial power of Tiwanaku

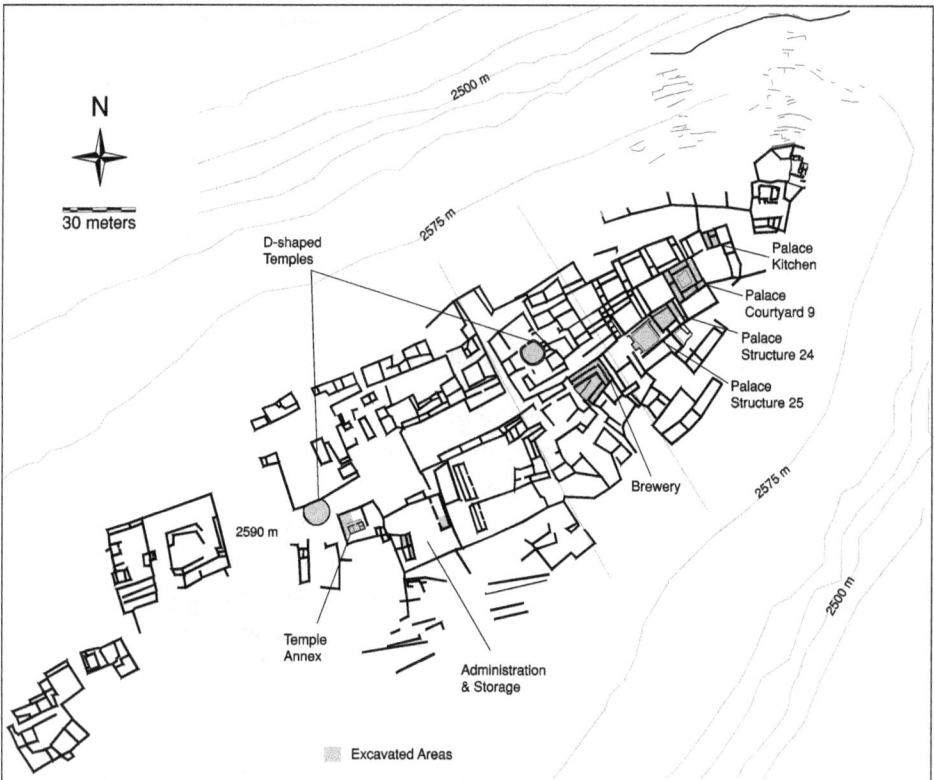

Figure 6.2. Cerro Baúl. Plan by Patrick R. Williams.

from the Lake Titicaca region began to demonstrate a strong presence in the region (Williams 2001).

Aside from the architectural presence at Cerro Baúl, the marker of Wari influence over the Middle Osmore Valley is the intensive investment in agricultural terracing and canal construction associated with their influx (Williams 2003). Williams outlines how the Wari transformed the area into an region of enhanced agricultural production. This intensive agricultural investment is important to our argument, because it likely included a strong agroforestry component that included the *S. molle* tree. The tree's potential in the region may partially explain the Wari's political and agricultural interest in the Osmore Valley (Ansión 1986; Goldstein and Coleman 2004; Kramer 1957; Terrell et al. 2003).

The complex of sites at Cerro Baúl consists of several sectors with forty individual building groups (rooms, patios, kitchens, etc.) that have been individually excavated. On the Cerro Baúl summit, we found several loci of intensive feasting and ritual that were associated with the final Wari activities at the site. The most important locus may be a feasting hall and kitchen complex on the summit that we refer to here as the Brewery structure (Moseley et al. 2005)(Fig. 6.2). The mass production of alcoholic beverages occurred in this location, and the majority of the evidence points to the production of *Schinus molle* drinks.

Archaeobotanical Recovery and Potential Beverage Ingredients at Cerro Baúl

Archaeologists often cite poor preservation as a reason for not sampling organic remains in the neotropics. Parts of Peru, however, are home to some of the driest deserts in the world. In coastal areas, preservation is excellent. While preservation is better along the coast of Peru, it varies from excellent to good in our study area. We have recovered, so far, over 200,000 plant remains representing thirty families and a variety of small (<4.0 mm) inorganic and organic remains. Our continuing excavations at Cerro Baúl include an intensive archaeobotanical sampling strategy that requires the collection of 1.0 liter of soil per square meter of excavated occupation floors and the excavation and volumetric sampling of entire features. This methodology has led us to a solid understanding of the terminal state of Middle Horizon settlement of the area from a macrobotanical perspective. Given the arid nature of the area's soils, we dry-sieved the sediments using a standard set of geological meshes (4.0-mm, 2.0-mm,

1.0-mm, and 0.425-mm mesh sizes) and to date have examined more than 600 square meters of the excavated areas. While there is always error implicated in archaeological sampling, our numbers here attest to the presence and relative abundance of plants used in the past.

The archaeobotanical evidence recovered at Cerro Baúl indicates that the potential existed for the production of beverages from a variety of resources (Table 6.3). For example, remains of a relatively large *Chenopodium* sp. (1.5–2.0 millimeters), corresponding in size with pre-Hispanic domesticated species, were recovered from the Brewery area (Bruno and Whitehead 2003). However, their small quantity (n = 11) suggests that brewing activities did not focus on the production of *Chenopodium* spp. fermented beverages. This can also be said for other grains and fruits, including corn (Table 6.3).

Of particular interest is our *Z. mays* evidence. Ostensibly, Cerro Baúl was an important settlement in the pre-Hispanic Andes, and the ritual consumption of food and drink was likely associated with political consolidation of power at the site (Moseley et al. 2005). Yet, one need only look at the meager evidence for consumption of maize throughout the site (Table 6.3) to intuit that something other than corn beer dominated beverage production at the site. Corn is present in the Cerro Baúl assemblage, including at least two varieties of *Zea mays*, an eight-row and a ten-row variety. Corn remains at the site, however, make up less than 1 percent of the total Cerro Baúl archaeobotanical assemblage (n = 410). We have relatively few whole cobs present (n = 4); most of the corn materials are in the form of fragmented carbonized cobs (n = 105) or cupules (n = 117), and the number of individual grains is likewise not noteworthy (n = 140). Most grains are small and found in hearth contexts. Some of the maize in the assemblage, the flour and flint types, could have been used for fermented beverage production (see Table 6.1). The *Zea mays* remains from the Brewery contexts, however, equal just 156 of the total determinations at Cerro Baúl and make up only 1 percent of the archaeobotanical assemblage in the Brewery area. Furthermore, investigation of starch grain presence among the Brewery's grinding stones reported by Moseley et al. (2005) indicates that tubers and chile peppers, and *not Z. mays*, were ground on the implements. These findings indicate that something other than corn was fermented.

This is not to suggest that maize was socially insignificant during this period. More corn was found in elite Baúl contexts than in the rest of the site, suggesting that its consumption connoted high status in some ways. Nevertheless, remains of husking, stored grains, or other processing remains are very few, and the indication is that corn did not figure promi-

Table 6.3. Fermentable Fruits and Grains Recovered at Cerro Baúl

Family	Determination	Plant part	Brewery	Palace Courtyard 9	Palace Structure 24	Palace Structure 25	Temple Annex	Off-summit domestic unit #30	Off-summit domestic unit #32	Total
Anacardiaceae	*Schinus molle*	Stem	4,337	122	341	11	270	0	4	5,085
		Seed	5,524	2,427	30,918	509	3,818	4	3	43,203
Cactaceae	cf. Cactaceae	Seed	2	0	4	4	0	21	5	36
		Stem	0	0	2	0	0	0	0	2
	Echinocactus sp.	Seed	40	0	0	0	29	4	10	83
	Echinopsis sp.	Seed	0	16	130	12	0	13	4	175
	Haageocereus sp.	Seed	0	4	2	1	0	46	1	54
	Opuntia sp.	Seed	0	1	73	2	0	0	0	76
Chenopodiaceae	*Chenopodium* sp.	Seed	1,061	321	1,454	403	307	5	31	3,582
Cucurbitaceae	cf. Cucurbitaceae	Seed	1	3	15	0	6	0	0	25
		Fruit	0	3	0	0	0	0	0	3
	Cucurbita sp.	Seed	1	8	0	0	2	0	0	11
	Lagenaria sp.	Fruit	0	21	0	37	0	0	0	58
		Seed	1	103	9	0	9	0	0	122
Fabaceae	*Acacia* sp.	Seed	9	2	0	0	0	0	0	11
	Arachis sp.	Fruit	2	0	0	0	0	0	0	2
		Seed	0	0	3	0	0	0	0	3
	cf. Fabaceae	Fruit	0	33	1	5	27	0	1	67
		Seed	7	24	8	1	9	0	0	49
	Phasaeolus lunatus	Seed	1	6	0	0	0	0	0	7
	Phaseolus sp.	Seed	28	3	6	0	0	0	0	37
Poaceae	*Zea mays*									
	10-row	Fruit	0	1	0	0	0	0	0	1
	8-row	Fruit	0	3	0	0	0	0	0	3
	Cob fragment	Fruit	72	3	4	2	23	0	1	105
	Cupule	Fruit	44	8	27	0	38	0	0	117
	Embryo	Seed	18	11	6	9	0	0	0	44
	Seed	Seed	22	28	58	3	29	0	0	140
Grand total			11,170	3,151	33,061	999	4,567	93	60	53,090

nently in the daily lives of people working and living on the site summit. Palace Courtyard 9, for example, had a relatively large amount of corn, but that corn represented less than 2 percent of the overall assemblage in the area (n = 54). This is consistent with the idea that the role of corn rose in importance later in the Andes, during the Late Intermediate and Late Horizon periods (Hastorf and Johannessen 1993). At Cerro Baúl, a beverage from another plant, *Schinus molle*, was likely involved in the performance, presentation, and reinforcement of ethnic identity.

Schinus Molle Fermented Beverages at Cerro Baúl

The most prevalent plant remains, in terms of both ubiquity and density, are seeds and fruit stems from the *Schinus molle* tree (n = 54,637).[3] In nearly every context examined, these seeds were present, although the quantities varied significantly. Additionally, processing remains from *S. molle* berries and drupes, for example, small, short stems, were abundant in a number of garbage and fire-use features. Although a number of known uses exist for the fruit of *S. molle*, our evidence suggests that it was used in the production of a fermented beverage.

Schinus molle

The *S. molle* plant is native to the region and is known locally as molle in Spanish, Aymara, and Quechua, the dominant languages of the area. It is known as the California pepper tree in the United States among English speakers. *S. molle* is ecologically successful in marginal environments, such as poor soils and saline aquifers (Kramer 1957). At present, local farmers in the arid Moquegua and Locumba valleys use the tree to line canals and create hedgerows along property boundaries. It is easily propagated through vegetative means and is a prized selection for firewood and construction materials. Williams (Terrell et al. 2003: 342–343) argues that *S. molle* was one of the critical elements in the agricultural system during the Middle Horizon. Ansión (1986) identifies *S. molle* as one of the principal trees used in Inca agroforestry.

The plant has a variety of other uses. The bark and leaves are used for their antiseptic and fever-reducing properties, and the seeds are often used as a substitute for black pepper and occasionally to adulterate pepper being sold in markets. The essential oils in *S. molle* are often used as insect repellant, and leaves, branches, and fruits are often placed in or near middens to reduce invertebrate infestation (Brack Egg 1999). These same oils are used as common remedies for sore throats and colds. The oils in the timber also give the wood natural resistance to insect activity, and for this reason, the wood is often preferred as a primary building material (Kramer 1957). *S. molle* was one of the most culturally useful plants before the Spanish Conquest (Cabieses 1993; Kramer 1957). Garcilaso de la Vega (1829) documents Andean populations' use of the seeds as a condiment in the Inca period. The Spanish were thrilled with its discovery and transported trees throughout the Pacific Rim within fifty years of conquest (Cabieses 1993). The tree is referred to as "el Perú" or "*peruil*" in a number of American and Asian contexts to this day. While these uses of the plant may be the reason that we find seeds and other parts archaeologically, there is no known published or observed use of *S. molle* fruits in quantity except for making a fermented beverage.

S. Molle and Chicha de Molle

When ripe, the berries produce enough water-soluble sugar for fermented beverage production. Guaman Poma indicates that, during the Inca period, fresh *S. molle* fruits were included in annual offerings made to huacas and *apus* (ancestor shrines within the Inca landscape) during the months of December and February (Guaman Poma 2005: 177, 192). While fruit can be found on *S. molle* trees at all times of the year (Goldstein and Coleman 2004), it is most abundant during the early months of the Andean summer, January and February. This may explain why the *S. molle* is not mentioned as a traditional Inca offering during other months of the year. Garcilaso de la Vega notes in several places, including in a chapter dedicated solely to the uses of *S. molle*, that it was used as an offering and in the production of a fermented beverage. This beverage was, on occasion, served in tandem with corn-based fermented beverages, including at feasting events (Garcilaso de la Vega 1829; see also Olivias W. 2001).

Unfortunately, the production steps to make chicha de molle were not detailed by the Spaniards. Sufficient ethnographic data from the valley, nonetheless, provide the basis for an experimental reconstruction of the brewing process (see Goldstein and Coleman 2004). Here, we highlight three important processes that produce different patterns of *S. molle* remains: fruit collection, processing, and boiling.

During the summer months, *S. molle* berries are abundant, to the point that trees bow with the weight of the fruits. We estimate that about 4,000

S. molle berries are required to produce twenty liters of chicha. We argue that widespread participation in fruit gathering would have been necessary for large events. Fruit from several trees would need to be harvested to produce the large quantities needed for a feast, requiring considerable labor. People working in their field systems could have collected wood, leaves, and berries at the same time for household needs. Thus, molle harvesting could have been conducted concurrently with other daily or seasonal agricultural tasks.

The second phase of production requires a winnowing process to separate the papery skins and small stems from each individual fruit. Ancient separation methods are unknown, but wind-driven winnowing or use of a cloth sieve are possibilities, as they have been successfully used ethnoarchaeologically (Goldstein and Coleman 2004). The winnowing process frees the individual seeds with their resin pockets from the papery and bitter-tasting outer coating, as well as from the small peduncles, or stems. Archaeologically, this would have left separate deposits of stems and paper apart from the seeds themselves. To locate possible processing contexts in our excavations, we separated the stems from the seeds in our analysis (Tables 6.3–6.6).

The third step of production is the boiling process. For beverage production, large quantities of warm or boiling water are essential.[4] Additionally, fuel and vessels for producing and containing large quantities of hot water would be needed at the site. Although water near the summit of Baúl was once more abundant than it is today (Williams 2001), there is no evidence of wells or other natural sources of water on the summit itself.

The three stages of the *S. molle* beverage production process have archaeological signatures, including archaeobotanical remains, fermenting jars, serving vessels (ceramic and gourd), and large dedicated firing areas (Table 6.4). Analyzing these can help us to interpret the social and political role of *S. molle* beverage production at Cerro Baúl.

Our study focuses on the elite precinct on the summit: the Brewery building, a feasting center and kitchen; the Palace, an elite residential structure that comprises administrative and support units, the Palace Courtyard 9, Palace Structure 24, and Palace Structure 25—and the Palace Kitchen; and the Temple Annex, an administrative and storage building (Fig. 6.2). We compare these areas of elite activity on the summit with nonelite household buildings off the summit that represent contemporary occupation but have no physical continuity with the elite precinct on the summit

6.4. Material Correlates of Alcohol Production in the Andes

Moore (1989)	Shimada (1994)	Goldstein & Shimada (n.d.)	Evidence for fermented beverages at Cerro Baúl
Large storage vessels		Porrones	Large cooking/storage vessel remains
Dregs		Z. mays cob & kernel remains	Parched seeds of S. molle, processed fruit stems
Grinding stones		Grinding stones	Present in contexts adjacent to brewing locales, but not necessary for S. molle beverages
Z. mays cobs		Z. mays cobs	Relatively few
Bags/textiles		Loom, Gossypium sp. seeds, spindle whorls, textiles	Some burned utilitarian textiles in brewery contexts, Gossypium sp. seeds, spindle whorls
Mate or gourd (Lagenaria sp. or Crescentia sp.) vessels		Lagenaria sp., seeds & vessels	Lagenaria sp. seeds & vessels in brewing & consumption contexts
Stirring implements	Cooking facilities adjacent to production facilities	Cooking facilities adjacent to production facilities	Dedicated & technologically distinct cooking facilities adjacent to feasting contexts
Different drinking vessels of similar forms		Variation in ceramic bowls	Variety of kero styles emulating & some identical to Ayacucho elite styles

Table 6.5. *Schinus molle* Remains at Cerro Baúl

Structure	Room Type	Feature	Stem	Seed	Total
Brewery	Brewing hearth	3	0	2	2
		4	17	1,004	1,021
		6	1,529	290	1,819
		7	14	21	35
		8	2	316	318
		9	6	207	213
		10	4	40	44
		11	276	268	544
		12	0	4	4
		13	6	55	61
		15	1,095	562	1,657
		Floor	1,388	2,753	4,141
Brewery total			4,337	5,520	9,857
Palace Kitchen	Room F	1	0	60	60
		Floor	0	5,611	5,611
	Room G	Floor	0	6	6
Palace Kitchen total				5,677	5,677
Palace Courtyard 9	Patio	5	0	748	748
	Room B	8	0	29	29
		Floor	0	1	1
	Room F1	4	0	13	13
		5	0	3	3
		5,3	0	1	1
		Floor	47	683	730
	Cuy pen	Floor	1	107	108
	Room G	Floor	74	109	183
Palace Courtyard 9 total			122	1,694	1,816
Palace Structure 24	Room A	2	4	242	246
		8	8	7,371	7,379
		9	0	71	71
		11	2	4	6
		12	3	67	70
		14	0	6	6
		4A	42	10,030	10,072
		4B	26	12,278	12,304
		4C	1	78	79
		Floor	235	468	703
	Room B	Floor	9	149	158
	Room C	3	0	6	6
		5	0	21	21
		8	0	18	18
		10	1	7	8
		11	3	15	18
		12	0	1	1
		Floor	7	86	93
Palace Structure 24 total			341	30,918	31,259

Palace Structure 25	Room A	2	0	3	3
		Floor	8	429	437
	Room A2	6	0	1	1
		Floor	0	51	51
	Room A3	Floor	3	25	28
Palace Structure 25 total			11	509	520
Temple Annex	Admin. Room	1	0	2	2
		3	0	2	2
	Large Receiving Room	1	1	21	22
		2	0	396	396
		3	0	308	308
		4	0	3	3
		5	2	32	34
		Floor	3	210	213
	Store Room C1	2	5	6	11
		4	2	2	4
		5	7	6	13
		7	4	0	4
		10	2	2	4
		Floor	6	13	19
	Store Room C2	7	2	0	2
		9	5	0	5
		12	0	1	1
		Floor	19	11	30
	Store Room D1	1	7	392	399
		Floor	8	1	9
	Store Room D3	1	34	508	542
		2	44	415	459
		Floor	119	1,487	1,606
Temple Annex total			270	3,818	4,088
Summit buildings total			5,081	48,140	53,221

(Table 6.5). The variable distribution of *S. molle* across these structures not only identifies the existence of intensive *S. molle* beer production but also suggests that its production and consumption played an important political and social role in the Wari colony.

Wari Elite Activity and *S. molle* Beverage Production

We recovered tens of thousands of *Schinus molle* seeds from several discrete features on the summit of Cerro Baúl associated directly with Wari material culture and architecture (Table 6.5). The distribution of *S. molle* seeds falls into patterns in four modalities recovered from discrete garbage-deposition features of exclusively *S. molle* seeds and floors littered with production remains. Although the moderate preservation of botanic remains at Cerro Baúl may have reduced the amount of seeds and other *S. molle* remains preserved, the relative quantities provide a robust illustration of distinct contexts of beverage production.

Modality 1: Large-scale Production

The first modality consists of deposits of more than 1,000 seeds. These large single-episode seed deposits are uniformly associated with kitchen contexts within the summit Palace complex. These deposits most likely represent the remains of large-scale beverage production. The distribution of these deposits in many different types of structures, however, demonstrates that the production of this fermented beverage occurred in various contexts, suggesting that its consumption played multiple roles on the summit. Structures that contained deposits in the order of the first modality include Palace Structure 24, the Palace Kitchen, and the Palace Structure 1 Brewery.

The highest quantity of seeds occurs in three different garbage pits in Palace Structure 24 and the Palace Kitchen buildings (each with individual deposits of more than 5,000 seeds). Palace Structure 24, Room A (ca. 10 × 4 meters), is associated with an elite, limited-access patio area where ritual/political activities may have taken place. A single central hearth is located in the center of the adjacent Room B (ca. 15 × 15 meters). Room A was used intensively as a garbage-deposition area, and we see two discrete instances of more than 10,000 seeds deposited.

The Palace Kitchen (ca. 5 × 7 meters) building represents a small independent cooking complex adjacent to the elite living compound and the Palace Courtyard 9 area. The Palace Kitchen, in contrast to the deposits in Palace Structure 24, presents no single deposit that can be identified as a trash deposit, but the remains of some 5,000 seeds were recovered from across the floor.

The next-highest number of *S. molle* seeds occurs in Structure 1 Brewery. In the 2004 season, Williams, Nash, and Moseley revisited contexts associated with what had been termed the "beer hall" by Feldman (Moseley et al. 1991; Moseley et al. 2005). The hall, what we now call the Brewery, is associated with a large open patio (ca. 8 × 15 meters) that contained the feasting debris from a single episode (Moseley et al. 2005). Of particular interest is a long room, interpreted as the brewing kitchen, where at least ten 1.5-meter-diameter hearth features were placed at 1.0-meter intervals along the north wall. Each hearth contained the remains of large cooking vessels, oxidized floors, and lenses of ash. Although the building was used for an extensive period of time, each of the hearths appears to have been used simultaneously for an event just prior to abandonment (Moseley et al. 2005).

Table 6.5 illustrates the high numbers of *S. molle* seeds (ca. 1,000 and lower per cooking hearth) and stems that were found in pits adjacent to these hearth features. Many of the seeds recovered are ostensibly carbonized but not covered in ash, a potential indicator that these materials were not used as fuel. Instead, material remains indicate that the cooking fires used a mixture of camelid dung and wood fuel. We interpret the high quantities of seeds found in most of the features as dregs or postproduction debris and therefore suggest that their abundance indicates a preference for brewing *S. molle*–based fermented beverages in these contexts. The floor area surrounding these cooking features includes some 2,700 seeds. Interestingly, the total number of stems (n = 4,337) recovered from the room accounts for 78 percent of the seeds (n = 5,524) present. It is the only context in which we find a nearly equivalent count of both seeds and stems in the same building (Table 6.3). This trend indicates that, in the case of the Brewery beverage preparation, the berries were likely cleaned and cooked in the same location. Additionally, other kitchen/domestic activities occurred in the same areas.[5]

In examining the individual contexts of each Modality 1 deposit, it is clear that different types of *S. molle* beverage production were occurring on the summit. In Palace Structure 24 and the Palace Kitchen, seed deposits occur in conjunction with other production refuse; the production events that took place in these contexts were most likely folded into other economic tasks and served the inhabitants or guests of the Palace complex. The abundance of *S. molle* trash in the kitchen area may indicate that group cooking for communal affairs occurred in the Palace Kitchen. The deposits of *S. molle* trash in the Palace Structure 24 garbage pits may relate to feasting on a lesser scale than that represented by the Structure 1 Brewery remains.

In the Structure 1 Brewery, on the other hand, we find a single room dedicated to processing *S. molle* seeds and beverage manufacture, where a series of productive steps occurred in a single locale, for a single purpose. Although the most striking context of intensive production is in this structure, this is not to say that it played the most important role in beverage manufacture at the site. The feasting debris in the patio within the Structure 1 Brewery, the hearths with associated jars in the Brewery kitchen, and the archaeobotanical data from throughout the Structure 1 Brewery complex suggest that the remains recovered from the Brewery building kitchen were the result of preparations for a feast just prior to the abandonment of Cerro Baúl (Moseley et al. 2005). This is in contrast to the deposits recovered from Palace Structure 24 and the Palace Kitchen, which appear to have been associated with multiple events and probably on a more frequent basis. Moreover, the events that generated the quantities of postproduction remains in Palace Structure 24 likely represent grand-scale events earlier in the Middle Horizon.

Modality 2: Household / Suprahousehold Production and Consumption

The second mode of *S. molle* deposits is between 200 and 500 *S. molle* seeds per single feature. The Palace Courtyard 9 complex (ca. 20 × 20 meters) came equipped with its own rooms for food processing that were adjacent to the large courtyard area and distinct from the Palace Kitchen rooms to the northeast of Palace Courtyard 9. These rooms, F and G (both ca. 4 × 10 meters), were used for preparation for less-intensive affairs and have discrete garbage deposits of fewer than 500 seeds. These smaller deposits probably relate to smaller-scale production events.

The patios and room configurations of the Palace Courtyard 9 and Palace Structure 25 (a large open space with a dais [12 × 12 meters] adjacent to the Palace Courtyard 9) exhibit distinct layouts. The patios of Palace 9 and Palace Structure 25 (a patio and dais (12 × 12 meters) adjacent to the Palace structure) present a different pattern from that of rooms F and G. In addition to deposits of *S. molle* seeds, both Patio Courtyard 9 and Palace Structure 25 contain *Lagenaria* sp. fragments (Table 6.3). Known also as *mate* or *potos* (Camino 1987), the cleaned and dried fruits of *Lagenaria* sp. (gourds) have long been used in the Andes as drinking and serving vessels for fermented beverages. The seeds of *Lagenaria* sp., however, were recovered only from Palace Structure 24 deposits (Table 6.3). This suggests that gourd vessel production (i.e., cleaning, scraping, and drying) occurred here and not in Palace Structures 25 or 9, where these vessels were likely used. Likewise, ceramic drinking bowls only occur in Palace Patio 9 and Palace Structure 25 (Costion et al. 2004). This evidence suggests that a specific consumption activity, probably ceremonial and involving individuals from beyond the immediate Palace complex, took place in these two patio areas.

The second modality of deposits of *S. molle* in the Cerro Baúl contexts probably represents household or suprahousehold production for consumption at the household or affine level, much as people produce *chicha de jora* today (Camino 1987). This level of production need not be associated directly with festival or feasting activities. Ethnographically and historically, people produce chicha at the household level for daily consumption or trade in kind at the interhousehold level (Camino 1987; see Bowser and Patton 2004 for Amazonian example). It is within these ethnographic contexts that Camino (1987), Gillin (1973), and Schaedel (1988) describe the use of *Lagenaria* sp. or mate vessels. Overall, evidence from this second modality demonstrates that the preference for this beverage goes beyond the ritual large-scale production demonstrated by the first modality. There was a preference for the beverage among elites in their households and for ceremonial use.

Administrative and Household Scales of *S. molle* Beverage Production

The third and fourth modalities are found much more widely throughout the site of Cerro Baúl and its annexes. The third modality of *S. molle* deposits includes counts of n<300 seeds. These deposits occur in floor and general intrusive garbage features, with the highest numbers being associated with abandoned rooms and intrusive middens (Table 6.5). Of particular interest is the occurrence of mostly third-level modality features within the Temple Annex (ca. 25 × 25 meters)—an administrative and storage structure adjacent to a "D"-shaped structure interpreted as a Wari ancestor shrine, a hallmark of Wari imperial architecture. The Temple Annex consists of a large receiving room (ca. 10 × 25 meters) flanked on the north and south by a series of three storage rooms (ca. 3 × 5 meters) on both sides. To the western end of the building is a small administrative room with a dedicated hearth attached to it and also one of the few burials recovered at the site. The only large deposit is in Store Room D3, one of the storage rooms on the side of the patio. The heavy presence of *S. molle* in Store Room D3 (floor and features, n = 2,607), most of which was on the floor (n = 1,606), may indicate that this room was a temporary storage structure for *S. molle* associated with events taking place in the ritual areas of the site. This structure represents 63 percent of the *S. molle* deposit in the Temple Annex, with the remaining 37 percent coming from the large receiving hall, where third-modality *S. molle* depositions occur as intrusive garbage pits in the entrance to the room. The meaning of these deposits is not understood but may be related to activities related to ritual associated with the opening or closing of the room.

Finally, the fourth modality of *S. molle* occurs as isolated remains across floors at the site n<100 in every context. Additionally, we have occurrences of the stems from the *S. molle* fruits that occur coincidentally with deposition on floors as well as in intrusive garbage features of *S. molle* seeds (Table 6.5). Most notable is the vast discrepancy between *S. molle* deposits on the summit and nonelite, perhaps local, domestic contexts on the slopes of Cerro Baúl. The two excavated domestic units (30 and 32) on the slopes are long, rectangular platforms (ca. 20 × 10 meters) that feature an enclosed patio and a small covered residential area at one end. Domestic Units 30 and 32 have almost no *S. molle* (n = 4 and n = 7, respectively; see Table 6.6). In each case, the incidence of *S. molle* in each housing unit represents less than 1 percent of the total assemblage (Domestic Unit 30 [n = 443]; Domestic Unit 32 [n = 1,853]).

It is significant that *S. molle* is present in these contexts at all, since Nash's (2002) work on the local elite compounds on the summit of Cerro Baúl's neighbor, Cerro Mejía, indicates that *S. molle* seeds were not present in these archaeological contexts. The lack of *S. molle* remains indicates that indigenous elites, while clearly tied through trade and political control to Wari-based elites on the Baúl summit through their material culture, may have prepared little to none of the beverage themselves. The nonparticipation of what we believe to be a culturally Wari activity could be interpreted as local elite resistance to ethnically Wari political power and activities associated with assertion of that control.

We believe that the fourth modality represents the communitywide effort necessary to collect the raw materials, that is, thousands of berries, to

Table 6.6. *Schinus molle* Presence at Cerro Baúl

Structure	Room	Feature	Stem	Seed	Total
Domestic Unit #30	Room C	Floor	0	1	1
Domestic Unit #32	Room A	Floor	4	3	7
Domestic structure total			4	4	8

produce large quantities of the *S. molle* beverage. Although the dispersed remains of *S. molle* across the site indicate that the berry was not altogether limited to elite access, its limited quantity outside of the summit complex suggests that the production of this fermented beverage was. Given the labor requirements for beverage production, it is likely that members from some of the households at Cerro Baúl and its surrounds collected the seeds from the downslope areas for the summit production. *S. molle* trees were probably located away from residences in the lower valley and irrigated areas around the summit. Nonelite agriculturalists working in the valley likely had the easiest access to these trees, as they do today, and probably were responsible for transporting fruits to their households for preprocessing, that is, removal of stems and skins. The cleaned products were then taken to the Baúl summit for use in beer production. This would explain the lack of stems recovered in the majority of summit deposits. The presence of stems in the Brewery and the Temple Annex contexts may indicate more elite control over the collection and use of *S. molle* in specific instances.

We are not suggesting full-time dedication of labor to the collection of *S. molle* fruits; rather, we propose that the collection of berries was probably an occasional expectation of certain household members, seasonally performed in anticipation of commensal events taking place on the summit, whether or not these people were themselves invited. Likewise, the occasional collection of *S. molle* firewood, leaves for medicinal purposes, and tracking in of dirt could explain the very low incidence of the seeds in archaeological contexts. The easiest explanation for the small but pervasive quantities of *S. molle* remains across the site is that berries were collected widely in the valley for beverage production at the summit and occasional condiment use in elite and non-elite contexts.

We interpret the limited to nonextant evidence of *S. molle* seeds as a clear indication that outside of Wari elite contexts the local population was not engaged in producing this beverage for their own consumption. Although locals used the tree in agroforestry, construction, and as fuel, as people still do today, they did not produce the beverage in a domestic setting. Whether this was a factor of elite control or merely of personal preference is difficult to determine; given the extensive presence of the *S. molle* tree, its numerous medicinal properties, and its reputation as an excellent fuel source, however, it seems probable that, if people *could* have collected these tree parts in larger quantities, they would have. The presence of limited *S. molle* fruits may in fact represent resistance to elite control over a prized commodity.

Schinus molle Fermented Beverage Production as a Cultural Indicator at Cerro Baúl

The *Schinus molle* and other plant remains recovered from the Cerro Baúl area point to a tradition of fermented beverage production from *S. molle* fruits rather than corn. Our research has allowed us to trace the production of *S. molle* beer through its production process. This sequence is similar, in broad strokes, to the production sequence of other Andean fermented beverages that have been described archaeologically (Goldstein and Shimada i.p.; Hastorf and Johannessen 1993; Moore 1989; Shimada 1994). Moreover, the details in our analysis illustrate that molle fermented beverage production entailed a variety of social and cultural processes that played an important role in the social dynamics of the period.

Our understanding of the material correlates of fermented beverage production comes from modern and historical contexts where corn-based fermented beverages were and remain the preference. Most ethnohistorical and ethnographic data focus on large-scale neighborhood brewing systems for corn beverages, traditionally referred to as *tavernas* (Camino 1987). Brüning (1989), Camino (1987), Gillin (1973), Huertas V. (1999), and Schaedel (1988), for example, all discuss the presence of tavernas in extended households on the north coast. These are areas where corn beers and other cooked foods, like roast meats, are produced for suprahousehold consumption, similar to the communal cooking of food between households and across neighborhoods that Weismantel also describes (1998). In contrast, *S. molle* beverage production at Cerro Baúl apparently was not an integral part of the daily nonelite domestic and supradomestic economy. Instead, access to molle beer seems to have been restricted to the elite, and it was usually enjoyed at special events associated specifically with contexts on the Cerro Baúl summit.

While reports of *S. molle* beverage production exist in some of the Chilean archaeological literature (Dauelsberg 1972; Erices 1975), comparable data sets are limited for the southern Andes and Middle Horizon periods. Two correlates exist in the Osmore Drainage. Paul Goldstein (1993) excavated a brewing facility at the Tiwanaku site of Omo (M-12) farther down the Osmore drainage (see Fig. 6.1). The architectural form of the Omo facility resembles the brewing facilities found in the elite household context and ritual contexts at Cerro Baúl (Palace Courtyard 9 and Palace Structure 25). Although large batches of fermented beverages were made in the Omo facility (Goldstein 1993: 36), it is unlikely that Wari-type *S. molle* beverages were produced there, because no seeds were recovered from this context (P. Goldstein, personal communication 2004).

The second example comes from the site of La Yaral, a Late Intermediate Period (AD 900–1000) Chiribaya site in the Lower Osmore Drainage (see Fig. 6.1). Rice recovered a potential *S. molle* fermented beverage brewery at a nonelite domestic structure with a separate fermenting room and a large hearth associated with the corner of a potential exterior courtyard. The fermenting room is strewn with charred *S. molle* seeds, the potential dregs of production (Rice 1993: 78–80). While both the Omo and La Yaral contexts are similar in some ways to those found at Baúl, the intensity seen in the Cerro Baúl Brewery appears to have no contemporary or later correlates in the valley.

The Structure 1 Brewery feature is unique in its capacity and dedication to fermented beverage production (Moseley et al. 2005). In the Brewery we have all of the material correlates of production on a large scale (Table 6.4), but, unlike the household-level production that has been observed in north coastal Peruvian ethnography and history, this context is unique. The closest correlate that we have is areas described at the Late Intermediate site of Chan Chan by Topic (1990). Topic describes craft-production areas directly adjacent to Chimor palaces that included areas of fermented beverage production and distribution. This later Chimú example is particular in that beverage production areas are set aside as distinct architectural spaces attached to craft production areas that were subordinate to middle-echelon elite control. These areas ostensibly are not communal feasting loci attached to the beverage production center, as is the case at Cerro Baúl.

Finally, the elite household contexts of production at Cerro Baúl, and Palace Structure 25 and the Temple Annex are both dissimilar to other reported archaeological production contexts for the Andes. This reality highlights the differences between beer production and consumption at Baúl and the two kinds of beer production most often thought of as typical in the Andes—the Inca and north coastal traditions. While the production of *S. molle* fermented beverages at Baúl shares material production correlates with these examples, the spatial and architectural elements are unique. Inca, Chimú, Tiwanaku, Chiribaya, and Wari brewing and drinking practices each had distinctive features.

Conclusion: Fermented Beverages in Perspective across Space and Time

The ubiquity of *S. molle* seeds across Cerro Baúl, coupled with the corresponding lack of seed use by locals, points to molle's use as a social and ethnic marker. Molle may have been a marker of Wari identity throughout the central Andes during the Middle Horizon. This idea is supported by macrobotanical remains of *S. molle* recovered from similar contexts at Conchopata, a Wari elite compound in the Ayacucho heartland (Cook and Glowacki 2003; Sayre and Whitehead 2003). Additionally, Williams (i.p.) has noted the apparent geographical correlation between the Wari road infrastructure throughout the Andes, sites with Middle Horizon Wari-style ceramics, and toponyms that include the Quechua word *molle*, a word that has *S. molle* as its only referent. This evidence, combined with our Cerro Baúl data, indicates that *S. molle* fermented beverages played an essential role in organizing and legitimizing elite activities, perhaps including the extraction of labor from nonelite households; this role was similar to that *Z. mays* beer played during Inca times and continues to play among the Quechua-speaking populations today. Moreover, molle beer was an integral part of Wari cuisine, it served as a marker of Wari ethnicity that likely served to represent their traditional and elite way of life.

Our vision of Andean prehistory has often been biased toward Inca and historical periods because these are better documented. Transformed by colonialism (Mintz 1985) and postcolonialism (Fanon 1969; also see Hayashida, this volume), however, these historical traditions are sometimes poor windows into earlier cultural activities. This chapter highlights the need to address multiple lines of archaeological evidence in order to evaluate perceived modern and historical continuities that are projected into the past. Our hope is that our interpretations of *S. molle* archaeobotanical evidence at the site of Cerro Baúl will open a broader discussion of the role and realities of ancient fermented beverage production. Ultimately, we aim to stimulate further archaeological investigations in the Andes that illustrate the diversity of non-Inca and non-Spanish cultural traditions in the Andean past.[6]

Notes

1. See Guaman Poma (2005: 255) for historical references.

2. A similar mechanism of transforming the ordinary into the extraordinary is visible with the combinations of plant materials used in indigenous healing practices today on the Peruvian north coast (Sharon 1978).

3. Of the contexts compared here, *S. molle* counts are slightly smaller (n = 48,288).

4. All Andean fermented beverages demonstrate considerable variety in the techniques used for production. Based on informant interviews and participant observation in production, Goldstein and Coleman (2004) report that boiling is required to produce *S. molle* fermented beverages. Some historical (Garcilaso de la Vega 1829; Pardo B. 2004) and archaeological (Cook and Glowacki 2003) works from the region, however, describe using only hot or warm water, instead of boiling water, for *S. molle* beverage production. The presence of fire in the contexts explored here and the large quantities of parched *S. molle* seeds led us to the conclusion that heating of the liquid was integral to production in Cerro Baúl.

5. Additionally, across the different features in the brewing kitchen we recovered *Erythoxylon coca* (n = 1, one of 3 found at the site), *Gossypium* sp. (cotton: n = 127, 80 percent of all *Gossypium* sp. seeds found at the site), and an overall diversity of plant families (n = 22, mean for the site = 12). Relative to the presence of cottonseeds, this is a likely indicator of the seasonal activity of cotton harvesting and cleaning. The activities of cotton cleaning and coca chewing were likely simultaneous with the cooking process and may indicate the cultural complementarity of these activities. We also believe that the coincidence of cotton cleaning and the abundance of *S. molle* beverage production as a potential seasonal indicator mean that the events taking place occurred during the Andean summer (February–March), the optimal harvest time for both cotton and molle.

6. Fieldwork at Cerro Baúl received funding through grants from the Bruno Foundation, the Heinz Family Foundation, the National Science Foundation, and the National Endowment for the Humanities, Dr. Michael Moseley and Dr. P. Ryan Williams, primary investigators. We thank Rosana Quispe Valencia and Evelyn López Sosa for laboratory work in the Museo Contisuyo. We thank the Museo Contisuyo, Moquegua, Peru, for logistical support. Sofía Chacaltana added editorial and content information. Additional thanks are extended to Dr. Lee A. Newsom, without whom the paleoethnobotanical research would not have happened.

References Cited

Acosta, P. José de
1954 [1590] *Historia natural y moral de las Indias*. In *Obras del P. José de Acosta*, Pedro F. Mateos, ed. Biblioteca de Autores Españoles. Madrid: Ediciones Atlas, Real Academia Española.

Allen, Catherine J.
1988 *The Hold Life Has: Coca and Cultural Identity in an Andean Community.* Washington, D.C: Smithsonian Institution Press.

Ansión, Juan
1986 *El árbol y el bosque en la sociedad andina.* Lima: Food and Agricultural Organization of the United Nations/INFOR.

Antúñez de Mayolo R., S. E.
1981 *La nutrición en el antiguo Perú.* Lima: Banco Central de Reserva del Perú, Fondo Editorial.

Bowser, Brenda, and John Patton
2004 Domestic Spaces as Public Places: An Ethnoarchaeological Case Study of Houses, Gender, and Politics in the Ecuadorian Amazon. *Journal of Archaeological Method and Theory 11(2): 157–181.*

Brack Egg, Antonio
1999 *Diccionario enciclopédico de plantas útiles del Perú.* Lima: United Nations Development Program.

Bruman, Howard J.
2000 *Alcohol in Ancient Mexico.* Salt Lake City: University of Utah Press.

Brüning, Heinrich
1989 [1922] Lambayeque: Estudios monográficos. Compiled by J. Vreeland. Lima: Sociedad de Investigación de la Ciencia y Arte Norteño, Consejo Nacional de Cienca y Tecnología.

Bruno, Maria, and William T. Whitehead
2003 Chenopodium Cultivation and Formative Period Agriculture at Chiripa, Bolivia. *Latin American Antiquity* 14(3): 339–356.

Cabieses, Fernando
1993 *Apuntes de medicina tradicional: La racionalización de lo irracional.* Lima: Consejo Nacional de Cienca y Tecnología.

Camino, Lupe
1987 *Chicha de maíz: Bebida y vida del pueblo Catacaos.* Piura: Centro de Investigación y Promoción del Campesinado.

Cárdenas, Martín
1989 *Manual de plantas económicas de Bolivia.* 2nd edition. La Paz: Amigos de los Libros.

Cobo, Bernabé
1964 [1653] *Historia del Nuevo Mundo.* Biblioteca de Autores Españoles, vols. 91–92. Madrid: Ediciones Atlas.

Cook, Anita, and Mary C. Glowacki
2003 Pots, Politics, and Power: Huari Ceramic Assemblages and Imperial Administration. In *The Archaeology and Politics of Food and Feasting in Early States and Empires*, Tamara L. Bray, ed., pp. 173–202. New York: Kluwer Academic/Plenum.

Costian, Kirk, Veronique Belislé, and Ana Miranda Quispe
2004 Wari Ceramics at Cerro Baúl: A First Look at Function and Space. Paper pre-

sented at the 69th Annual Meeting of the Society for American Archaeology, Montreal.

Cummins, Thomas B. F.

2002 *Toasts with the Inca: Andean Abstraction and Colonial Imagery of Queros*. Ann Arbor: University of Michigan Press.

Cutler, Hugh C., and Martín Cárdenas

1947 Chicha, a Native South American Beer. *Botanical Museum Leaflets* (Harvard University) 13(3): 33–60.

Dauelsberg, Percy

1972 Arqueología del Departamento de Arica. In *Enciclopedia de Arica*, pp. 161–178. Santiago: Enciclopedias Regionales.

De Jaegher, Christian, and Antonio H. Valverde

1991 *Tecnología campesina del maíz: Comunidad campesina de Simirís-Piura*. Piura: Central Peruana de Servicios.

Douglas, Mary

1987 *Constructive Drinking: Perspectives on Drink from Anthropology*. New York: Cambridge University Press.

Erices, Sergio

1975 Evidencias de vegetales en tres cementerios prehispánicos, Arica, Chile. *Chungará* 5: 65–71.

Fanon, Frantz

1969 *The Wretched of the Earth*. London: Penguin.

Garcilaso de la Vega, El Inca

1829 [1609] *Historia de la conquista del Nuevo Mundo*. Vol. 3. Madrid: Imprenta de los Hijos de Doña Catalina Piñuela.

Gillin, John

1973 [1947] *Moche: A Peruvian Coastal Community*. Smithsonian Institution Institute of Social Anthropology Publication no. 3. Westport: Greenwood.

Goldstein, David, and Robin Christine Coleman

2004 *Schinus Molle L.* (Anacardiaceae) Chicha Production in the Central Andes. *Economic Botany* 58(4): 523–529.

Goldstein, David J., and Izumi Shimada

I.p. Feeding the Fire: Food, Metal, and Ceramic Production in the Middle Sicán Period (950–1050 CE). In *From Subsistence to Social Strategies: New Directions in the Study of Daily Meals and Feasting Events*, Elizabeth Klarich, ed. Boulder: University of Colorado Press.

Goldstein, Paul

1993 House, Community, and State in the Earliest Tiwanaku Colony: Domestic Patterns and State Integration at Omo M12, Moquegua. In *Domestic Architecture, Ethnicity, and Complementarity in the South-Central Andes*, Mark Aldenderfer, ed., pp. 25–41. Iowa City: University of Iowa Press.

Goody, Jack

1982 *Cooking, Cuisine, and Class: A Study in Comparative Sociology*. Cambridge: Cambridge University Press.

Guaman Poma de Ayala, Felipe
2005 [1615] *Nueva crónica y buen gobierno*. Lima: Fondo de Cultura Económica.
Guillet, David
1979 *Agrarian Reform and Peasant Economy in Southern Peru*. Columbia: University of Missouri Press.
Hastorf, Christine A., and Sissel Johannessen
1993 Pre-Hispanic Political Change and the Role of Maize in the Central Andes of Peru. *American Anthropologist* 95(1): 115–138.
Horkheimer, Hans
1973 *Alimentación y obtención de alimentos en el Perú prehispánico*. Lima: Universidad Nacional Mayor de San Marcos.
Huertas V., Luis
1999 *La costa peruana vista a través de Sechura: Espacio, arte y tecnología*. Lima: Prom Perú.
Hui, Yiu H.
2004 *Handbook of Food and Beverage Fermentation Technology*. New York: Marcel Dekker.
Kramer, Floyd L.
1957 The Pepper Tree, *Schinus molle L. Economic Botany* 2(4): 322–326.
La Barre, Weston
1938 Native American Beers. *American Anthropologist* 40: 224–234.
Mayer, Enrique
2002 *The Articulated Peasant: Household Economies in the Andes*. New York: Westview.
Mintz, Sidney W.
1985 *Sweetness and Power: The Place of Sugar in Modern History*. New York: Penguin.
Mitchell, William P.
1991 *Peasants on the Edge: Crop, Cult, and Crises in the Andes*. Austin: University of Texas Press.
Moore, Jerry D.
1989 Pre-Hispanic Beer in Coastal Peru: Technology and Social Context of Prehistoric Production. *American Anthropologist* 91(3): 682–695.
Moseley, Michael E., Paul S. Goldstein, Robert A. Feldman, and Luis Watanabe
1991 Colonies and Conquest: Tiwanaku and Huari in Moquegua. In *Huari Administrative Structure: Prehistoric Monumental Architecture and State Government*, William H. Isbell and Gordon F. McEwan, eds., pp. 93–119. Washington, D.C: Dumbarton Oaks.
Moseley, Michael E., Donna J. Nash, Patrick R. Williams, Susan de France, Ana Miranda Q., and Mario Morales
2005 Burning Down the Brewery: Establishing and Evacuating an Ancient Imperial Colony at Cerro Baúl, Peru. *Proceedings of the National Academy of Sciences* 102(48): 17264–17271.

Murra, John

2001 Maíz, tubérculos y ritos agrícolas. In *El mundo andino: Población, medio ambiente y economía*. John Murra, ed., pp. 143–152. Lima: Pontificia Universidad Católica del Peru.

Nash, Donna J.

2002 The Archaeology of Space: Places of Power in the Wari Empire. Doctoral dissertation, University of Florida.

Nicholson, G. Edward

1960 Chicha Maize Types and Chicha Manufacture in Peru. *Economic Botany* 14(4): 290–299.

Olivias W., Rosario

2001 *La cocina de los Incas*. Lima: Universidad de San Martín de Porres.

Pardo B., Oriana

2004 Las chichas en el Chile precolombino. *Chloris Chilensis* 7(2), http://www.chlorischile.cl., accessed June 8, 2007.

Rice, Don S.

1989 Osmore Drainage, Peru: The Ecological Setting. In *Ecology, Settlement, and History in the Osmore Drainage*, Don S. Rice, Charles Stanish, and Phillip R. Scarr, eds., vol. 1, BAR International Series no. 545, pp. 17–33. Oxford: British Archaeological Reports.

1993 Domestic Architecture and Residential Organization at La Yaral. In *Domestic Architecture, Ethnicity, and Complementarity in the South-Central Andes*, Mark Aldenderfer, ed., pp. 66–82. Iowa City: University of Iowa Press.

Salas, Jorge A.

2002 *Diccionario mochica-castellano castellano-mochica*. Lima: Universidad de San Martín de Porres.

Sayre, Matthew, and William Whitehead

2003 New Paleoethnobotanical Evidence from Conchopata: A Huari Site. Paper prepared for the symposium Recent Work at Conchopata, 68th Society for American Archaeology Annual Meeting, Milwaukee.

Schaedel, Richard

1988 *La etnografía muchik en las fotografías de H. Brüning 1886–1925*. Lima: Ediciones COFIDE.

Schultes, Richard Evans, and Robert F. Raffauf

1990 *The Healing Forest: Medicinal and Toxic Plants of the Northwest Amazonia*. Portland: Dioscorides.

Sharon, Douglas

1978 *Wizard of the Four Winds*. New York: Free Press.

Shimada, Izumi

1994 *Pampa Grande and the Mochica Culture*. Austin: University of Texas Press.

Sokup, Jaralsov

1970 *Vocabulario de los nombres vulgares de la flora peruana y catálogo de los géneros*. Lima: Editorial Salesiana.

Staller, John E.

2006 The Social, Symbolic and Economic Significance of *Zea mays* L. in the Late Horizon Period. In *Histories of Maize: Multidisciplinary Approaches to the Prehistory, Biogeography, Domestication, and Evolution of Maize*, John E. Staller, Robert H. Tykot, and Bruce F. Benz, eds., pp. 449–465. New York: Academic Press.

Terrell, John E., James P. Hart, Sibel Barut, Nicolleta Cellinese, Antonio Curet, Tim Denham, Chapurika M. Kusimba, Kyle Latinis, Rahul Oka, Joel Palka, Mary E. Pohl, Kevin O. Pope, Patrick R. Williams, Helen Haines, and John E. Staller

2003 Domesticated Landscapes: The Subsistence Ecology of Plant and Animal Domestication. *Journal of Archaeological Method and Theory* 10: 323–368.

Topic, John R.

1990 Craft Production in the Kingdom of Chimor. In *The Northern Dynasties: Kingship and Statecraft in Chimor*, Michael E. Moseley and Anne Cordy-Collins, eds., pp. 145–146. Washington, D.C.: Dumbarton Oaks.

Weismantel, Mary J.

1998 *Food, Gender, and Poverty in the Ecuadorian Andes*. New York: Waveland.

Williams, Patrick R.

2001 Cerro Baúl: A Wari Center on the Tiwanaku Frontier. *Latin American Antiquity* 12(1): 67–83.

2003 Hydraulic Landscapes and Social Relations in the Middle Horizon Andes. In *The Reconstruction of Archaeological Landscapes through Digital Technologies*, Maurizio Forte and Patrick R. Williams, eds., pp. 163–172. BAR International Series, vol. 1151. Oxford: British Archaeological Reports.

In press Wari and Tiwanaku Borderlands. In *Tiwanaku: Papers of the New World Art Symposium 2005, Denver Art Museum*.

Williams, Patrick Ryan, and Donna J. Nash

2002 Imperial Interaction in the Andes: Huari and Tiwanaku at Cerro Baúl. In *Andean Archaeology I: Variations in Sociopolitical Organization*, William H. Isbell and Helaine Silverman, eds., pp. 243–265. New York: Kluwer Academic/Plenum.

Yacovleff, E., and F. L. Herrera

1935 El mundo vegetal de los antiguos Peruanos. *Revista del Museo Nacional* (Lima) 4: 33–34.

7

Tiwanaku Influence on Local Drinking Patterns in Cochabamba, Bolivia

Karen Anderson

> They all say, bring us chicha from Cochabamba.
> —*Herminia X*

The Tiwanaku polity, centered at the site of Tiwanaku in the Andean highlands (Fig. 7.1), developed into a state-level society around AD 500 and lasted until about AD 1100. With the rise of the state, a distinctive Tiwanaku style developed that included a new and complex ceramic assemblage. The transition to this new assemblage occurred quickly and spread throughout the heartland of Tiwanaku. One of the most common new forms was a tall, finely made drinking cup, the kero, generally agreed to have been used for drinking fermented beverages such as maize or quinoa beer. The high frequency of keros found in a wide variety of Tiwanaku contexts attests to the popularity and widespread consumption of beers at all social levels.

While beer could be made from many grains and fruits (see Goldstein, Coleman Goldstein, and Williams and Hayashida, this volume), the evidence suggests that maize beer (which I call *chicha* in this chapter) was the beer of choice during Tiwanaku hegemony. Prior to Tiwanaku, maize was found in limited quantities in the southern Lake Titicaca basin. However, with the advent of the state, the distribution of maize increased substantially, especially at Tiwanaku, where it was found in surprisingly high quantities, considering the difficulty of growing it in the high-elevation environment (Wright et al. 2003: 393, 402).

Goldstein (2003) argues that the popularity of maize chicha was a driving force in Tiwanaku's political economy—one that pushed it outward to-

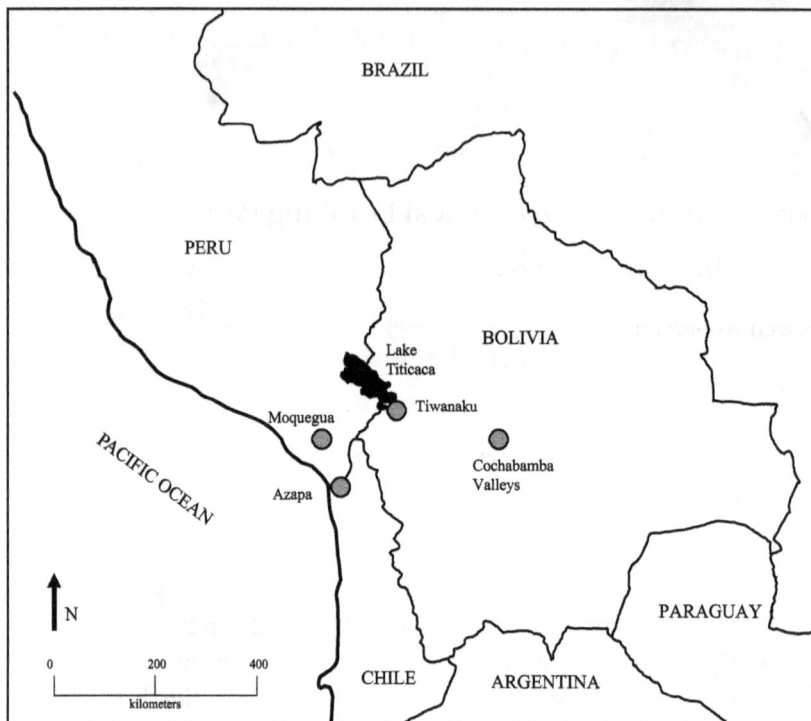

Figure 7.1. The south-central Andes showing Tiwanaku and peripheries. Map by the author.

ward lower-elevation maize-growing areas, such as Moquegua and Cochabamba, outside its heartland. He thinks that maize chicha was so significant that he has coined the phrase "chicha economy" to describe the phenomenon. Hastorf and her colleagues (Hastorf et al. 2006) support the idea of an expanding chicha economy. They examined highland maize remains and identified three major maize varieties at Tiwanaku during the Middle Horizon. One is consistent with maize found at Moquegua, another is consistent with varieties found at Cochabamba, and the last is yet to be identified.[1]

When Tiwanaku colonists arrived in Moquegua, they brought the chicha economy to an area that had no clear preexisting drinking tradition (Goldstein 2003). Goldstein claims the widespread evidence for drinking in Moquegua during the Middle Horizon is due to the spread of Tiwanaku's "mania for maize beer" (2003: 144), with Tiwanaku drinking vessels and paraphernalia adopted as an important part of the correct way to serve and drink this new beverage. Thus, in Moquegua, the spread of chicha drinking and drinking vessels were introduced simultaneously, and it is impossible to separate the two.

Cochabamba is the center of maize and chicha production in modern Bolivia (see Fig. 7.1). The region has long been known to have had significant Tiwanaku influence (Bennett 1936; Byrne de Caballero 1984; Céspedes Paz 2000; Céspedes Paz et al. 1994; Rydén 1959). As in other Tiwanaku-influenced areas, Cochabamba's artifacts commonly include Tiwanaku-style drinking vessels. However, Cochabamba is distinct in that drinking fermented beverages was a long-standing local tradition *prior* to the arrival of Tiwanaku. Thus, in Cochabamba we have a unique opportunity to examine the power and attraction of Tiwanaku drinking paraphernalia and practices *independent* of the introduction of drinking itself.

In this chapter, I examine the social power of the Tiwanaku-style drinking tradition in the Cochabamba setting, I focus in this chapter primarily on drinking vessels, including changes in style, archaeological context, and importance. I find that significant changes occurred in local drinking practices when Cochabamba was integrated into the Tiwanaku political economy.

I present new data from extensive excavations at the site of Piñami (Anderson 2006, 2007a; Céspedes Paz 2000), supplemented by data from the site of Quillacollo (Anderson and Céspedes Paz 1998; Céspedes Paz et al. 1994), both long-term habitation mounds in the Central Valley of Cochabamba that were continuously occupied during this pivotal time period. Household and mortuary data from these sites demonstrates that Tiwanaku drinking practices were closely emulated in Cochabamba. Local customs of drinking fermented beverages changed dramatically, and the new practices served to integrate Cochabamba into the Tiwanaku political economy. Tiwanaku-style drinking customs were practiced throughout the Middle Horizon in Cochabamba, demonstrating that drinking rituals were important to the expansion and long-term stability of the Tiwanaku state in this region.

Drinking and Social Change

Food and drink are not just about a physical need for survival; rather, the ways in which they are prepared, served, and consumed are integral to social practices that affirm, contest, and transform social identities. Many researchers have noted that fermented beverages are unusually important

in political interactions and are generally considered to confer higher prestige and to be more essential in politically charged contexts than are other
drinks (Bowser 2000, 2002; Dietler 1990, 2001, 2003; Dietler and Hayden
2001). Thus, the consumption of alcoholic beverages often becomes a
highly ritualized and politicized practice.

While any vessel that can hold liquid can be used for drinking fermented
beverages, the use of specialized drinking vessels accentuates the ceremony of the occasion (Hayden 2001). Highly elaborated drinking vessels
are common in societies of all scales. By their form and decoration, serving
vessels are useful for displaying symbolic messages of identity, rank, belief,
social relationships, and political alliance—messages that are conveyed to
all participants during drinking.

In his seminal article, Dietler (1990) discusses how new beverages and
drinking customs may radically affect the political economy of a recipient
society and details circumstances under which drinking practices would
most likely be emulated. He shows that emulation is dependent on a variety
of social factors, including whether there was a preexisting drinking practice; whether access to the drink or drinking paraphernalia is restricted; the
social relationship between the donor and recipient; the intensity of interactions; and the prestige of the adopted drinking traditions. Dietler asserts
that, when new drinking practices, rather than a new beverage, are introduced, these practices are adopted by the recipients either to differentiate
groups or to forge symbolic ties between them (Dietler 1990: 379). "Complete adoption of drinking patterns and beliefs of a donor society is likely
to occur only when contacts are close and pervasive, and when . . . cultural
identity [of the recipient] comes to be defined vis-à-vis the donor society"
(Dietler 1990: 378). Thus, changes from Cochabamba-style drinking traditions to those that highly emulate Tiwanaku would suggest that the people
of Cochabamba were symbolically associating themselves with Tiwanaku
and actively adopting a Tiwanaku cultural identity. It would also suggest
close interactions among local residents and people of Tiwanaku origin or
heritage.

While many archaeologists have emphasized the importance of elite
drinking behaviors, especially in feasting contexts, it is important to note
that drinking practices among the nonelite at the household level can also
have political ramifications. Bowser's work is helpful for understanding this
process (Bowser 2000, 2002, 2004; Bowser and Patton 2004). Her work was
in a small-scale multiethnic community in Ecuador where manioc chicha is

the staple beverage, women make and decorate their family's chicha bowls, and chicha is served daily to family and visiting guests. Bowser found that politics are conducted in household contexts during formal and informal visiting, and these visits are a critical venue for community decision making and consensus building. Chicha vessels are very important in these contexts. They are part of the social etiquette of hospitality and reciprocity, and the designs portrayed on the vessels subtly signify current political alliances and in-group/out-group information that other members of the community can "read" quite effectively. It may thus be at the intimate level of the household that the decisions of individuals to adopt or resist social change can be best seen.

For our purposes, where new drinking practices and associated material culture rather than a new drink were introduced, examination of what was emulated, in what contexts, and to what extent can give us insight into the social processes and motivations of the people of Cochabamba as they adopted, transformed, and later abandoned specific Tiwanaku drinking practices.

Drinking Traditions at Tiwanaku

The southern Lake Titicaca basin was home to the Tiwanaku polity (ca. AD 500–1100), the only state-level society to develop in the south-central Andes. By the Late Formative 2 period (ca. AD 300–500), before the foundation of the state, the site of Tiwanaku already had a substantial residential population and a monumental ceremonial core (Janusek 2004; Kolata 1993; Stanish 2003). However, the pre-state Qeya-style ceramics in use at the time included few decorated vessels, and those few were found primarily in ritual contexts rather than residential areas (Janusek 2003: 50; 2004: 120). While kero forms were present in the Qeya assemblage, they have been found only in very low frequencies and were rare at Tiwanaku itself (Janusek 2003).

Around AD 500, the Tiwanaku state emerged, accompanied by the new state art style and an abrupt change in the ceramic assemblage in the Tiwanaku heartland (Janusek 2003: 56). State ceramics included many new forms (see Janusek 2003: 57, fig. 3.27), and the assemblage as a whole was visually striking, with a red base color, polychrome decoration, and bold and distinctive iconography. The vessels were distinctive to the touch, being very thin, evenly made, smooth, burnished, and quite hard. Decorated

Tiwanaku serving ware was not restricted to use by elites, but instead was used throughout the Tiwanaku heartland from the ceremonial core to small hamlets. While the greatest technical virtuosity and some forms and motifs apparently were reserved for the elite (Couture 2002; Couture and Sampeck 2003; Janusek 2003), the majority of serving ware forms—including drinking cups, bowls, small pitchers, and jars—are found in all site types.

Decorated Tiwanaku serving ware was not merely available, but was common (Alconini 1993; Bermann 1990, 1994; Goldstein 1989, 2005; Janusek 1994, 2002, 2003; Rivera Casanovas 1994, 2003). Excavation of domestic areas within Tiwanaku has produced serving ware percentages ranging from 19 to 25 (Janusek 2004: 130), and surface collections at subsidiary sites in the Titicaca basin have produced 7 to 35 percent serving wares (Janusek 2004: 130). The high percentage of these vessels found in domestic contexts shows that access to these vessel types was not restricted to elites; rather, use of these vessels was part of general domestic practices and an important element of Tiwanaku identity in the heartland.

Despite general consistency in frequency and stylistic attributes, the Tiwanaku style includes subtle but visible differences between regions and even between neighborhoods within the capital (Janusek 2002, 2003, 2004; Rivera Casanovas 1994, 2003). This localized variation, together with evidence of ceramic production in areas outside the ceremonial core, indicates that many of the Tiwanaku serving wares were locally produced rather than controlled and produced by elites.

Tiwanaku Drinking Vessels

In the Tiwanaku assemblage, there is no form that stands out as more symbolic of the Tiwanaku state than the kero (Goldstein 2003, 2005; Janusek 2003). The kero is a finely made drinking cup used for fermented beverages (Goldstein 2003; Janusek 2003). Keros are more ostentatious than a typical cup, and their size suggests that they were designed for public display. Janusek reports that a typical kero at Tiwanaku stands 16 to 20 centimeters high and opens to a rim diameter of 12 to 18 centimeters (mean = 14 centimeters) (Janusek 2003: 60). It is a tall hyperboloid form, similar to a modern tumbler, often with a single or double raised horizontal band two-thirds of the way up the vessel. Keros also tend to be more finely finished and highly burnished than other serving ware forms and portray complex iconography (Janusek 2003: 60–61).

In terms of frequency, keros are one of the most common serving ware forms found in Tiwanaku domestic contexts, often representing up to 30 percent of total serving wares (Couture 2002: 209, 277; Janusek 2002: 46; Rivera Casanovas 1994). While elites tended to have more finely made drinking vessels (Couture 2002), the high frequencies of drinking vessels and brewing jars found in nonelite domestic contexts shows that elites neither controlled access to drinking nor had a monopoly on feasting. Instead, chicha drinking using Tiwanaku-style keros was a common practice.[2]

Pre-Tiwanaku Drinking Traditions at Cochabamba

The Cochabamba valleys are located approximately 300 to 400 kilometers east of Tiwanaku, nestled in the eastern slopes of the Andes (Fig. 7.2). These large, fertile valleys have temperature and rainfall patterns ideally suited for growing maize and other mesothermal crops that are difficult to grow at higher elevations. Both the later Inca and Spanish empires con-

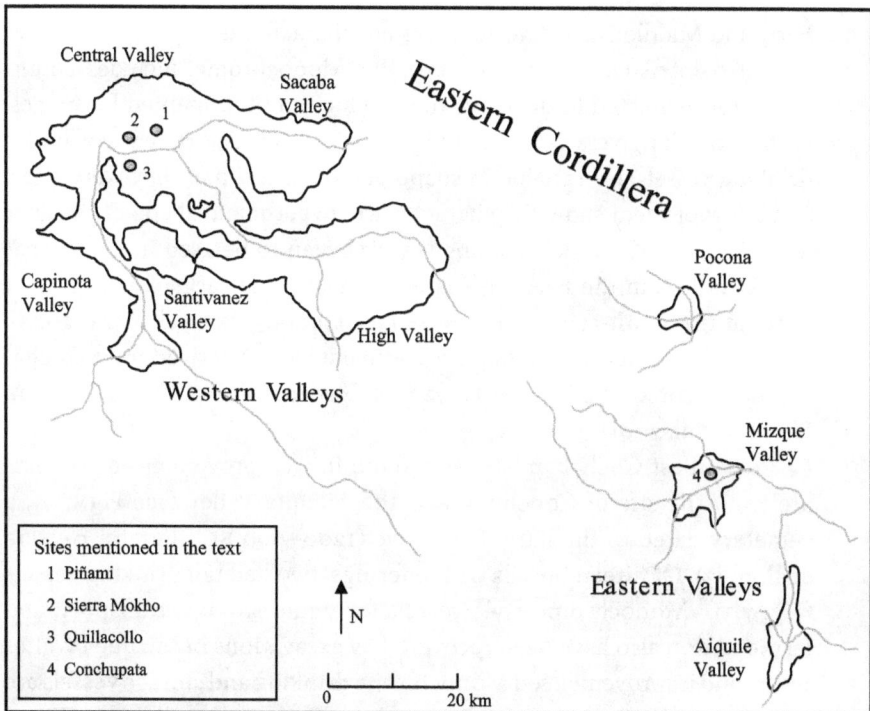

Figure 7.2. The Cochabamba valleys. Map by the author.

trolled the Cochabamba valleys for their agricultural productivity (Wachtel 1982), and it is not surprising that we would find evidence of Tiwanaku interests there as well.

The Formative (~1600 BC–AD 600)

To better understand the impact of Tiwanaku on local drinking customs, it is important to examine the evidence for drink in Cochabamba prior to the Middle Horizon. The Formative in Cochabamba was a long period of local development starting with the beginning of ceramic production in the region. People lived in sedentary villages of round, single-room houses and subsisted predominately on farming and hunting (Brockington et al. 1995; Gabelmann 2005; Pereira Herrera et al. 2001). Settlement patterns show numerous small villages located primarily along rivers. There is also evidence of long-distance exchange of elite goods, such as marine shells, at this time (Brockington et al. 1995; Gabelmann 2005).

Early and Middle Formative (~1600 BC–AD 200)

Early and Middle Formative ceramics are characterized by slipped vessels with no painted decoration. This style, the "Monochrome," includes a number of forms related to drinking and production of fermented beverages, such as drinking vessels and liquid storage and transport jars. Formative drinking vessels are variable in shape but are taller than they were wide, and a few of them show the characteristic hyperboloid shape of the later kero (Fig. 7.3). Kero-like drinking vessels began to be used in the Cochabamba valleys in the Early Formative, considerably earlier than in other areas of the south-central Andes (Goldstein 2003; Janusek 2003, 2004), and it has been suggested that the Tiwanaku kero is derived from Cochabamba precursors (Céspedes Paz 2000; Céspedes Paz et al. 1994; Pereira Herrera et al. 2001).

The earliest Cochabamba keros found in well provenienced contexts are from the site of Conchupata in the Mizque Valley (see Fig. 7.2), a cemetery dated to the Early Formative (1200–600 BC) (Pereira Herrera et al. 1992). Of fifteen burials with offerings, two had tall drinking vessels (Fig. 7.3).[3] Monochrome-style vessels for liquid storage, transport, and fermentation also have been recovered by excavations in Mizque (Walter 1966), and unprovenienced Monochrome drinking and storage vessels are included in the Cochabamba Archaeological Museum collection (David Pereira Herrera, personal communication, 2004).[4] Overall, Monochrome drinking vessels are rare in frequency and come from mortuary rather

COCHABAMBA DRINKING VESSELS FORMS BY TIME PERIOD		
Time Periods and styles	Drinking Vessel Forms	Pitcher forms (Vessels in black are likely related to chicha drinking, vessels in grey are less so)
Formative Monochrome Styles		
Late Formative painted ware styles		
Middle Horizon Cochabamba-Tiwanaku style		
Late Intermediate Period Local styles		

Figure 7.3. Principal Cochabamba drinking vessel forms and most common pitcher form by time period. The pitcher forms shown for the Late Formative and Middle Horizon are grey to show that their relationship to serving chicha is less secure than for the Late Intermediate Period. The Formative Monochrome drinking vessels shown are from (*left to right*) Cliza (Walter 1966), Conchupata (Pereira Herrera et al. 1992), and Mayra Pampa (Pereira Herrera et al. 2001). The others are from the excavations at Pinami.

than domestic contexts (Anderson and Céspedes Paz 1998; Brockington et al. 1985; Brockington et al. 1995; Céspedes Paz et al. 1994; Gabelmann 2005).

Whether the fermented beverages used in the Formative were made of maize or other plants is still uncertain, because no detailed botanical studies have been done in Cochabamba. However, some macrobotanical evidence from Early and Middle Formative sites in the greater Cochabamba region suggests that maize was of limited importance, whereas another grain crop, *tarwi*, was more common (Pereira Herrera et al. 2001: 173).

Late Formative (~AD 200–600)

The Late Formative is an important time period, though it is still poorly understood. It is defined by the appearance of distinctive ceramic styles with painted geometric iconography that co-occurred with the Monochrome style. These new regional painted styles include the Tupuraya, Sauces, Quillacollo, and Mojocoya styles (Anderson and Céspedes Paz 1998; Céspedes Paz et al. 1994; Dollerer 2004; Ibarra Grasso 1965; Ibarra Grasso and Querejazu Lewis 1986; Pereira Herrera and Brockington 2005). These styles continued to be used throughout the Late Formative and into the early Middle Horizon.

Whether these painted styles were a product of local development, trade networks, or colonists from other areas is unknown. However, kero forms were identified in all except the Quillacollo style. Late Formative painted keros vary less in shape than do Monochrome vessels, ranging from straight-sided to slightly flared (Fig. 7.3) (Dollerer 2004). In addition to drinking vessels, the Late Formative assemblages include a variety of utilitarian vessels that were clearly for liquid storage and transport. Yet, as in the Early and Middle Formative, kero-shaped drinking vessels continue to be rare (Brockington et al. 1985; Céspedes Paz et al. 1994; Dollerer 2004).

Little botanical evidence is available for the Late Formative, so it is not known which plants were most likely used for fermentation.

Formative Summary

The presence of kero-shaped drinking vessels, together with vessels likely used for liquid storage, transport, and fermentation during the Formative Period suggests that fermented drink was a Cochabamba tradition hundreds of years before drinking vessels were used in the highlands around Tiwanaku. However, Formative drinking vessels are found in very low frequencies, primarily in mortuary contexts.

The limited contexts and numbers of kero-like drinking vessels do not necessarily imply that consumption of fermented beverages was restricted to special contexts or uses. Certainly, beers could have been served in more multipurpose forms of pottery, such as bowls, or in vessels made from wood or gourds, which do not preserve well. In any case, throughout the Formative, kero-like drinking vessels were not part of regular domestic practice, but instead, were associated more with specific ceremonial contexts and possibly only available to certain individuals.

Middle Horizon Drinking Traditions in Cochabamba
(AD ~700–1100)

The inception of the Middle Horizon in Cochabamba is defined by the rapid and widespread appearance of Tiwanaku-style ceramics. The prevalence of the state style has long been documented; however, the implications for the nature of Tiwanaku interaction with Cochabamba are still debated, and the issue remains a key research focus. Models include direct control (Céspedes Paz 2000; Kolata 1993), indirect control, exchange (Browman 1984, 1997), religious proselytization, independent colonies or colonists, and diffusion of the Tiwanaku ceramic style with little social impact (Higueras-Hare 1996).

Previous work in the region has been limited. Early excavations by Bennett (1936), Rydén (1959), and Walter (1966) documented strong Tiwanaku influence in the valleys. Based on Tiwanaku material from Arani, Bennett characterized Cochabamba as having a "derived Tiwanaku" style that was not true "Classic" Tiwanaku, a characterization that has been used to support a theory that Cochabamba was politically independent of Tiwanaku. There have been a number of publications on the Cochabamba-Tiwanaku relationship (Byrne de Caballero 1984; Céspedes Paz 2000; Céspedes Paz et al. 1994; Higueras-Hare 1996); of these, the models used by Céspedes Paz and Higueras-Hare are the most dissimilar. Based on ceramic data and site-type changes throughout the valley system, Céspedes Paz (2000) favors a model of Cochabamba as a directly controlled colony of an expansive Tiwanaku state. In contrast, based on evidence showing few changes in land use or settlement location in the Capinota and Mizque valleys during the Middle Horizon, Higueras-Hare posits a "status quo" model, suggesting that Tiwanaku had very little social or political impact on Cochabamba.

Excavations in the Central Valley of Cochabamba

The data presented here come from excavations in the Central Valley of Cochabamba (see Fig. 7.2), the largest, most fertile valley in the Cochabamba system and the one geographically closest to Tiwanaku. If the Tiwanaku polity wanted to invest heavily in the Cochabamba valleys for its agricultural productivity, the Central Valley would have been the best candidate.

The evidence for Tiwanaku influence in Cochabamba comes primarily from our extensive excavations at the site of Piñami (Anderson 2004, 2006, 2007a, 2007b).[5] Like the site of Quillacollo, Piñami was a long-term habitation mound that reached 4.5 meters in height and 2 to 3 hectares in area. The site was occupied from the Late Formative to the Colonial Period. Piñami is exceptional for having the most extensive Tiwanaku-era occupation yet identified in the Cochabamba valleys. Piñami was originally thought to be a Middle Horizon cemetery due to the density of burials found in earlier excavations (Céspedes Paz 2000), but our excavations have revealed approximately 3 meters of superimposed Middle Horizon domestic occupations with burials, as well as more than a meter of post–Middle Horizon occupations. Thus, Piñami provides mortuary and household data spanning the Middle Horizon and Late Intermediate periods, allowing us to see changes in local drinking vessels at a single site from the beginning to the end of Tiwanaku hegemony.

Evidence from Piñami provides a more detailed understanding of local subsistence during the Middle Horizon and shows that farming, primarily of maize, and camelid herding were the most common activities, supplemented by raising cuy, hunting, collecting, and fishing.

Based on macrobotanical evidence and preliminary isotope analysis of human remains (Corina Kellner, personal communication, 2007), the evidence for heavy maize use during the Middle Horizon is strong. However, we still cannot say if this represents intensified production over the Late Formative due to increased demand for maize in the highlands or whether maize was already heavily produced during the Late Formative.

Middle Horizon Chronology (~AD 600–1100)

The Middle Horizon in Cochabamba has been divided into two phases (Céspedes Paz 2000): the Illataco Phase, a short transitional phase between local and Tiwanaku patterns; and the Piñami Phase, a longer period of strong, established Tiwanaku association.[6] The beginning of the Illataco Phase is marked by the first appearance of Tiwanaku-style ceramics.[7]

The Illataco Phase

In general, the Illataco Phase seems to have been one of increasingly open trade networks (Anderson 1999; Anderson and Céspedes Paz 1998; Céspedes Paz 2000), as demonstrated by the increased variety in ceramic styles found together, which includes Tiwanaku imports, regional imports, continuation of local Late Formative painted styles, and a new local style called Cochapampa, a hybrid style that incorporates some modified Tiwanaku motifs (Céspedes Paz 2000). The local version of the Tiwanaku state style, "Cochabamba-Tiwanaku," began to be produced early in this phase and became the dominant local style over time.

Analysis of the ceramic drinking vessels during this transitional phase hints that drinking vessels and practices may have been key in local adoption and emulation of Tiwanaku. During the Illataco Phase, keros became common in domestic contexts, a pattern quite different from that found in the Formative contexts, where they were rare to nonexistent. Early in the Illataco Phase, keros included both imported Tiwanaku vessels (identified based on macroscopic examination of paste, temper, and paint colors) and local-style keros, particularly the Cochapampa and Sauces styles. Toward the end of the Illataco Phase, local-style serving wares decreased in frequency, and the Cochabamba Tiwanaku style became more common. During this transition, Tiwanaku-style kero forms were adopted earlier and more consistently than were other Tiwanaku-style serving forms, such as bowls (Table 7.4).

The Piñami Phase

By the Piñami Phase, the Cochabamba-Tiwanaku style was produced exclusively in western Cochabamba (Anderson and Céspedes Paz 1998; Céspedes Paz 2000; Céspedes Paz et al. 1994). Since there is some variety in the Cochabamba-Tiwanaku style found throughout the larger valley system, I will refer to Cochabamba-Tiwanaku ceramics from Central Valley sites as Central Valley Cochabamba-Tiwanaku (CVCT). The CVCT style generally follows the same canons of color, iconography, symmetry, and layout as vessels found at Tiwanaku. CVCT-style vessels, like their highland counterparts, were finely made. They were more symmetrical in shape, harder, more uniformly burnished, and required substantially more effort to produce than the Cochabamba Late Formative styles. It was clearly important that CVCT vessels not only use Tiwanaku iconography but also look and feel like Tiwanaku fineware as well. However, like other regions that adopted Tiwanaku serving wares, Cochabamba expressed regional difference through form preferences, slight differences in color hues, and preferred icons.

Domestic Contexts

Drinking Vessel Frequency

One of the clearest indicators of the impact of Tiwanaku is the frequency of serving/ceremonial ware in the CVCT style, which increased to lev-

els similar to those found at Tiwanaku habitation sites in the Titicaca basin. For example, at the sites of Piñami and Quillacollo, decorated sherds
increased from less than 5 percent of the total assemblages in the Late
Formative to 5 to 10 percent in the transitional Illataco Phase, then to 25
percent for the Early Piñami Phase. Total serving ware frequency for the
Early Piñami Phase (painted and nonpainted sherds) reached 35 percent of
the total assemblage. This is similar to the percentages reported for excavations at Tiwanaku discussed above (Janusek 2004: 130) and clearly shows
an important change in the local drinking and eating customs.

Of the CVCT serving ware found in domestic contexts, drinking vessels
and bowls were the two most common types. Drinking vessels were highly
represented in the serving ware, averaging 25 to 40 percent of the total.

Drinking Vessel Forms

Not only were drinking vessels common, but also there were a variety of
sizes and form variants, suggesting a range of associated drinking rituals.
Of these, the three most common drinking vessel forms in the CVCT style
were a standard kero, similar in proportion to those found at Tiwanaku, a
taller thinner kero, and the vaso embudo, or funnel-shaped cup. All three
of these drinking vessel forms had the capacity to hold substantial amounts
of liquid, averaging 810, 1225, and 675 ml, respectively (Table 7.1). Both
the tall kero and the vaso embudo are uncommon at Tiwanaku and are
characteristic of Cochabamba-Tiwanaku drinking vessels (Figs. 7.4 and
7.6) (Janusek 2003).

Table 7.1. Drinking Vessel Dimensions and Volumes

Drinking vessel	Average height (cm)	Average rim diameter (cm)	Average difference between height & rim diameter (cm)	Average volume (ml)	Number of vessels
Middle Horizon/ Tiwanaku forms					
Standard *kero* cup	16.2	14.3	1.9	810	17
Tall *kero* cup	21.0	16.0	5.0	1,225	14
Vaso embudo	17.3	13.6	3.7	675	22
Pitcher	16.1	7.6	8.5	990	2
Late Intermediate forms					
Kero cup	12.4	10.0	2.4	315	15
Pitcher	24.7	11.7	13.0	4,300	6
Modern gourd bowls	--	--	--	380	10

Figure 7.4. *Keros* from Cochabamba. Center *kero* shows the tall, thinner Cochabamba Tiwanaku version of the *kero* compared to two standard *keros*. Note that all rim diameters are the same. Photo by the author.

Figure 7.5. Extra-large *kero* from Cochabamba. The *kero* on the left is extra-large (25 cm tall, rim diameter 18 cm, volume 1.5 liters), and the *kero* on the right is a standard-size *kero* from Pinami (16.2 cm tall, rim 15 cm). The extra-large vessel is from the excavation by Walter (1966) in the Mizque valley (collection UMSS Archaeological Museum in Cochabamba) but is consistent with rim diameters from extra-large *keros* from the western valleys. Photo by the author.

Figure 7.6. Three *challadores*—a local Cochabamba drinking vessel form. Each was found in burials at Piñami in the western Central Valley. All show Tiwanaku iconography and banding. Photo by the author.

The tall kero has a rim diameter similar to that of the standard kero but is taller and had a thinner middle section (Table 7.1). Some of these tall keros reach extra-large proportions of up to 25 centimeters in height, 18 centimeters in diameter, and 1.5 liters in volume (Fig. 7.5). The extra-large keros were uncommon at Piñami, and due to their size were most likely used in feasting contexts (Hayden 2001).

The vaso embudo was the only non-Tiwanaku form adopted into the CVCT fineware assemblage. This funnel-shaped vessel was common in local styles east and south of the Central Valley of Cochabamba (Anderson 1997; Dollerer 2004; Ibarra Grasso 1965; Ibarra Grasso and Querejazu Lewis 1986; Janusek 2003; Pereira Herrera and Brockington 2005). The form has an extremely small base such that it cannot be set down (Figure 7.6),[8] and is sometimes referred to as a *challador* (offering vessel), since many were made with holes in their bases such that any liquid would spill out continuously. Despite the non-Tiwanaku antecedents of the vaso embudo, when it was adopted as part of the CVCT, this form was decorated using Tiwanaku iconography and technology (Fig. 7.6).

Summary of Middle Horizon Domestic Evidence

CVCT-style serving wares quickly replaced local serving wares. Kero forms transitioned to the CVCT style more completely at an earlier date than did other vessel types, suggesting that Tiwanaku-style drinking rituals were important in the early process of assimilation.

Tiwanaku-style drinking vessels became an essential part of the domestic assemblage and were found in all households in high percentages. This change—from low percentages of keros to high percentages and from specific and restricted contexts to being ubiquitous—shows that not only Tiwanaku ceramic styles were being adopted but also the associated Tiwanaku practices and values. Tiwanaku-style drinking vessels were seen as necessary in household hospitality rituals. Overall, this denotes a high degree of acceptance and emulation of Tiwanaku drinking traditions, signifying a change to a local Tiwanaku-centered identity.

However, as at Tiwanaku itself, local variation was found. Some drinking vessels in use in Cochabamba were more diagnostically Cochabamba than others, yet even with these more characteristically Cochabamba forms, the Tiwanaku colors, iconography, and finishing techniques predominated. These new traditions, once adopted, were strong, and Tiwanaku symbols and drinking customs remained in Cochabamba until the demise of the state.

Mortuary Contexts

Mortuary data provide a different way to understand how Tiwanaku drinking customs were adopted in western Cochabamba. By relating drinking vessels to individuals in mortuary contexts, we can examine not only whether there were changes in drinking vessel frequency and style preferences, but also whether these preferences were patterned with regard to sex, age, and status. Additionally, mortuary traditions tend to be quite conservative, so transitions in offering customs may be indicative of significant ideological and ritual shifts that transcend the quotidian domestic sphere.

Frequency of Tiwanaku-style Drinking Vessels

To consider Tiwanaku impact on local mortuary patterns, we turn again to the evidence from Piñami (Anderson 2007a). Our excavations produced forty-one burials with undisturbed offerings. These can be separated into two temporal groupings: twenty-eight "Early" burials from the end of the Illataco Phase through the Early Piñami Phase contexts; and thirteen "Late" burials from Late Piñami Phase contexts. Pottery offerings were primarily serving wares such as drinking vessels (keros and challadores), serving bowls, pitchers, small jars, and ritual vessels, as well as utilitarian vessels such as small cooking pots (Fig. 7.7).

Figure 7.7. Adult female gravelot that includes two drinking vessels—one *kero* and one *challador*. Photo by the author.

Ceramic drinking vessels, especially kero forms, were common as grave offerings throughout the Middle Horizon (Table 7.2). Of the twenty-eight early burials, twenty-seven had ceramic offerings, averaging 4.2 vessels per burial. Twenty-eight percent of these ceramic offerings were drinking vessels, and 59 percent of burials with ceramic offerings had at least one drinking vessel. Late burials contained substantially fewer offerings (Table 7.2), drinking vessels still comprised 25 percent of the total ceramic offerings and were found in 57 percent of burials with any ceramic grave goods.

The early gravelots included both local and Tiwanaku-style offerings. Subdividing the early gravelots by ceramic style, we find that gravelots with only local-style offerings were much less likely to include drinking vessels than were those with some or all Tiwanaku-style offerings. Of the six burials with only local offerings, just one had a drinking vessel (17 percent), whereas for the ten burials with all Tiwanaku offerings, 70 percent had at least one drinking vessel; for the eleven burials with mixed Tiwanaku and local offerings, 72 percent had at least one drinking vessel (Table 7.3).

Subdividing the vessels from the early burials by vessel type demonstrates that the Tiwanaku style was more closely associated with keros than was any other vessel form aside from ritual vessels. Eighty-five percent of the all the keros from Early burials were Tiwanaku style. Likewise, vasos embudos were predominately Tiwanaku (73 percent). By comparison, non–drinking vessel forms, such as jars and bowls (tazones), were less commonly made in Tiwanaku style (e.g., only 36 and 48 percent, respectively; Table 7.4).

Table 7.2. Middle Horizon Burial Patterns and Drinking Vessels, Piñami

Time period	Total burials	Burials with offerings	Burials with offerings with drinking vessels	Total vessels	Drinking vessels	Average vessels/ burial
Early Middle Horizon	28	27	16 (59% of 27)	117	33 (28% of 117)	4.2
Late Middle Horizon	13	7	4 (57% of 7)	16	4 (25% of 16)	1.2
Total	41	34	20 (59% of 34)	133	37 (28% of 133)	3.3

Table 7.3. Drinking Vessel Frequency in Early Middle Horizon Burials, Piñami

Style of vessels in burials	Number of burials	Burials with drinking vessels	Number of vessels in burials	Number of drinking vessels in burials
Local style only	6	1 (17% of 6)	14	1 (7% of 14)
Tiwanaku style only	10	7 (70% of 10)	42	11 (26% of 42)
Mixed styles (local, Tiwanaku, and hybrid)	11	8 (72% of 11)	61	21 (34% of 61)

Table 7.4. Vessel Style in Early Middle Horizon Burials, Piñami

Style	Drinking vessel form		Other vessel forms				Total vessels by style
	Kero	Vaso embudo	Ritual	Bowl	Jar or pitcher	Utilitarian	
Tiwanaku	17 (85%)	11 (73%)	3 (100%)	13 (48%)	13 (36%)	0	57 (48%)
Hybrid	1 (5%)	0	0	2 (7%)	12 (33%)	0	15 (13%)
Local	2 (10%)	4 (27%)	0	7 (26%)	5 (14%)	0	18 (15%)
Undetermined	0	0	0	5 (19%)	6 (17%)	17 (100%)	28 (24%)
Total vessels	20	15	3	27	36	17	118

Drinking Vessels by Age Category

To identify variation by age category, we looked at all the undisturbed single-occupant burials at Piñami. Of these, we were able to determine the age of thirty-two individuals, including sixteen adults, three adolescents, eight children, and five infants (Yoshida 2005) (Table 7.5). The data show that drinking vessels were appropriate grave offerings for all age categories. Adults had a somewhat higher number of drinking vessels than did subadults, but this appears to simply reflect that adults received more total offerings. Overall, there is no statistically significant difference between the presence of drinking vessels and age category.

Drinking Vessels and Status

Drinking vessels do appear to be related to status distinctions. Early burials with offerings contained on average 4.2 pottery vessels per burial; drink-

Table 7.5. Relationship of Age and Drinking Vessels, Piñami

Age category	Burials/age category	Burials with offerings	Average number of vessels/burial		Burials with drinking vessels
			All burials	Burials with offerings	
Adult	16	15	3.9	4.1	12
Adolescent	3	2	1.6	2.5	2
Child	8	5	1.6	2.6	3
Infant	5	3	2.0	3.3	1

ing vessels were 28 percent of the total. However, two of these burials appear to have had higher status than the rest. They both had substantially higher-than-average grave goods (twelve each of mixed styles), tombs with the most ornate construction techniques (stone walls, stone cover), and other types of offerings not found in other burials, such as strings of small green beads and metal plaques. The greater number of offerings in these burials was not proportionate in all vessel categories. Instead, we found significantly more drinking vessels than other vessel types, with 6 drinking vessels (50 percent of all offerings) in one tomb, and 7 (58 percent) in the other (n = 117, chi sq = 9.48, df = 1, p = .002).

Interestingly, in each instance, the drinking vessels included four identical or almost identical drinking vessels deposited in pairs, one inside the other. Pairs of cups have been found in mortuary, offering, and feasting contexts in other Andean archaeological sites (Bray 2003: 104–105; Cook and Glowacki 2003: 195–196; Pärssinen 2005; Rydén 1959), and pairs of cups are still used in the Andes today as part of feasting events where the host retains one cup and provides the other to each guest in turn (see Allen, this volume; Cook and Glowacki 2003). The sets of cups in the higher-status burials at Piñami may have been used in similar feasting events hosted by higher-status individuals, supporting the theory that feasting and drinking using special drinking cups was an important part of social competition in Middle Horizon Cochabamba.

Women and Drinking Vessels

Sex could be positively or probably determined in sixteen burials with eight females and eight males (all adults except for one adolescent female and one adolescent male) (Yoshida 2005). Generally, both men and women were buried with drinking vessels. However, examination by time period shows that male burials were found with drinking vessels throughout the Middle Horizon, but there was temporal variation with regard to females.

Each of the five Early female burials included drinking vessels, from one to three vessels each (see Fig. 7.8), but none of the three Late Piñami female burials had drinking vessel offerings. While this is a small sample, it does show that women clearly had access to chicha and chicha vessels during the Illataco through Early Piñami phases, and it suggests that drinking rituals may have become more exclusively the domain of socially competitive men through time.

This is a similar pattern to that found at other Tiwanaku sites, where apparently there were gender differences in access to drinking vessels. For example, the Tiwanaku colony of Moquegua, Peru, and the Tiwanaku site of Iwawi to the west of Tiwanaku show clear differences in grave offerings based on sex. At Moquegua, Goldstein notes that for twenty-six individuals for whom sex could be determined, drinking vessels (keros) were found only in burials of men and juveniles of undetermined sex (Goldstein 2005: 254). At Iwawi, only male burials contained keros, and none were found in female burials. (JoEllen Burkholder, personal communication, 2006).[9] Isotope analysis of the Moquegua burials shows this gender-based difference applied to diet as well; men consumed more maize and meat than did women, while women consumed more leguminous plants (Goldstein 2005: 254; Sandness 1992: 54).

Together, the analyses of grave goods and isotope data suggest that chicha drinking was primarily a male activity (Goldstein 2005: 254). This is reminiscent of the Inca pattern at Mantaro, where a by-product of imperial expansion to Mantaro was the disruption of prior gender equality, resulting in males having greater access to chicha and meat (Goldstein 2003; Hastorf 1991).

The consistent evidence from Iwawi and Moquegua suggests that the male-female dichotomy may reflect gender roles in the Tiwanaku capital. If this is the case, Cochabamba individuals showed independence from Tiwanaku drinking norms for women during the Illataco through Early Piñami phases, likely as a continuation of Cochabamba Formative drinking traditions. The lack of drinking vessels in Late Piñami Phase female burials may suggest increasing gender inequities over time in Cochabamba, in keeping with Tiwanaku practices.

Summary of Middle Horizon Mortuary Evidence

The mortuary data both corroborate and complement the evidence from domestic contexts. Like the domestic data, mortuary evidence clearly shows the importance of drinking vessels. The majority of tombs excavated, regardless of age, status, or (initially) gender, had at least one drinking vessel. Clearly, these vessels were highly valued as grave offerings, were readily accessible, and were not restricted to elites or any other single group.

The Tiwanaku style appears to have been adopted more broadly and rapidly on drinking vessels, especially keros, than on other vessel types. During the transition, other vessels often continued to follow local decorative styles and techniques of manufacture, whereas the preference for Tiwanaku-style keros was marked from the start. This evidence suggests that the ceremonial aspects of Tiwanaku, particularly ritualized drinking practices, were central to the transition from local to Tiwanaku practices in Cochabamba.

The high percentages of drinking vessels in higher-status tombs and the presence of special paired cups suggest that higher-status individuals held special responsibilities in feasting, again emphasizing the importance of ceremonial drinking to social competition and hospitality.

The gender data point out one important way that Cochabamba did not initially follow Tiwanaku norms. For an extended period of time, drinking vessels were considered appropriate grave offerings for women, probably in keeping with preexisting local gender roles. Over time, this association may have been reduced in ways more reflective of gender inequities at the Tiwanaku capital.

Post-Tiwanaku Drinking Patterns

The Late Intermediate Period (~AD 1100–1450)

The Tiwanaku polity dissolved about AD 1100. With this political dissolution, there was a dramatic shift in settlement patterns at and around the site of Tiwanaku. The population at the capital was greatly reduced, and numerous small hamlets formed in the basin and throughout the region (Janusek 2004; Kolata 1993; Mathews 2003). The state ceramic style—including Tiwanaku iconography, technology, and various vessel forms—was decisively abandoned. Dedicated drinking vessels such as keros disappeared completely, and the main serving ware form that remained in use was a rounded multipurpose bowl (Janusek 2003).

In the Cochabamba region, the change was substantial though less dramatic. Although numerous sites such as Piñami and Quillacollo continued to be occupied, there was nevertheless a change in settlement patterns, with the appearance of many new sites in defensible locations (Gyarmati and Varga 1999).

The change in ceramic styles was notable. Material culture that heavily referenced Tiwanaku, represented by the use of Tiwanaku state symbols, was abandoned and replaced by new ceramic forms with geometric iconography (Céspedes Paz 1982; Ibarra Grasso 1965; Ibarra Grasso and Querejazu Lewis 1986; Muñoz Collazos 1993) (Fig. 7.8). Manufacturing techniques for ceramics became less labor intensive, with less time and energy put into hardness, symmetry, vessel-wall thinness, smoothing, and burnishing.

Unlike at Tiwanaku, dedicated drinking vessels in Cochabamba remained an important part of the domestic assemblage, though the social importance of their use appears to have declined. At Piñami, Late Intermediate drinking vessels and pitchers are found in domestic contexts, including households and middens. However, there is a reduction in the quantity of serving ware and the percentage of drinking cups in the total ceramic assemblage. Céspedes Paz (2000) reports a Late Intermediate burial at Piñami with offerings of a small kero and pitcher, so it is clear that drinking vessels were still used as grave offerings. However, given the low number of

Figure 7.8. Typical Ciaco-style Late Intermediate Period serving pitcher and drinking cup. The pitcher holds 4.5 liters, enough to fill 15 average-size cups. Photo by the author.

published studies of Late Intermediate burials, the importance of drinking vessels in burials during this period remains uncertain.

As for vessel forms, challadores disappeared during this period while hyperboloid kero shapes continued to be used in a modified form. The hyperboloid drinking vessels differed from their Middle Horizon counterparts in size, shape, and decoration (see Fig. 7.3). The new kero-cup was much smaller on average—only 12.4 centimeters tall with a rim diameter of 10.0 centimeters (Table 7.1).

Vessel volumes also were greatly reduced. Late Intermediate cups held only 220 to 450 ml (average ~315 ml), down to almost a fourth of the capacity of the Cochabamba-Tiwanaku tall kero (average volume 1,225 ml) or half the typical challador (average volume 675 ml).[10] The reduction in drinking vessel size was paralleled by a greater emphasis on serving pitchers. Pitchers, decorated with the same slips and designs as the cups, increased in both size and frequency during the Late Intermediate Period. Pitchers could be quite large, with interior volumes of 3–5 liters, which could easily hold enough liquid to fill 9–15 average Late Intermediate cups (Fig. 7.8). The pitchers were very likely used to serve chicha.[11]

Late Intermediate Summary

During the Late Intermediate, Cochabamba discontinued its strong connection to the highlands. The people abandoned Tiwanaku iconography and many ceramic forms, and they did not follow the new post-Tiwanaku highland traditions. Drinking cups were down-sized. Large serving pitchers and matching small cups usurped the prominent position formerly occupied by the ostentatious Tiwanaku drinking vessels.

In Cochabamba, as in other Tiwanaku peripheries like Moquegua (Goldstein 2003), the abandonment of Tiwanaku styles and traditions did not mean abandonment of drinking traditions. Instead, new traditions were formed that maintained the importance of drinking in the domestic arena.

Discussion

Despite Cochabamba's preexisting drinking traditions and kero forms, Tiwanaku drinking practices and vessels radically influenced Cochabamba traditions. Drinking vessels decorated with Tiwanaku symbols were quickly employed in Cochabamba and became part of a consistent pattern of ritual commensalism at the domestic level that lasted hundreds of years. The fact that Tiwanaku drinking customs, vessel forms, and technology of manufacture were adopted in Cochabamba much as at Tiwanaku itself is highly suggestive that there was intense day-to-day interaction between the groups, possibly via colonists from Tiwanaku.

What was it about Tiwanaku drinking traditions that made local affiliation easy and rapid? My thesis is that, in addition to the strong symbolic importance of materials related to Tiwanaku and their ideological power, it was both the increased importance of drinking and the inclusiveness of Tiwanaku drinking traditions that were appealing, greatly facilitating the integration process. This pattern of Tiwanaku inclusiveness is found at Cochabamba and is a characteristic of the Tiwanaku state; at the capital, in the greater Lake Titicaca basin, and at Moquegua, drinking vessels in the Tiwanaku tradition are common in households and burials, a pattern quite dissimilar to that found in the Wari and Inca empires (Bray 2003; Cook and Glowacki 2003).

The importance of this should not be underestimated. Instead of a practice restricted to the elite or to feasting contexts, the new custom of chicha drinking at the household level using special drinking vessels had the effect of integrating the entire local population quickly and effectively into the Tiwanaku sphere, and, to paraphrase Dietler (1990: 378), Cochabamba cultural identity came to be defined vis-à-vis Tiwanaku society.

Returning to Bowser's ethnoarchaeological data, we can project how this chicha transformation could have taken place household by household. From Bowser's work, I have presented two key themes. First, substantial local politics takes place at the household level during formal and informal visits. Second, beer is always served during these visits, and the bowls used for serving beer contain messages via stylistic elements that signify information imparted to guests about the household's political group, ethnic identification, and factional affiliations (Bowser 2000, 2002). Examining the data from Cochabamba in this light, we can see that, while there was a drinking tradition prior to Tiwanaku, there was not a tradition of universal chicha drinking at the household level using finely crafted ceramic drinking vessels. Thus, contact with colonists or traders from Tiwanaku who brought the tradition with them would have had a great impact, especially in rituals of reciprocal hospitality. The evidence shows that, early in the transition process, local drinking vessels increased in frequency, suggesting that locals were participating in the new drinking customs, initially using their own style of vessels or imported vessels from Tiwanaku. However, almost immediately after the new drinking customs were introduced, CVCT drinking vessels became increasingly more common.

Thus, at the household level, people were sending messages to others in their community of their acceptance not only of Tiwanaku drinking practices but also of Tiwanaku ideology and political affiliation. In the game of social competition, Tiwanaku material culture and attendant practices were clearly perceived as of higher status and socially advantageous. The result was a rapid transformation of local identity to one that referenced Tiwanaku definitively. This Tiwanaku identity lasted for hundreds of years.

Post-Tiwanaku we see a second rapid transformation as Tiwanaku identity is rejected. Tiwanaku iconography and color schemes, some of the most salient characteristics of the state style, were abandoned completely. Serving forms were substantially altered, with changes that included the downplaying of individual drinking cups and accentuation of the shared serving pitcher. However, these changes were not so complete as to indicate a complete rejection of Middle Horizon drinking practices. Instead, we find that drinking using special vessels continued to be a significant Late Intermediate domestic practice in Cochabamba. It is likely that some of the same social processes of competitive hospitality and factional alliance-building that helped make Tiwanaku acceptance rapid also served in the post-Tiwanaku era to quickly end Tiwanaku referents and to transition forms and iconography to those that symbolized local identities.

In sum, Tiwanaku drinking customs promoted social cohesion at the household level, at home, and abroad, using paraphernalia heavily coded with state symbols. So powerful was this tradition that it radically changed Cochabamba, an area with a preexisting chicha tradition in which the drink was nothing new. Drinking practices and vessels were part of important rituals that alternately served to promote rapid social transformation and to undergird social stability.[12]

Notes

1. During the Middle Horizon, maize increased substantially in distribution, especially at Tiwanaku, where maize was the second most important domestic edible crop found (Wright et al. 2003: 390). This is surprisingly high considering the difficulty of growing it in the high-elevation environment and suggests "substantial long-distance import" of maize (Wright et al. 2003: 402). In addition, isotopic evidence confirms maize-related dietary change in the Middle Horizon. Goldstein notes

that isotope analysis from Moquegua burials shows that pre-Tiwanaku people had much less maize in their diet than Tiwanaku-period populations (Goldstein 2003). Preliminary isotopic analysis by Berryman, Blom, and Tykot (2007) of burial populations from Tiwanaku, Khonko Wankane, and Lukurmata confirms that during the Late Formative people had limited access to maize, but during the Middle Horizon the amount of maize in the diet increased substantially for some individuals (up to 70 percent) and remained similar to Formative levels in the others. While the pattern is not completely clear-cut in all sectors, some of the highest levels of dietary maize were found in individual burials found in elite sectors of Tiwanaku, indicating some elite control of maize. In the Late Intermediate Period, levels of dietary maize return to Formative levels.

2. There are vessel forms as well as some motifs that appear mostly in elite contexts, notably, the flaring-rim bowl (*escudilla*) and a curved-base tazón (Alconini Mújica 1993; Couture 2002; Couture and Sampeck 2003; Janusek 2002: 46), and in general the vessels found in elite areas were higher quality than those found in nonelite residential areas (Couture 2002; Janusek 2002: 43–44).

3. Excavation at the site of Mayra Pampa, an Early Formative site in the Mizque Valley, produced a burial with an unusual double kero (see Fig. 7.3) (Pereira Herrera and Brockington 2000; Pereira Herrera et al. 2001).

4. The frequencies and contexts of storage and fermentation vessels have not been published.

5. Funding for the research was provided by a National Science Foundation Dissertation Improvement Grant, a National Geographic Society Emergency Grant, and the University of California Research Expedition Programs. Support and collaboration for the project in Bolivia was provided by the Instituto de Investigaciones Antropológicas y Museo Arqueológico de la Universidad Mayor de San Simón, Cochabamba. This project has been a multiyear collaborative effort. Special thanks to museum director and project supervisor, David M. Pereira Herrera, and Project Piñami codirector, archaeologist Zulema Terceros Céspedes, and to the neighbors of Barrio Quechisla. Also thanks to archaeologist Gori Tumi Echevarría López, physical anthropologist Bonnie Yoshida, and to the other Bolivian and American archaeologists who worked on the project.

6. There are few C-14 dates for the Middle Horizon in Cochabamba, so it is not currently possible to correlate the Illataco and Piñami phases with the chronology of the Tiwanaku capital.

7. Imported serving ware vessels were identified based on a combination of factors, including differences in paste and temper, paint pigment colors, and iconography. The most diagnostic attributes indicating imported wares were nonlocal temper and paste types, particularly gold mica and high-sand-content pastes. Imported Tiwanaku vessels were more common in the Illataco and Early Piñami phases than in the Late Piñami phase.

8. Determining frequencies of standard versus tall keros from fragments is difficult due to the overlap of rim diameter ranges and shape similarity. However, it is

clear that kero forms were much more common than vaso embudo forms in both domestic and mortuary contexts.

9. Burkholder states that at Iwawi small jars with flaring rims ("*florero*" forms) were found only in female burials. She suggests that this vessel type could have been used for drinking chicha among women (JoEllen Burkholder, personal communication, 2008).

10. Since few whole Late Intermediate Period drinking vessels were found in our Piñami excavations, sizes and volumes are based on measurements taken from the general collection of the Universidad Mayor de San Simón Archaeological Museum in Cochabamba with the kind consent of the museum's director, David Pereira Herrera. The Late Intermediate vessels used were comparable to whole vessels and fragments found in excavation in style attributes and rim and base diameters.

11. This is a new development, distinct from the Tiwanaku Period, where serving ware pitchers occurred infrequently and had a volume capacity of ~1 liter, just sufficient to fill a single kero (see Table 7.1), and were less likely to be directly associated with serving chicha.

12. Thanks to Justin Jennings and Brenda Bowser for inviting me to participate in this volume and for their patient and detailed editing of this paper. Special thanks to Corina Kellner, JoEllen Burkholder and Carrie Ann Berryman, Deborah E. Blom, and Robert H. Tykot for their kind permission to cite some of their unpublished data or conference papers. Thanks as well to reviewers Jerry Moore and George Gumerman for their helpful comments. Any errors are my own.

References Cited

Alconini Mújica, Sonia
1993 La cerámica de la Pirámide Akapana y su contexto social en el estado de Tiwanaku. Licenciatura thesis, Universidad de San Andrés.
Anderson, Karen
1997 Omereque: A Middle Horizon Ceramic Style of Central Bolivia. Master's thesis, University of California, Santa Barbara.
1999 Tiwanaku Political Economy: The View from Cochabamba. Paper presented at the 64th Annual Meeting of the Society for American Archaeology, Chicago.
2004 Desarrollo local y el impacto Tiwanaku: El Formativo Tardío hasta el Intermedio Tardío en el valle central de Cochabamba. Paper presented at the I Congreso de Arqueología de Bolivia, La Paz.
2006 Tiwanaku Impact on the Cochabamba Region: Household Evidence from Piñami. Paper presented at the 71st Annual Meetings of the Society for American Archaeology, San Juan.
2007a Variety and Transformation: Tiwanaku Impact on Local Mortuary Practices at Piñami, Cochabamba, Bolivia. Paper presented at the 72nd Annual Meetings of the Society for American Archaeology, Austin.
2007b The Cochabamba Tiwanaku Style: How "Derived" Was It? Paper presented at

the Southern Andean Iconographic Series Colloquium in Pre-Columbian Art and Archaeology, Universidad de Chile.

Anderson, Karen, and Ricardo Céspedes Paz
1998 Tiwanaku and the Local Effects of Contact: The Late Formative to Middle Horizon Transition in Cochabamba, Bolivia. Paper presented at the 63rd Annual Meeting of the Society for American Archaeology, Seattle.

Bennett, Wendell C.
1936 Excavations in Bolivia. *Anthropological Papers of the American Museum of Natural History* 35(4): 329–507.

Bermann, Marc
1990 Prehispanic Household and Empire at Lukurmata, Bolivia. Doctoral dissertation, University of Michigan.
1994 *Lukurmata: Household Archaeology in Prehispanic Bolivia*. Princeton: Princeton University Press.

Berryman, Carrie Ann, Deborah E. Blom, and Robert H. Tykot
2007 Paleodietary Insight into the Rise of the State in the Southern Titicaca Basin: The View from Khonkho Wankane. Paper presented at the 72nd Annual Meeting of the Society of American Archaeology, Austin.

Bowser, Brenda
2000 From Pottery to Politics: An Ethnoarchaeological Case Study of Political Factionalism, Ethnicity, and Domestic Pottery Style in the Ecuadorian Amazon. *Journal of Archaeological Method and Theory* 7(3): 219–248.
2002 The Perceptive Potter: An Ethnoarchaeological Study of Pottery, Ethnicity, and Political Action in Amazonia. Doctoral dissertation, University of California, Santa Barbara.
2004 The Amazonian House: A Place of Women's Politics, Pottery, and Prestige. *Expedition* 46(2): 18–23.

Bowser, Brenda J., and John Q. Patton
2004 Domestic Spaces as Public Places: An Ethnoarchaeological Case Study of Houses, Gender, and Politics in the Ecuadorian Amazon. *Journal of Archaeological Method and Theory* 11(2): 157–181.

Bray, Tamara L.
2003 To Dine Splendidly: Imperial Pottery, Commensal Politics, and the Inca State. In *The Archeology and Politics of Food and Feasting in Early States and Empires*, Tamara L. Bray, ed., pp. 93–142. New York: Kluwer Academic/Plenum.

Brockington, Donald L., David M. Pereira Herrera, Ramón Sanzetenea Rocha, and María de los Ángeles Muñoz Collazos
1995 Estudios arqueológicos del Período Formativo en el sur-este de Cochabamba. In *Cuadernos de Investigación*, Serie Arqueología 8. Cochabamba: Universidad Mayor de San Simón.

Brockington, Donald L., David M. Pereira Herrera, Ramón Sanzetenea Rocha, Ricardo Céspedes Paz, and Carlos Pérez L.
1985 Informe preliminar de las excavaciones arqueológicas en: Sierra Mokho y

Chullpa Pata (Período Formativo). In *Cuadernos de Investigación,* Serie Arqueología 5. Cochabamba: Universidad Mayor de San Simón.

Browman, David

1984 Tiwanaku: Development of Interzonal Trade and Economic Expansion in the Altiplano. In *Social and Economic Organization in the Prehispanic Andes,* David Browman, Richard Burger, and Mario Rivera, eds., pp. 117–142. British Archaeological Reports, International Series 194. Oxford: British Archaeological Reports.

1997 Political Institutional Factors Contributing to the Integration of the Tiwanaku State. In *Emergence and Change in Early Urban Societies,* Linda Manzanilla, ed., pp. 229–243. New York: Plenum.

Byrne de Caballero, Geraldine

1984 El Tiwanaku en Cochabamba. *Arqueología Boliviana* 1: 67–72.

Céspedes Paz, Ricardo

1982 La cerámica incaica en Cochabamba. In *Cuadernos de Investigación.* Serie Arqueología 1, Universidad Mayor de San Simón (January): 1–57.

2000 Excavaciones arqueológicas en Piñami. *Boletín de INIAN—Museo.* Serie Arqueología 9, Universidad Mayor de San Simón (March): 1–14.

Céspedes Paz, Ricardo, Karen Anderson, and Ramón Sanzetenea

1994 Report on the Excavation at the Parochial Building, Quillacollo, Bolivia. Cochabamba: Museo Arqueológico de La Universidad Mayor de San Simón.

Cook, Anita, and Mary Glowacki

2003 Pots, Politics, and Power: Huari Ceramic Assemblages and Imperial Administration. In *The Archaeology and Politics of Food and Feasting in Early States and Empires,* Tamara L. Bray, ed., pp. 173–202. New York: Kluwer Academic/Plenum.

Couture, Nicole

2002 The Construction of Power: Monumental Space and an Elite Residence at Tiwanaku, Bolivia. Doctoral dissertation, University of Chicago.

Couture, Nicole, and Kathryn Sampeck

2003 Putini: A History of Palace Architecture at Tiwanaku. In *Tiwanaku and Its Hinterland: Archaeology and Paleoecology of an Andean Civilization,* vol. 2, *Urban and Rural Archaeology,* Alan Kolata, ed., pp. 226–263. Washington, D.C.: Smithsonian Institution Press.

Dietler, Michael

1990 Driven by Drink: The Role of Drinking in the Political Economy and the Case of Early Iron Age France. *Journal of Archaeological Anthropology* 9: 352–406.

2001 Theorizing the Feast: Rituals of Consumption, Commensal Politics, and Power in African Contexts. In *Feasts: Archaeological and Ethnographic Perspectives on Food, Politics, and Power,* Michael Dietler and Brian Hayden, eds., pp. 65–114. Washington, D.C.: Smithsonian Institution Press.

2003 Clearing the Table: Some Concluding Reflections on Commensal Politics and Imperial States. In *The Archaeology and Politics of Food and Feasting in Early*

States and Empires, Tamara L. Bray, ed., pp. 271–282. New York: Kluwer Academic/Plenum.

Dietler, Michael, and Brian Hayden (eds.)

2001 Digesting the Feast—Good to Eat, Good to Drink, Good to Think: An Introduction. In *Feasts: Archaeological and Ethnographic Perspectives on Food, Politics, and Power*, Michael Dietler and Brian Hayden, eds., pp. 1–20. Washington, D.C.: Smithsonian Institution Press.

Dollerer, Cristof

2004 Proyecto Tupuraya: Informe preliminar sobre los trabajos arqueológicos y documentación de los estilos cerámicos tupuraya y sauces como los dos desarrollos tránsitos entre el Formativo y la Época Tiwanaku en Cochabamba, Bolivia. Cochabamba: Universidad Mayor de San Simón, Instituto de Investigaciones Antropológicas y Museo Arqueológico.

Gabelmann, Olga

2001 Choroqollo—Producción de cerámica e intercambio de bienes durante el Período Formativo: Un ejemplo del Valle Santiváñez, Cochabamba. *Textos Antropológicos* 13(1–2): 197–229.

2005 Proyecto Santa Lucía 2003/04: Organización social, producción de cerámica e intercambio en el Período Formativo en el valle alto de Cochabamba. In *Jornadas Arqueológicas 2004*, pp. 51–73. Sucre: Universidad Mayor de San Francisco Xavier.

Goldstein, Paul S.

1989 Omo, a Tiwanaku Provincial Center in Moquegua, Peru. Doctoral dissertation, University of Chicago.

2003 From Stew-Eaters to Maize-Drinkers: The Chicha Economy and the Tiwanaku Expansion. In *The Archaeology and Politics of Food and Feasting in Early States and Empires*, Tamara L. Bray, ed., pp. 143–172. New York: Kluwer Academic/Plenum.

2005 *Andean Diaspora: The Tiwanaku Colonies and the Origins of South American Empire*. Gainesville: University Press of Florida.

Gyarmati, Janos, and András Varga

1999 *The Chacaras of War: An Inka State Estate in the Cochabamba Valley, Bolivia*. Budapest: Museum of Ethnography.

Hastorf, Christine A.

1991 Gender, Space, and Food in Prehistory. In *Engendering Archaeology*, Joan M. Gero and Margaret W. Conkey, eds., pp. 132–159. Cambridge: Basil Blackwell.

Hastorf, Christine A., William T. Whitehead, Maria C. Bruno, and Melanie Wright

2006 The Movements of Maize into Middle Horizon Tiwanaku, Bolivia. In *Histories of Maize: Multidisciplinary Approaches to the Prehistory, Linguistics, Biogeography, Domestication and Evolution of Maize*, John Staller, John Tykot, and Bruce Benz, eds., pp. 429–448. Oxford: Elsevier.

Hayden, Brian

2001 Fabulous Feasts: A Prolegomenon to the Importance of Feasting. In *Feasts:*

Archaeological and Ethnographic Perspectives on Food, Politics, and Power, Michael Dietler and Brian Hayden, eds., pp. 23–64. Washington, D.C.: Smithsonian Institution Press.

Higueras-Hare, Álvaro

1996 Prehispanic Settlement and Land Use in Cochabamba, Bolivia. Doctoral dissertation, University of Pittsburgh.

Ibarra Grasso, Dick Edgar

1965 *Prehistoria de Bolivia*. La Paz: Los Amigos del Libro.

Ibarra Grasso, Dick Edgar, and Roy Querejazu Lewis

1986 *30,000 años de prehistoria en Bolivia*. La Paz: Los Amigos del Libro.

Janusek, John Wayne

1994 State and Local Power in a Prehispanic Polity: Changing Patterns of Urban Residence in Tiwanaku and Lukurmata, Bolivia. Doctoral dissertation, University of Chicago.

2002 Out of Many, One: Style and Social Boundaries in Tiwanaku. *Latin American Antiquity* 13(1): 35–61.

2003 Vessels, Time, and Society: Toward a Ceramic Chronology in the Tiwanaku Heartland. In *Tiwanaku and Its Hinterland: Archaeology and Paleoecology of an Andean Civilization*, vol. 2, *Urban and Rural Archaeology*, Alan Kolata, ed., pp. 30–89. Washington, D.C.: Smithsonian Institution Press.

2004 *Identity and Power in the Ancient Andes: Tiwanaku Cities through Time*. New York: Routledge.

Kolata, Alan

1993 *The Tiwanaku: Portrait of an Andean Civilization*. Cambridge: Blackwell.

Mathews, James Edward

2003 Prehistoric Settlement Patterns in the Middle Tiwanaku Valley. In *Tiwanaku and Its Hinterland: Archaeology and Paleoecology of an Andean Civilization*, vol. 2, *Urban and Rural Archaeology*, Alan Kolata, ed., pp. 112–128. Washington, D.C.: Smithsonian Institution Press.

Muñoz Collazos, María de los Ángeles

1993 *El Intermedio Tardío en Cochabamba: Arqueología y etnohistoria*. Licenciatura thesis, Instituto Nacional de Antropología e Historia, Mexico City.

Pärssinen, Martti

2005 Tiwanaku: Una cultura y un estado andino. In *Pariti: Isla, misterio y poder. El tesoro cerámico de la cultura Tiwanaku*, Antti Korpissari and Martti Pärssinen, eds., pp. 17–37. La Paz: Republic of Bolivia and Republic of Finland.

Pereira Herrera, David M., and Donald L. Brockington

2005 *Mojocoya y greyware: Interacción e intercambios entre la Amazonia, Chaco y Andes*. Cuadernos de Investigación, Serie Arqueología no. 10. Cochabamba: Universidad Mayor de San Simón, Instituto de Investigaciones Antropológicas y Museo Arqueológico.

Pereira Herrera, David M., and Donald L. Brockington (eds.)

2000 *Investigaciones arqueológicas en las tierras tropicales del Departamento de Cochabamba—Bolivia*. Cochabamba: Universidad Mayor de San Simón.

Pereira Herrera, David M., María de los Ángeles Muñoz Collazos, Ramón Sanzetenea Rocha, and Donald L. Brockington
1992 *Conchupata: Un panteón formativo temprano en el valle de Mizque.* Cuadernos de Investigación, Serie Arqueología no. 7. Cochabamba: Universidad Mayor de San Simón, Instituto de Investigaciones Antropológicas y Museo Arqueológico.
Pereira Herrera, David M., Ramón Sanzetenea Rocha, and Donald L. Brockington
2001 Investigaciones del Proyecto Arqueológico Formativo en Cochabamba, Bolivia. *Textos Antropológicos* 13(1–2): 167–182.
Rivera Casanovas, Claudia
1994 Ch'iji Jawira: Evidencias sobre la producción de cerámica en Tiwanaku. Licenciatura thesis, Universidad Mayor de San Andrés.
2003 *Ch'iji Jawira: Evidencias sobre la producción de cerámica en Tiwanaku.* Cochabamba: Universidad Mayor de San Simón.
Rydén, Stig
1959 *Andean Excavations II: Tupuraya and Cayhuasi: Two Tiahuanaco Sites.* Monograph Series no. 6. Stockholm: Ethnographical Museum of Sweden.
Sandness, Kari
1992 Temporal and Spatial Dietary Variability in the Osmore Drainage, Southern Peru: The Isotope Evidence. Master's thesis, University of Nebraska, Lincoln.
Stanish, Charles
2003 *Ancient Titicaca: The Evolution of Complex Society in Southern Peru and Northern Bolivia.* Berkeley & Los Angeles: University of California Press.
Wachtel, Nathan
1982 The Mitimas of Cochabamba Valley: The Colonization Policy of Huayna Capac. In *The Inca and Aztec States, 1400–1800*, George A. Collier, R. I. Rosaldo, J. D. Wirth, eds., pp. 199–235. New York: Academic Press.
Walter, Heinz
1966 *Beiträge zur Archäologie Boliviens.* Baessler Archiv, Neue Folge (4). Berlin: Dietrich Reimer.
Wright, Melanie F., Christine A. Hastorf, and Heidi A. Lennstrom
2003 Pre-Hispanic Agriculture and Plant Use at Tiwanaku: Social and Political Implications. In *Tiwanaku and Its Hinterland: Archaeology and Paleoecology of an Andean Civilization*, vol. 2, *Urban and Rural Archaeology*, Alan Kolata, ed., pp. 384–403. Washington, D.C.: Smithsonian Institution Press.
Yoshida, Bonnie
2005 Preliminary Results of Anatomical Analyses of the Burials from Piñami, Bolivia. Unpublished, 2005 field season.

8

Pots, Brewers, and Hosts

Women's Power and the Limits of Central Andean Feasting

Justin Jennings and Melissa Chatfield

Among their many possible functions, feasts are events that create and maintain social capital by perpetuating a durable network of relationships that link actual and potential resources (after Bourdieu 1986: 248). Social capital is important in the Andes and in other regions of the world because reciprocity forms the backbone of the economy (Dietler 1996: 92–97; Dietler 2001: 66; Earle 1991: 3; Hayden 2001: 38; Mayer 2002; Perodie 2001: 187). A host's generosity, measured in part by the amount of food and drink served at the feast, creates a network of indebted participants (social capital) that the host can later call on for labor, agricultural products, or other services. The smaller the required labor force to produce food and drink at an event, the less social capital a host needs to expend before a feast takes place.

Chicha, a fermented beverage made out of maize, manioc, molle, and/or other plants (Goldstein, Coleman Goldstein, and Williams, this volume; Hayashida, this volume) was likely fundamental to feasts in many regions of the central Andes by at least the Early Intermediate Period (200 BC–AD 750) (see, e.g., Cavero Carrasco 1986: 23–30; Gero 1990, 1992; Hastorf 1991; Hastorf and Johannessen 1993; Lau 2002; Moore 1989; Morell 2002; Shimada 1994; Stanish 1994). One of the easiest ways to increase yields per brewer is to increase the size of the brewing and fermenting vessels used (Jennings 2005; Perlov, this volume). Professional brewers (chicheras) today, for example, can produce more than double the typical household rate of chicha, because they use large brewing and fermenting vessels (170 liters or more in volume). Using bigger pots, therefore, could allow for the accumulation of more social capital by increasing production rate per brewer.

Despite the advantages of bigger pots for hosts, however, beer for feasts today is usually brewed in smaller pots that are typically found in household
assemblages (80 liters or less in volume) (Chávez 1985: 163; Cleland and
Shimada 1998: 116; Hildebrand and Hagstrum 1999: 33; Sillar 2000: 151–155,
177). Both small and large brewing and fermenting jars are common in the
prehistoric central Andes.

This chapter examines the use of smaller pots for household-level feasting in the central Andes today in order to explore the implications for the
production and use of big beer pots for state-sponsored feasts in the past.
We argue that smaller pots are used today because women often produce
chicha in the home. A shift in vessel size is outside the interests of these
women for three reasons. First, the material, social, and technical demands
of making large vessels stress the capabilities of most households. Second,
significant increases in vessel size render jars increasingly less mobile, and
thus cumbersome, for a single woman to use within the home. Finally, and
most important, the use of smaller beer pots in the home allows women
to have significant control over feasting events by serving independently
produced beer. We argue that these factors restricting vessel size likely
operated in the past as well.

Scholars have long noted a gendered asymmetry in central Andean
feasting, as has been noted in other areas of the world (Dietler and Hayden
2001: 11). Men, especially since the Spanish Conquest (Silverblatt 1987), often hold the highest political offices, which benefit from large-scale feasts,
while women frequently do much of the brewing and other culinary work
that makes feasts possible (Allen 2002: 96–98; Bolin 1998: 179; D'Altroy
2002: 195–196; Hamilton 1998: 64–65). Although the relationship between
the men, who tend to host the feasts, and the women, who actually rally
the resources, is seemingly exploitative on the surface, women are deeply
integrated into the political process through their own social networks and
private (and, on rare occasions, quite public) conversations with husbands
and male relatives (Allen 2002: 97; Hamilton 1998; see Bowser 2000 and
2004 for Amazonian examples).

Women's influence is based in part on their collective control over the
production and distribution of the beer and other items consumed at feasts
(Allen 2002: 97). Since beer often spoils in less than a week, a host cannot stockpile it over the course of several months or years (Jennings 2005,
but see Hayashida, this volume). The social positions of hosts are therefore dependent upon maintaining themselves in the good graces of a large
number of independent household brewers who must be called upon to

produce at one time the massive quantities of beer consumed at events. Diffused rather than centralized production of critical feasting supplies keeps political ambitions in check because of the dependency of political leaders on a number of female brewers and on household labor in general; a host's crowning feast swiftly turns into an embarrassment if beer arrives late, sour, or in insufficient quantity. Since household dynamics and goals are apt to restrict vessel size, we argue that smaller brewing and fermenting vessels are an indication of diffused production.

In central Andean prehistory, most possible brewing and fermenting vessels fit within the volume range of typical household pots used today, and these ancient pots are found in domestic contexts (see, e.g., Goldstein 1993: 35; Goldstein 2005: 235; Isbell 1977: 68–71; Julien 2004: 93–94; Miller 2004: 132–135; Moore 1989: 692; Segura Llanos 2001: 72–96; Silverman 1993: 245–250). If these smaller pots are the result of similar production and feasting patterns, then women may have held significant collective political power through their control over the production and distribution of beer.

Yet there are also very large pots found in the ancient Andes. These pots, employed, for example, in the Moche, Wari, and Inca states, rival in size the 170-liter pots used by chicheras today (Perlov, this volume) and are often found in contexts that suggest specialized mass production of alcohol (Chapdelaine 1997: 32; D'Altroy and Hastorf 1992: 265; Goldstein, Coleman Goldstein, and Williams, this volume; Isbell and Grouleau, i.p.; Miller 2004: 133; Morris 1979: 28, 32; Shimada 1994: 144, 169, 208, 222). Although some women in a community undoubtedly benefited from specialized production, a host with access to big pots would no longer need to lean as heavily on community participation to prepare a feast; he or, more rarely, she could depend instead on fewer people to produce a lot of beer in one place. The use of big pots for centralized production, therefore, could have undercut women's collective political power by making dispersed household chicha production less critical to feasting preparations.

The dynamics of ceramic production, brewing, and feasting discussed in this chapter are relevant only to stratified communities in the central Andes where domestic production occurs in peasant households that are composed primarily of members of a nuclear family. Life in these communities is rapidly changing through market penetration, urban migration, state intervention, and other factors. Moreover, there is considerable regional variability in central Andean lifeways, which affects the way that pots are made, beer is produced, and feasts are held (Goldstein, Coleman Goldstein, and Williams, this volume; Hayashida, this volume; Orlove and Schmidt 1995; Ravines and Villiger 1989). Nonetheless, there are broadly similar ways that people carry out these activities within the constraints of the domestic mode of production in the central Andes, and some evidence suggests that these customs have deep roots (see Jennings and Bowser, this volume, for a discussion of continuities and changes).

We generalize across a region in this chapter, and then we project these generalizations into the past. While we are aware of the dangers of inter-preting the past based on ethnographic examples (Hayashida, this volume; Isbell 1995; Quilter 1996: 308), we feel that an understanding of the full implications of the relationship between feasting and domestic production is possible only when we have "households with faces" (see Tringham 1991). We tentatively draw these faces through ethnographic analogies that are buttressed by archaeological evidence.

Making Pots, Brewing Beer, and Throwing Feasts in the Domestic Mode

In the central Andes, the peasant, or campesino, household has long been the fundamental unit of production (Mayer 2002; Murra 1985). Although families are largely self-sufficient, some degree of specialization often oc-curs. One household, for example, might regularly produce chicha to be exchanged with other families, while another might specialize in ceramics production. Nonetheless, their activities are constrained within a domestic mode of production. In order to understand the relationship between ves-sel size, feasting, and political power, we need to understand how pots are made, beer is brewed, and feasts are thrown within this mode of produc-tion practiced by different campesino households that is in this region. In this section, we describe the traditional methods used in the central Andes today and argue that similar methods likely were used in the region by those earlier societies that lacked specialized brewing facilities.

Making Pots

By definition, traditional pottery production in the central Andes is orga-nized at the household level (see, e.g., Litto 1976; Sillar 2000). Although molds or the paddle-and-anvil finishing technique are used in some places (see, e.g., Cleland and Shimada 1998; Ravines and Villiger 1989; Sabogal

Figure 8.1. Itinerant potters from the community of Pumpuri, Bolivia, burnishing wide-mouth jars. Photo courtesy of Bill Sillar.

Weisse 1980), most domestic potters of the central Andes use a coil method of vessel formation followed by a scraping finishing technique (Sillar 2000: 55–58). Households produce a wide variety of vessel forms, with the pots finished, dried, and decorated in and around the home, and then fired in an open fire nearby (Fig. 8.1).

Ceramic production tends to be gendered in the central Andes (Arnold 1993; Camino 1985; Chávez 1985; Sillar 2000; Spahni 1966; Tschopik 1946: 537). In general, men mine clay and temper, mix clay, and form vessels (especially larger vessels); women are often in charge of finishing and decorating most vessels; and all family members participate in the firing (Arnold 1993; Camino 1985; Chávez 1985; Sillar 2000). It is not uncommon for men and women, however, to perform tasks that transgress gender roles or for all family members to work together during labor crunches (Hagstrum 1989: 32; Sillar 2000: 67).

The ceramics used in chicha production are among the largest vessels fabricated in the domestic context. There are two basic forms used in the central Andes to make beer—open, and constricted-orifice jars (often called *rakis* and *urpus*, respectively).[1] Karen Mohr Chávez details how these vessels are made in the Cuzco region (1985: 188–192), and her description gives a sense of the basic steps usually taken to make these types of vessels. In order to construct a half-meter-tall raki, a potter collects locally available clay and temper and mixes them with water inside his home (men make rakis in Chávez' study area). The clay is placed into a potter's plate, which serves as a mold for the base of the vessel, and a thick coil is added around the top. The potter widens and flattens the coil using his hands and then joins the coil and base using a triangle-shaped stone tool. Next, the potter adds four more rings using a similar process and then takes the pot outside to dry for two hours. After this initial drying, the potter adds seven additional rings to the pot, finishes the raki's interior with a stone, and then takes the vessel outside to dry for three hours. He then brings the vessel back inside to scrape, smooth, and polish the exterior and to add both the handles and the neck of the vessel. The vessel is then dried inside for seven to fourteen days before final drying occurs outside for about a week.

After the vessel is slipped and painted, it is fired in the open patio of the house. A circular firing area is covered with dung to a depth of thirty centimeters. Household members place rakis, urpus, and other large vessels on a bed of sherds above the dung and then stack smaller vessels on top. A wall of stone and adobe (thirty to fifty centimeters high) is constructed around the vessels, and the space between the wall and the pots is filled with dung or firewood. The mound is then covered in grass, and the grass is finally covered in dung. After a few stones are removed for ventilation, a household member lights the pile, and the pottery is fired from two to five hours, depending on the size of the batch.[2]

Chávez' description differs in some details from potting techniques elsewhere in the central Andes, but the basic steps and rhythm of the domestic production of beer vessels are similar (see, e.g., Arnold 1993; Camino 1985; Litto 1976; Ravines and Villiger 1989). We know that most possible brewing and fermenting jars were formed in the prehistoric Andes by coiling using similar tools and then fired in open-fire settings (Anders et al. 1998: 243; Hayashida 1999: 344; Lunt 1988: 493; Pozzi-Escott et al. 1998: 263; Shimada 1998a). Therefore, we suggest that many of today's constraints on domestic ceramic production of these vessels, in terms of material procurement, fabricating techniques, drying time, and other factors, are broadly similar to those faced by potters in the past.

Brewing Beer

Chicha is an umbrella Spanish term for any indigenously brewed alcoholic beverage in the Americas, and there are a wide variety of plants, such as manioc, molle, and peanuts, that can be used to brew it (Gómez Huamán

1966: 49–50; Nicholson 1960: 290–291; Vázquez 1967: 266–270). In the central Andes today, chicha is commonly produced using maize, and, as a result, most of the comparative ethnographic information published on feast preparation describes maize beer production. We therefore consider the details of domestic maize chicha brewing in this section. Steps for making other kinds of chicha are, of course, different, but all of the brews need to be heated, cooled, and then fermented (Goldstein and Coleman 2004; La Barre 1938). Similar functional needs often lead to similar designs, and the pots used in alcohol production share similar forms across the central Andes (Cutler and Cárdenas 1947; Hayashida, this volume; Jennings 2005; Nicholson 1960; Perlov, this volume)

Chicha brewing is primarily a female activity (Allen 2002: 152; Camino 1987: 39–42; Cutler and Cárdenas 1947: 37; Gómez Huamán 1966: 35; Holmberg 1971: 200; Orlove and Schmidt 1995: 276; Perlov, this volume;

Figure 8.2. A woman with a set of typical household *chicha* storage vessels in the Cotahuasi Valley of southern Peru. Photo by the author.

Rodríguez O. and Solares S. 1990: 31; Skar 1993: 41; but see Hayashida, this volume).

Men and children help in the brewing process—for example, they often harvest the maize or other ingredients, gather firewood, or help in some of the other tasks throughout the brewing process—but women zealously maintain their control over all aspects of the production process (Allen 2002: 151–153; Condori Mamani and Quispe Huamán 1996: 55; Perlov, this volume). Beer is generally made in and around the home, and fermentation occurs inside or in shaded areas. Since beer was consumed on a daily basis until recently, all households owned beer vessels that were constantly in use (Allen 2002: 114–126; Holmberg 1971; Simmons 1962) (Fig. 8.2).

Maize beer is made by masticating maize flour or by allowing the maize to germinate and then grinding the grains into flour. For the remainder of the brewing process, the recipe is largely the same. The flour is placed into a raki and then hot water is added, or the flour and water are boiled at a low temperature over the fire. Depending on the recipe, this mixture is alternatively heated and cooled over the course of one to three days (Cutler and Cárdenas 1947: 45–47; Gillin 1947; Manrique Chávez 1997: 308–309; Mújica Lengua and Godós Alcázar 2004: 50; Nicholson 1960: 296). Water is constantly added to the raki during this period, as evaporation readily occurs from the open-mouthed vessel, and certain parts of the mixture, such as the sediment and the caramel-like upper layer, are removed to make other products (Cutler and Cárdenas 1947: 45–46). The mixture is then transferred to an urpu, where it cools and ferments.

Fermentation is initiated from the yeasts in the unwashed jar or by throwing previously brewed chicha in with the new batch. The liquid begins to ferment quickly and may begin to bubble violently after a few hours. The fermentation occurs in one to six days, depending on elevation and environment (Cutler and Cárdenas 1947: 47), although three to four days is typical. Maize beer sours rapidly and usually spoils in under seven days.

Chicha brewing has been a female activity since at least the fifteenth century (Hastorf 1991; Marcoy 1873: 57; Morris 1979: 28; but see Rostworowski 1977: 241, and Hayashida, this volume), and maize beer is prepared today using methods similar to those described in detailed accounts from the eighteenth to the early twentieth centuries (Anonymous 1961: 13; Camino 1987: 39–42; Gómez Huamán 1966: 43–44; Hocquenghem and Monzón 1995: 112; Llano Restrepo and Campuzano Cifuentes 1994: 24–25; Ruiz 1998: 81; Tschiffely 1933: 48–49; Wiener 1993: 731–732). Although we have no recipes for maize beer before the Spanish Conquest, production technologies recovered in archaeological excavations strongly suggest that maize beer has been made in a similar fashion since at least the Early Intermediate Period (200 BC–AD 750) (Gero 1990, 1992; Moore 1989; but see Hayashida, this volume). Emerging information about chicha made from molle (Goldstein, Coleman Goldstein, and Williams, this volume) suggests that recipes for this beverage also may have changed little over time.

Throwing Parties

Major feasts occur throughout the year in the Andes during holidays, funerals, work projects, and other occasions (Bolin 1998). The events are important means of defining social hierarchies and obligatory relationships (Isbell 1974: 112) and are essential to acquiring the means for performing tasks that require the labor and resources of large segments of a community (Martel 1974). There are often customary guidelines for what should be served, when it should be presented to guests, and to whom items should be given (Martel 1974: 100–101), but in general, a good feast needs to fill bellies and make people "stumbling drunk" (Gelles 2000: 103). If the hosts are perceived as stingy, then they risk losing prestige and access to the labor from guests (Isbell 1978: 177; Martell 1974: 88, 104). Households might once in a generation be responsible for a major feast, and the occasion is an opportunity to generate considerable prestige in the community if carried out successfully (Allen 2002: 151; Meyerson 1990: 123). Although males tend to publicly sponsor feasting events (Gose 1994: 138; Isbell 1978: 170; Martel 1974), the success or failure of a feast is at least equally dependent upon a wife's ability to solicit sufficient beer and food through her social network (Hamilton 1998: 169).

The relationships between the hosts and chicha producers are often quite complicated (Isbell 1974: 113), but are guided in large part by the reciprocal bonds of *ayni* or *minka* exchanges. The most common form of exchange, ayni, is a delayed reciprocal labor exchange between members of a community. The sponsors will return this labor, in this case, chicha brewing, at a later time (Isbell 1978: 167; Mayer 2002: 109), and a "strict accordance is kept of debts and credits" (Isbell 1978: 168). In terms of social capital, gains from hosting the feast are tempered by subsequent ayni obligations (Mayer 2002: 116).

Minka is the second form of labor exchange. Minka laborers are often recompensed for their work with rights and gifts, but there is no obligation for the sponsors to return their labor at a later time (Allen 2002: 72–74;

Isbell 1978: 167–177; Mayer 1974, 2002: 108–112). Minka exchanges are asymmetrical transactions between people of different social or economic groups (Mayer 2002: 110; Trawick 2003: 100–108). The food, drink, and gifts received by the laborer never fully recompense her work, and the host's generosity at the feast asserts power over minka partners (Gose 1994: 11; Mayer 2002: 110). Minka exchanges, therefore, allow hosts to more easily extend their social capital. Pots, maize, and other materials can also be brokered in community feasting events through ayni and minka partners, resulting in the same social debt (Sillar 2000: 106–110; Weismantel 1988: 176).

The food and drink consumed at a feast may be prepared on-site or in the home. In most cases, soup, stew, or other items are initially prepared in the home and then brought to the event (Allen 2002: 152; Bastien 1978: 177). At the feast, food may be reheated, arranged, and served. Since beer takes at least a week to prepare and ferment, chicha is almost always prepared in the home and then transported to the event by a household (Meyerson 1990: 130). For example, women carried 120 liters of chicha to the festival of Yarqa Aspiy in the Ayacucho region of central Peru (Isbell 1978: 171). For particularly large events, women will nonetheless gather to produce alcohol on-site (Sillar 2000: 115). Women, however, tend to resist attempts to move feast preparation out of the home for long periods of time. Their schedules are already busy, and they can better control the timing, pace, and organization of affairs within their own household (Hamilton 1998: 139–141; Weismantel 1988: 175–179). Feast sponsors therefore must elicit promises of food and drink from many households and then wait for these goods to be assembled on the day of the event.

Dispersed preparation for feasts through the pooling of domestic production has not been extensively discussed for the prehistoric central Andes. As researchers have done in other regions (Bray 2003; Dietler and Hayden 2001), Andean archaeologists have focused on feasting events or on specialized facilities that were dedicated to feast preparation. Nonetheless, Peruvian data from Joan Gero's research in the Callejón de Huayllas (1990, 1992) and Christine Hastorf's work in the Mantaro Valley (1991) suggest that women's household labor was likely pooled for feasts, and the wide distribution of probable beer vessels across early sites indicates that pooling labor could have been a production strategy in the past (see, e.g., Goldstein 1993: 35; Goldstein 2005: 235; Isbell 1977: 68–71; Julien 2004: 93–94; Miller 2004: 132–135; Moore 1989: 692; Segura Llanos 2001: 72–96;

Silverman 1993: 245–250). The long-standing importance of reciprocity in the Andes (Mayer 2002) and reciprocity's ubiquity in organizing feasts around the world (Hayden 1996, 2001) also make it likely that feasts in the ancient Andes were organized at least in part through reciprocal bonds.

The Limitations of Domestic Production and Its Impact on Feasting Patterns

Today and in the past, large-scale feasts could be underwritten through the domestic production of pots and beer from households scattered across a region. Although some families in communities can produce more chicha than others because they have more pots, more family members, or more maize, there are limits to the productive capacities of households. Among other constraints, vessel weight, vessel production costs, household beer demands, and women's self-interest act to keep the size of the brewing and fermenting jars down. With access limited to smaller vessels, the host of a large feast must expend more and more social capital prior to the event to acquire the products of more and more households. This section explores a few of the factors that keep vessel size down.

Weight

Perhaps the most important limiting factor is weight. In the production sequence of making a beer pot, at least two adults are needed to move the pot back and forth as the vessel is dried and later fired (Chávez 1985: 188–192). The most difficult task is likely transporting the vessel outside to dry while the clay is still wet and then returning it to the home in order to apply the neck and handles to the body. A completed raki, for example, weighs at least 11.4–13.4 kilograms after firing (Chávez 1985: 188–192), and the vessel, although neckless, would likely weigh a bit more than this when wet. Although one person could carry the weight, the awkwardness of the shape and the plasticity of the vessel make it necessary for two people to carry it, with each person having one hand on the mold underneath the vessel and the second hand on the neck opening to balance the load (Chávez 1985: 190).

As vessel size increases, weight more than doubles, as does wall thickness. An 80-liter vessel, for example, might weigh as much as 20 kilograms and would become more cumbersome to handle. Larger vessels would likely become increasingly difficult for two people to carry reliably and might require the assistance of non-household members. Moreover, larger vessels would have a greater chance of cracking, breaking, or becoming deformed because of the difficulties associated with moving them during manufacture (Arnold 1985: 70).

A lone woman, perhaps with the help of her children, must also be able to manipulate the pots after they are fired, because men and adolescents are frequently away from the home throughout the day in the central Andes (Allen 2002: 60; Weismantel 1988: 175). During the brewing process, the rakis need to be tipped over and picked up several times. While an adult woman would have no problem lifting a 40 liter–capacity pot, she would likely struggle with the same pot while straining the liquid and transferring the chicha into fermenting jars. Since a liter of water weighs one kilogram, the woman would have to be able to tilt a vessel weighing more than 50 kilograms (not including the weight of the maize). An 80 liter–capacity vessel containing chicha would weigh more than 100 kilograms, and manipulating the vessel might necessitate help from other family members. Chicheras require the help of at least one to two other people to use their larger vessels (Nicholson 1960: 296; Perlov, this volume). A woman and her small children, however, must be able to handle chicha brewing alone, along with all other household tasks (Fig. 8.3).

Figure 8.3. Fermenting jars used by a *chichera* on the north coast of Peru to brew a total batch of about 600 liters. Photo courtesy of Frances Hayashida.

Weight would also be an issue in transporting vessels. Since the pack limit of llamas is quite low, humans traditionally carry heavy loads in the Andes (Rowe 1946: 237). In the Inca Empire, pottery jars were carried on the back with a rope that passed through the handles or underneath knobs on the jar (Rowe 1946: 237), and chicha jars continue to be carried in similar ways to this day (Julien 2004: 111; Tschopik 1950: 208). People can carry the largest vessels in this manner, since an empty 120-liter vessel might weigh as little as 45 kilograms. This vessel, however, could not be carried full of chicha.

While the ability of people to carry heavy loads over distances has been consistently underestimated by archaeologists (Malville 2001), 150 percent of body mass seems to be an average for experienced bearers (Malville 2001: 238). If Peruvian adults on average weigh about 56 kilograms (Frisancho 1976: 201), then 84 kilograms would be around the maximum that each individual could carry. A 120-liter vessel filled with chicha would weigh around 165 kilograms, an 80-liter vessel, about 108 kilograms, and a 40-liter vessel would weigh in at 53 kilograms. Most of the chicha vessels carried today do not exceed 40 liters in capacity (Litto 1976: frontispiece, 23), and Guaman Poma de Ayala's depictions also show smaller vessels being used at the time of the Inca Empire (1992: 204, 220, 262, 268).

Production Costs

The costs of increasing vessel size also would be an important factor limiting their production by households. As vessel size and wall thickness increase, the most obvious increase in cost is for materials. More clay, temper, and water must be collected to form the vessels. Additional wood, grass, and dung are needed to fully cover the vessels while firing them for a longer period of time (Rice 1987; Rye 1981; Shepard 1956). At least in the highlands, where raw materials are often found kilometers away from each other over rugged and steep terrain, the added time and labor to collect more of this material could necessitate an extra day of work and overtax household energy budgets (Arnold 1993: 65–66; Condori Mamani and Quispe Huamán 1996).

A large pot also requires significant increases in labor and time in order to mix the raw materials. Potters usually use foot trampling to mix extremely large batches of clay (Rice 1987: 119), and this also seems to be the case in the Andes (Chávez 1985: 168). The process is labor-intensive—one ethnographer reports that the process is over when the clay is smooth and the person sweats (Chávez 1985: 168)—and larger batches require more trampling time to mix thoroughly. Additional investment would be needed to roll thicker coils, and more coils would be needed to make the pot. Finishing and polishing the vessel would also be more work, and the potter's access to the interior of the vessel would become more difficult as size increased.

Finally, increased drying time would be perhaps one of the greatest increased stresses on household labor. Family members must routinely check on vessels and rotate them for even drying (Chávez 1985: 192; Rice 1987: 152). Moreover, the longer a vessel dries, the longer it will be exposed to potential damage by inclement weather, animals, or household members. Drying time varies according to climate and manufacturing technique (Arnold 1985), but in the same production context, bigger pots take significantly longer to dry than smaller pots (DeBoer and Lathrap 1979: 120, table 4.2; Specht 1972: 128). In the central Andes, drying times may differ by a week or more (Chávez 1985: 192; Litto 1976: 21).

Firing is the most critical stage of pottery production, since vessels are often broken, cracked, or deformed at this stage. Mórropan potters on the north coast of Peru, for example, must normally discard 4–8 percent of their vessels after firing, and losses of up to 90 percent are not uncommon (Cleland and Shimada 1998: 120). There are a wide variety of reasons for vessel damage, but undesired inclusions, incomplete mixing, improper joining, uneven drying, and variable firing temperatures are among the most common (Rice 1987; Shepard 1956).

The potential for damage increases with vessel size, because the chances of something going wrong in each step rises. The likelihood of faulty inclusions or incomplete mixing intensifies as more clay, temper, and water are mixed together at once. Potters have more difficulty joining one coil to the next in the interior of larger pots, and, of course, there is a larger surface area in which an error can be made. Larger vessels also have a greater chance of damage from some areas drying more slowly than others and are more likely to be left outside too long in the sun or to get wet. Finally, bigger vessels must be fired longer, which extends the riskiest part of production and endangers the results (Arnold 1985: 70; DeBoer and Lathrap 1979: 120, table 4.2; Rice 1987: 118, 128, 153; Vlade and Druc 1999: 107).

The lifespan of a ceramic vessel is dependent on its wall thickness, curing, transportability, as well as the amount and type of use it sees (Longacre 1981). In the Mantaro Valley of highland Peru, for example, a ceramic olla in daily use lasts an average of 1.77 years (Hildebrand and Hagstrum 1999: 36). Large jars (20–40 liters, called *fiestas grandes* in the Mantaro Valley) can last much longer, but this is only because they are so infrequently used (Hildebrand and Hagstrum 1999: 38). In general, larger pots last longer than smaller ones because they are heavier and more difficult to move (and thus used less often and kept in storage) (DeBoer and Lathrap 1979: 121, fig. 4.5; Nelson 1991: 174). Although the use-life of a large vessel, as an expensive piece of equipment in terms of the cost of energy required to produce it, might be extended with careful curing, beer pots are handled during brewing, transporting, and serving beer, and this movement exposes them to a greater risk of damage and breakage (Arnold 1985: 152–154). Although one can mend a cracked beer pot (B. Bowser, personal communication, 2006), many of the vessels used for dry storage in Andean households are damaged chicha jars that can no longer be used to brew and ferment beer (Sillar 2000: 108). Regardless of the length of the use-life, bigger vessels take more time, energy, and risk to make, and thus accidents are much more costly when they occur (Sillar 2000: 108).

Household Demand

Households typically own a wide array of ceramic forms that are used during the daily round of food preparation (Chávez 1985: 163–164; Hildebrand and Hagstrum 1999: 34; Sillar 2000: 104–105). Some of these vessels are traditionally dedicated to chicha production and used to create weekly or biweekly batches of beer. A constant supply of chicha is necessary because it is still an essential part of mobilizing labor (Mayer 2002), and, at least until recently (see Orlove and Schmidt 1995), it was consumed daily in the household. Potential household production rates therefore must match not only household consumption rates but also the common labor exchanges that occur throughout the year. In the first half of the twentieth century, adults typically consumed between two and three liters of chicha daily (Jennings 2005: 247). If the average household contains 2.2 adults (Figueroa 1984: 14), then the maximum amount of chicha needed in a week until recently would be forty-six liters (consumption rates for children are not discussed in the literature but appear to be minimal [Allen 2002: 5]).

A family also calls upon labor partners, often a handful of kin or close neighbors, throughout the year to manage certain household tasks. Generally, the number of participants is limited by the scale of the task to be completed—only so many people are required to roof a house or till a field—and conducted as an ayni exchange. The sponsors of the event are responsible for reciprocating labor at a later date and offering food and drink to invited laborers (Isbell 1978: 167; Mayer 2002: 109). Unlike larger feasts designed to gain social capital through excessive generosity, these small feasts act to maintain the status quo of an intimate group of exchange partners. The food and chicha provided are therefore a meal that matches typical daily consumption rates (Martel 1974; Mayer 2002: 109). A typical event might involve as many as eight individuals from outside the household over the course of two days (Allen 2002: 56; Mayer 2002: 113; Meyerson 1990: 39). If this two-day event were the largest event to occur during a normal year for a household, then the woman would have to produce 48 liters of chicha for an event, and a maximum of 94 liters for the week to cover both daily and event consumption.

On rarer occasions, a household would need to produce more chicha for a labor project. For example, Isbell (1978: 168) describes how fourteen men came together over four days to construct a house. If our calculations are correct, then a batch of up to 168 liters of chicha needed to be brewed by the household (or acquired from elsewhere).

If 94 liters per week is the maximum production rate needed for a household during a typical year, then it would make sense for women to possess culinary equipment to meet these demands. In the Mantaro Valley of central Peru, Hildebrand and Hagstrum (1999) found that an average household's cooking assemblage contained four or five small to medium-sized ollas (3.5–13.5 liters) and two larger ollas (21.1 liters). These assemblages of pots (fermenting jars were not included in their analysis) are similar to those noted elsewhere (Condori Mamani and Quispe Huamán 1996: 88; Sillar 2000: 107). The larger pots could be used to brew weekly batches of chicha, especially since home-brewed beer consumption has dropped significantly since the 1950s (Allen, this volume; Orlove and Schmidt 1995). Moreover, the family may own a couple of larger brewing and fermenting jars (approximately 40–50 liters each), which may be used a few times a year to support larger labor exchanges (Sillar 2000: 108). A woman's kitchen, therefore, is equipped to meet the annual needs of the household, and a few small jars (less than 100 liters in total capacity) meet these needs.

Women's Self-Interest

Women's interests might be the most important factor limiting vessel size. If men are the public face of the household, then women are the private power (Núñez del Prado Béjar 1975a). Although mutable, men and women have traditionally been assigned roles in the household, such as weaving, cooking, child rearing, seed planting, and, most important for our purposes, brewing (Núñez del Prado Béjar 1975a). Women tend to control the administration and distribution of household resources (Hamilton 1998: 169; Hastorf 1991: 134; Núñez del Prado Béjar 1975b: 624–626; Silverblatt 1987: 14). This resource control is perhaps most readily expressed when food and drink are served (Allen 2002: 59; Weismantel 1988: 179–180). A woman serving from the pot has a "veritable arsenal of tools for expressing her opinion of those she serves" by deciding who should be served first, how much he or she should be served, and what spoons, bowls, and/or cups each guest will be provided (Weismantel 1988: 179–180; see Bowser 2000 and 2004 for Amazonian examples). Women therefore take brewing and serving beer quite seriously. Brewing, like cooking, is traditionally central to their ethnic and gender identity (Weismantel 1988), and women's roles as brewers and servers of beer appear to go back at least to the Inca period (Murra 1980; Rowe 1946).

Men, of course, recognize the essential complementary contributions that women make to the household (Bolin 1998: 120–123; Hamilton 1998). A man therefore rarely forgets to thank his wife for his food (Allen 2002: 59), and he almost always, albeit often quietly, consults his wife before making important decisions regarding both the household and the community (Bolin 1998: 121). Males are most commonly the public sponsors of feasts and the loudest participants at these events, and women are often quiet and deferential to men at assemblies and other public events (Allen 2002: 98; Gose 1994: 138; Isbell 1978: 170; Martel 1974). Women collectively exert their influence over proceedings, however, and this power manifests itself through supplying and serving beer and food at the event (see, e.g., Allen 2002: 96–98; Colloredo-Mansfeld 1999: 150–159).

Because their power tends to be collectively implemented and hidden within the private sphere, women engage in the political process in ways that are closed to men (Allen 2002: 98; Núñez del Prado Béjar 1975a). In public, for example, husbands may be unable to refuse a request from a host for beer, but wives, in consultation with each other, determine the amount of beer that will be given and when the beer will arrive (Bolin 1998: 121). Since production is veiled behind the walls of dozens of homes, a host is dependent upon a process that is difficult to monitor. If not enough palatable beer arrives on the day of the feast, the host cannot solicit production of another batch of beer to cover the last-minute shortfall because of preparation and fermentation time. Women, therefore, influence public affairs, in part, by producing, transporting, and serving beer that has been made in the home (Fig. 8.4).

Figure 8.4. Guaman Poma's depiction of sowing in the Inca Empire. Note the woman in the rear serving *chicha* (1992: 250).

In sum, vessel weight, vessel production costs, production demands, and women's self-interest act to keep the size and number of vessels small. Smaller pots reflect the lifestyles and interests of nuclear families pursuing an agro-pastoral lifestyle. Forty-liter vessels are common in most households, and larger vessels, perhaps up to ninety liters, can be successfully made and used in a domestic context with little to no assistance from non-family members.

Nonetheless, size matters. Beyond eighty to ninety liters, households would find it riskier and, in some cases, beyond their abilities to produce and use these larger pots. The pots are more difficult and time-consuming to make, and they are more likely to break during drying and firing. The fired pots are clumsy to use, heavy to maneuver, and onerous, if not impossible, to transport. More important, smaller pots are an important means of ensuring women's influence over political activities by making feasts dependent upon the efforts of household labor across the entire community.

Big Pots and Big Shots in the Ancient Andes

Feasting has long been an important means by which social capital is gained and maintained within many societies (Hayden 1995, 1996, 2001). A feast is often the culmination of months of work by many people. The story of how food and drink arrived *to* the table is just as critical to our understanding of the past as the story of social behaviors *at* the table (Jennings et al. 2005). As in some other areas of the world (see, e.g., Arthur 2003; Holtzman 2001; Kahn 1986), feasting in the Andes has long been based on a seemingly asymmetrical relationship between largely male hosts and female laborers. It is in the very serving of food produced by their own hands, however, that women's power is collectively expressed in the home and at feasts.

There is sufficient evidence to suggest that past domestic production in many regions of the ancient Andes was broadly similar to traditional arrangements found in the region today. Pots tended to fit within the modern household ranges in terms of size and number, the bulk of culinary equipment was manufactured in domestic settings, and brewing often occurred in the home (Cobo 1990: 194; Goldstein 2005: 209; Moore 1989: 691; Shimada 1998b). Smaller beer pots were likely used because of pragmatic production and consumption limitations that were similar to those faced by households today, and also because small vessel size ensured that a host was dependent upon the collective will of the community for a feast's success.

Yet, examples of large pots that were part of specialized brewing facilities appear with the development of the first states (Chapdelaine 1997: 32; D'Altroy and Hastorf 1992: 265; Goldstein 2005: 207; Morris 1979: 28–32; Moseley et al. 2005: 17267; Shimada 1994: 144, 169, 208) (Fig. 8.5). Patrick Ryan Williams and his colleagues, for example, have uncovered a brewing facility at the Wari site of Cerro Baúl that boasts twelve 150-liter fermenting jars and a production capacity of approximately 1,800 liters (Moseley et al. 2005: 17267), and the cloistered women, or *mamacuna*, of the Inca Empire used similarly sized jars to produce the thousands of liters of chicha

Figure 8.5. An excavator carries an Inca-period *raki* from the site of Choquepuqio in southern Peru. The vessel's volume is approximately 120 liters. Photo courtesy of Gordon McEwan.

consumed at Inca feasts (Costin 2001: 235; Morris and Thompson 1985: 90).[3] Since chicha spoils quickly, production at these specialized facilities was probably episodic (Goldstein 2003: 162; Shimada 1994: 244), and labor was pooled only in the weeks preceding a feast. Nonetheless, we suggest that the presence of these facilities signals a sharp departure in feasting patterns. With larger pots, less community involvement was needed (see Fig. 8.3).

The emergence of specialized facilities in Andean states does not indicate the end of household brewing. All homes likely continued to make chicha for daily consumption and other household needs (Cobo 1990: 194; Goldstein 2005: 209; Moore 1989: 691), and homes could pool their resources to underwrite larger community events (Jennings 2005). Specialized facilities, however, freed hosts in a number of ways from some of the reciprocal ties that might have limited their gains in social capital. First, a host and his household with access to a specialized facility would need to call upon the labor of fewer individuals, and thus would accumulate fewer future obligations while collecting the same amount of beer. Second, the shrunken labor pool means that feasts would have become less like potlucks, because fewer guests contributed to each event. In fact, a gift that cannot be reciprocated puts a person in an inferior position (Mauss 1990: 65), and as the chicha output of specialized facilities increased, more and more people would have participated in events for which they had prepared little or no food and drink (Mayer 2002: 116). Finally, resistance to labor demands is most effective when it is disguised, low profile, diffuse, and undisclosed (Scott 1985, 1990). In a centralized production facility, the host could monitor and control brewers more easily than if household producers were dispersed throughout a community.

The full or partial exclusion of domestically produced food and beer would have been particularly crippling to women, whose participation in the political process was underwritten by their household production. "Flattened" by her overwhelming inability to reciprocate at the household level for a feast (Mauss 1990: 41), a woman's ability to influence extrahousehold politics in the community was seriously compromised as chicha brought to a feast became more of a token of allegiance than a viable contribution to the affair.

The disenfranchisement of women could explain isotopic evidence for lower maize consumption by women than men in the Tiwanaku and Inca states (Goldstein 2003: 164; Hastorf 1991: 152; Williams 2005). Once feasting was incorporated into these states, women apparently participated less actively in them, both as part of the hosting apparatus and as guests, and thus drank less beer (see, e.g., Hastorf 1991: 152). Today's campesino communities recognize their dependence on household production, and hosts make a strong effort to ingratiate themselves with the female and male participants who underwrite a feast (Isbell 1978: 168–170).

The idiom of reciprocity likely has deep roots in the Andes (Mayer 2002: 105), and at least the Inca Empire couched its rule within an "idealized system of reciprocity and redistribution" (Ramírez 2005: 225; also see Weismantel 1991: 874–875). In reality, the Incas, and earlier Andean states, strove to break aspects of production free from the more balanced reciprocal bonds that limited the accumulation of social capital by moving the production of some items out of the household (Mayer 2002: 116–118). While scholars have widely recognized the importance of feasting in the rise of social inequality, there has been considerably less emphasis on the leveling mechanisms embedded within feasting that may minimize status gains (see, e.g., Wiessner 1996). Diffused household production ensures that the social capital gained through the event is shared across a wide range of producers because of the commensurate social debt that the host accrues in order to assemble the food and drink for the feast. Moreover, hosts who are dependent upon a scattered workforce that lies outside of their direct control must act within accepted cultural patterns of behavior that likely lessen status differences between households. The use of larger pots in specialized facilities undermines this leveling mechanism and thus frees hosts from some of their reciprocal obligations. When this happens, a woman's political influence is significantly eroded in those cultures where her power flows from control over domestic production.

Notes

1. There are many different terms for vessel forms across the Andes. *Raki* and *urpu* are some of the most common Quechua terms for wide-mouthed and narrow-mouthed jars, respectively, and are often used in the central Andes. For the sake of convenience, we use these vessel form terms throughout the chapter.

2. We do not suggest that all beer pots are or were made by coiling and fired in open-fire settings. There is evidence in ethnographic and archaeological contexts for a formation technique combining molds and the paddle-anvil method on Peru's north coast (Cleland and Shimada 1998: 117–118; Hayashida 1999: 346), and kiln firing is also known archaeologically from the region (although it seems to have been used for firing smaller vessels) (Shimada 1998a).

3. Exact volume measurements for Inca vessels remain unpublished (but see Bray, this volume), but archaeological evidence from the Inca site of Choquepuquio yields a maximum vessel size of 180 liters (Gordon McEwan, personal communication, 2005).

References Cited

Abercrombie, Thomas A.

1998 *Pathways of Memory and Power: Ethnography and History among an Andean People.* Madison: University of Wisconsin Press.

Allen, Catherine J.

2002 *The Hold Life Has: Coca and Cultural Identity in an Andean Community.* 2nd edition. Washington, D.C.: Smithsonian Institution Press.

Anders, Martha, Susana Arce, Izumi Shimada, Victor Chang, Luis Tokuda, and Sonia Quiroz

1998 Early Middle Horizon Pottery Production at Maymi, Pisco Valley, Peru. In *Andean Ceramics: Technology, Organization and Approaches*, Izumi Shimada, ed. Museum of Applied Science Center for Archaeology, supplement to vol. 15, pp. 233–251. Philadelphia: University of Pennsylvania.

Anonymous

1961 [1720] Información anónima sobre la vida y costumbres del pueblo de Virú, Provincia de Trujillo, Departamento de la Libertad. *Revista del Archivo Nacional del Perú* 25(1): 10–25.

Arnold, Dean E.

1985 *Ceramic Theory and Cultural Process*. New York: Cambridge University Press.

1993 *Ecology and Ceramic Production in an Andean Community*. New York: Cambridge University Press.

Arthur, John W.

2003 Brewing Beer: Status, Wealth, and Ceramic Use Alteration among the Gamo of South-Western Ethiopia. *World Archaeology* 34: 516–528.

Bastien, Joseph W.

1978 *Mountain of the Condor: Metaphor and Ritual in an Andean Ayllu*. Prospect Heights: Waveland.

Blitz, John

1993 Big Pots for Big Shots: Feasting and Storage in a Mississippian Community. *American Antiquity* 58: 80–96.

Bolin, Inge

1998 *Rituals of Respect: The Secret Life of Survival in the High Peruvian Andes*. Austin: University of Texas Press.

Bourdieu, Pierre

1986 The Forms of Capital. In *Handbook of Theory and Research for the Sociology of Education*, John G. Richardson, ed., pp. 241–248. New York: Greenwood.

Bowser, Brenda

2000 From Pottery to Politics: An Ethnoarchaeological Study of Political Factionalism, Ethnicity, and Domestic Pottery Style in the Ecuadorian Amazon. *Journal of Anthropological Method and Theory* 7(3): 219–248.

2004 The Amazonian House: A Place of Women's Politics, Pottery, and Prestige. *Expedition* 46(2): 18–23.

Bray, Tamara L. (ed.)

2003 *The Archaeology of Food and Feasting in Early States and Empires*. New York: Kluwer Academic/Plenum.

Camino, Lupe

1985 Tarika, un centro alfarero. *Boletín de Lima* 6(35): 49–54.

1987 *Chicha de maíz: Bebida y vida del pueblo Catacaos*. Piura: Centro de Investigación y Promoción del Campesinado.

Cavero Carrasco, Ranulfo
1986 *Maíz, chicha y religiosidad andina*. Ayacucho: Universidad Nacional de San Cristóbal de Huamanga.

Chapdelaine, Claude
1997 Le Tissus urbain du site moche, una cité péruvienne précolombienne. In *À l'ombre du Cerro Blanco: Nouvelles découvertes sur la culture Moche, côte nord du Pérou*, Claude Chapdelaine, ed., pp. 11–82. Montreal: Université de Montréal.

Chávez, Karen L. Mohr
1985 Traditional Pottery of Raqchí, Cuzco, Peru: A Preliminary Study of Its Production, Distribution, and Consumption. *Ñawpa Pacha* 22–23: 161–210.

Cleland, Kate M., and Izumi Shimada
1998 Paleteada Potters: Technology, Production Spheres, and Sub-Culture in Ancient Peru. In *Andean Ceramics: Technology, Organization and Approaches*, Izumi Shimada, ed. Museum of Applied Science Center for Archaeology, supplement to vol. 15, pp. 111–150. Philadelphia: University of Pennsylvania.

Cobo, Bernabé
1990 [1653] *Inca Religion and Customs*. Translated and edited by Roland Hamilton. Austin: University of Texas Press.

Colloredo-Mansfeld, Rudi
1999 *The Native Leisure Class: Consumption and Cultural Creativity in the Andes*. Chicago: University of Chicago Press.

Condori Mamani, Gregorio, and Asunta Quispe Huamán
1996 *Andean Lives*. Ricardo Valderrama, Carmen Escalante Gutiérrez, Paul Gelles, and Gabriella Martínez Escobar, eds. Austin: University of Texas Press.

Costin, Cathy
2001 Production and Exchange of Ceramics. In *Empire and Domestic Economy*, Terence D'Altroy and Christine Hastorf, eds., pp. 203–242. New York: Kluwer Academic/Plenum.

Costin, Cathy, and Melissa B. Hagstrum
1995 Standardization, Labor Investment, Skill, and the Organization of Ceramic Production in Late Prehispanic Peru. *Latin American Antiquity* 60(4): 619–639.

Cutler, Hugh C., and Martín Cárdenas
1947 Chicha, a Native South American Beer. *Botanical Museum Leaflets* (Harvard University) 13(3): 33–60.

D'Altroy, Terence N.
2002 *The Incas*. Malden: Blackwell.

D'Altroy, Terence N., and Christine A. Hastorf
1992 The Architecture and the Contents of Inka Storehouses in the Xauxa Region. In *Inka Storage Systems*, Terry LeVine, ed., pp. 259–286. Norman: University of Oklahoma Press.

DeBoer, Warren R., and Donald W. Lathrap
1979 The Making and Breaking of Shipibo-Conibo Ceramics. In *Ethnoarchaeology: Implications of Ethnography for Archaeology*, Carol Kramer, ed., pp. 102–138. New York: Columbia University Press.

Dietler, Michael
1996 Feast and Commensal Politics in the Political Economy: Food, Power, and Status in Prehistoric Europe. In *Food and the Status Quest*, Polly Wiessner and Wulf Schiefenhövel, eds., pp. 87–125. Providence: Berghahn Books.
2001 Theorizing the Past: Rituals of Consumption, Commensal Politics, and Power in African Contexts. In *Feasts: Archaeological and Ethnographic Perspectives on Food, Politics, and Power*, Michael Dietler and Brian Hayden, eds., pp. 65–114. Washington, D.C.: Smithsonian Institution Press.

Dietler, Michael, and Brian Hayden
2001 Digesting the Feast—Good to Eat, Good to Drink, Good to Think: An Introduction. In *Feasts: Archaeological and Ethnographic Perspectives on Food, Politics, and Power*, Michael Dietler and Brian Hayden, eds., pp. 1–20. Washington, D.C.: Smithsonian Institution.

Earle, Timothy
1991 The Evolution of Chiefdoms. In *Chiefdoms: Power, Economy, and Ideology*, Timothy Earle, ed., pp. 1–15. New York: Cambridge University Press.

Figueroa, Adolfo
1984 *Capitalist Development and Peasant Economy in Peru*. New York: Cambridge University Press.

Frisancho, A. Roberto
1976 Growth and Morphology at High Altitude. In *Man in the Andes: A Multidisciplinary Study of High-Altitude Quechua*, Paul T. Baker and Michael A. Little, eds., pp. 180–207. Stroudsburgh: Dowden, Hutchinson, and Ross.

Gelles, Paul H.
2000 *Water and Power in Highland Peru: The Cultural Politics of Irrigation and Development*. New Brunswick: Rutgers University Press.

Gero, Joan M.
1990 Pottery, Power, and . . . Parties! *Archaeology* 43(2): 52–56.
1992 Feasts and Females: Gender Ideology and Political Meals in the Andes. *Norwegian Archaeological Review* 25: 15–30.

Gillin, John P.
1947 *Moche: A Peruvian Coastal Community*. Institute of Social Anthropology Publication 3. Washington, D.C.: Smithsonian Institution.

Glowacki, Mary, and Anita G. Cook
2003 Pots, Politics, and Power: Huari Ceramic Assemblages and Imperial Administration. In *The Archaeology and Politics of Food and Feasting in Early States and Empires*, Tamara L. Bray, ed., pp. 173–202. New York: Kluwer Academic/ Plenum.

Goldstein, David, and Robin Christine Coleman
2004 *Schinus Molle L.* (Anacardiaceae) Chicha Production in the Central Andes. *Economic Botany* 58(4): 523–529.

Goldstein, Paul

1993 House, Community, and State in the Earliest Tiwanaku Colony: Domestic Patterns and State Integration at Omo M12, Moquegua. In *Domestic Architecture, Ethnicity and Complementarity in the South-Central Andes*, Mark S. Aldenderfer, ed., pp. 25–41. Iowa City: University of Iowa Press.

2003 From Stew-Eaters to Maize-Drinkers: The Chicha Economy and the Tiwanaku Expansion. In *The Archaeology and Politics of Food and Feasting in Early States and Empires*, Tamara L. Bray, ed., pp. 143–172. New York: Kluwer Academic/ Plenum.

2005 *Andean Diaspora: The Tiwanaku Colonies and the Origins of South American Empire*. Gainesville: University Press of Florida.

Gómez Huamán, Nilo

1966 Importancia social de la chicha como bebida popular en Huamanga. *Wamani* 1(1): 33–57.

Gose, Peter

1994 *Deathly Waters and Hungry Mountains: Agrarian Ritual and Class Formation in an Andean Town*. Toronto: University of Toronto Press.

Guaman Poma de Ayala, Felipe

1992 [1615] *El primer nueva crónica y buen gobierno*, John V. Murra and Rolena Adorno, eds. Mexico City: Siglo Veintiuno.

Hagstrum, Melissa B.

1989 Comunidades alfareras especializadas del Vale del Mantaro. *Boletín de Lima* 11(61): 29–34.

Hamilton, Sarah

1998 *The Two-headed Household: Gender and Rural Development in the Ecuadorian Andes*. Pittsburgh: University of Pittsburgh Press.

Hastorf, Christine A.

1991 Gender, Space, and Food in Prehistory. In *Engendering Archaeology: Women and Prehistory*, Joan M. Gero and Margaret W. Conkey, eds., pp. 132–159. Cambridge: Blackwell.

Hastorf, Christine A., and Sissel Johannessen

1993 Pre-Hispanic Political Change and the Role of Maize in the Central Andes of Peru. *American Anthropologist* 95(1): 115–138.

Hayashida, Frances M.

1999 Style, Technology and State Production: Inka Pottery Manufacture in the Leche Valley, Peru. *Latin American Antiquity* 10(4): 337–352.

Hayden, Brian

1995 Pathways to Power: Principles for Creating Social Inequality. In *Foundations of Social Inequality*, T. Douglas Price and Gary Feinman, eds., pp. 15–85. New York: Plenum.

1996 Feasting in Prehistoric and Traditional Societies. In *Food and the Status Quest*, Polly Wiessner and Wulf Schiefenhövel, eds., pp. 127–148. Oxford: Berghahn Books.

2001 Fabulous Feasts: A Prolegomenon to the Importance of Feasting. In *Feasts: Archaeological and Ethnographic Perspectives on Food, Politics, and Power*,

Michael Dietler and Brian Hayden, eds., pp. 23–64. Washington, D.C.: Smithsonian Institution Press.

Hildebrand, John A., and Melissa B. Hagstrum
1999 New Approaches to Ceramic Use and Discard: Cooking Pottery from the Peruvian Andes in Ethnoarchaeological Perspective. *Latin American Antiquity* 10(1): 25–46.

Hocquenghem, Anne-Marie, and Susana Monzón
1995 *La cocina piurana: Ensayo de antropología de la alimentación.* Lima: Instituto de Estudios Peruanos.

Holmberg, Alan
1971 The Rhythm of Drinking in a Peruvian Coastal Mestizo Community. *Human Organization* 30(2): 198–202.

Holtzman, Jon
2001 The Food of Elders, the "Ration" of Women: Brewing, Gender, and Domestic Processes among the Samburu of Northern Kenya. *American Anthropologist* 103(4): 1041–1058.

Isbell, Billie Jean
1974 Parentesco andino y reciprocidad: Kukaq: Los que nos aman. In *Reciprocidad e intercambio en los Andes peruanos*, Giorgio Alberti and Enrique Mayer, eds., pp. 110–152. Lima: Instituto de Estudios Peruanos.
1978 *To Defend Ourselves: Ecology and Ritual in an Andean Village.* Prospect Heights: Waveland.

Isbell, William H.
1977 *The Rural Foundations for Urbanism: Economic and Stylistic Interaction between Rural and Urban Communities in Eighth-century Peru.* Urbana: University of Illinois Press.
1995 Constructing the Andean Past or "As You Like It." *Journal of the Steward Anthropological Society* 23(1–2): 1–12.

Isbell, William H., and Amy Grouleau
In press The Venerated Woman of Conchopata: A New Context for Feasting and Offering. In *From Subsistence to Social Strategies: New Directions in the Study of Daily Meals and Feasting Events*, Elizabeth A. Klarich, ed. Boulder: University Press of Colorado.

Jennings, Justin
2005 La Chichera y el Patrón: Chicha and the Energetics of Feasting in the Prehistoric Andes. In *Foundations of Power in the Prehispanic Andes*, Christina A. Conlee, Dennis Ogburn, and Kevin Vaughn, eds., pp. 241–259. Archaeological Publications of the American Anthropological Association, vol. 14. Washington, D.C.: American Anthropological Association.

Jennings, Justin, Kathy L. Antrobus, Sam J. Atencio, Erin Glavich, Rebecca Johnson, German Loffler, and Christine Luu
2005 "Drinking Beer in a Blissful Mood": Alcohol Production, Operational Chains, and Feasting in the Ancient World. *Current Anthropology* 46(2): 275–303.

Julien, Catherine

2004 Las tumbas de Sacsahuaman y el estilo Cuzco-Inca. *Ñawpa Pacha* 25–27: 1–125.

Kahn, Miriam

1986 *Always Hungry, Never Greedy: Food and the Expression of Gender in a Melanesian Society.* New York: Cambridge University Press.

La Barre, Weston

1938 Native American Beers. *American Anthropologist* 40: 224–234.

Lau, George

2002 Feasting and Ancestor Veneration at Chinchawas, North Highlands of Ancash, Peru. *Latin American Antiquity* 13(3): 279–304.

Litto, Gertrude

1976 *South American Folk Pottery.* New York: Watson-Guptill.

Llano Restrepo, María, and Marcela Campuzano Cifuentes

1994 *La chicha, una bebida fermentada a través de la historia.* Bogotá: Instituto Colombiano de Antropología.

Longacre, William A.

1981 Kalinga Pottery: An Ethnoarchaeological Study. In *Patterns of the Past: Studies in Honor of David L. Clark,* Ian Hodder, Glyn Isaac, and Norman Hammond, eds., pp. 49–66. Cambridge: Cambridge University Press.

Lunt, Sarah

1988 The Manufacture of Inca Aryballus. In *Recent Studies in Pre-Columbian Archaeology, Part II.* Nicolas J. Saunders and Olivier de Montmollin, eds. BAR International Series no. 421, pp. 489–511. London: British Archaeological Reports.

Malville, Nancy J.

2001 Long-distance Transport of Bulk Goods in the Pre-Hispanic Southwest. *Journal of Anthropological Archaeology* 20: 230–243.

Manrique Chávez, Antonio

1997 *El maíz en el Perú.* Lima: Consejo Nacional de Ciencia y Tecnología.

Marcoy, Paul

1873 *A Journey across South America.* London: Blackie and Son.

Martel, César Fonseca

1974 Modalidades de la Minka. In *Reciprocidad e intercambio en los Andes peruanos,* Giorgio Alberti and Enrique Mayer, eds., pp. 86–109. Lima: Instituto de Estudios Peruanos.

Mauss, Marcel

1990 *The Gift: The Form and Reason for Exchange in Archaic Societies.* New York: W. W. Norton.

Mayer, Enrique

1974 Las reglas de juego en la reciprocidad andina. In *Reciprocidad e intercambio en los Andes peruanos,* Giorgio Alberti and Enrique Mayer, eds., pp. 37–65. Lima: Instituto de Estudios Peruanos.

2002 *The Articulated Peasant: Household Economies in the Andes*. Boulder: Westview.

Meyerson, Julia

1990 *"Tambo": Life in an Andean Village*. Austin: University of Texas Press.

Miller, George

2004 An Investigation of Cuzco-Inca Ceramics: Canons of Form, Proportion, and Size. *Ñawpa Pacha* 25–27: 127–149.

Moore, Jerry

1989 Pre-Hispanic Beer in Coastal Peru: Technology and Social Context of Prehistoric Production. *American Anthropologist* 91(3): 682–695.

Morell, Virginia

2002 Empires across the Andes. *National Geographic* 201(6): 106–129.

Morris, Craig

1979 Maize Beer in the Economics, Politics, and Religion of the Inca Empire. In *Fermented Food Beverages in Nutrition*, Clifford F. Gastineau, William J. Darby, and Thomas B. Turner, eds., pp. 21–34. New York: Academic Press.

Morris, Craig, and Donald E. Thompson

1985 *Huánuco Pampa: An Inca City and Its Hinterland*. New York: Thames and Hudson.

Moseley, Michael E., Donna J. Nash, Patrick Ryan Williams, Susan D. deFrance, Anna Miranda, and Mario Ruales

2005 Burning Down the Brewery: Establishing and Evacuating an Ancient Imperial Colony at Cerro Baúl, Peru. *Proceedings of the National Academy of Sciences* 102(48): 17264–17271.

Mújica Lengua, Fidel Rudulpho, and Paula García Godós Alcázar

2004 Caracterización bioquímica y tecnológica de bebidas fermentadas tradicionales. *Jornado de Investigación Universitaria de la Universidad Nacional de San Cristóbal de Huamanga* 4: 47–56.

Murra, John V.

1980 *The Economic Organization of the Inka State*. Greenwich: JAI.

1985 "El Archipielago Vertical" Revisited. In *Andean Ecology and Civilization*, Shozo Masuda, Izumi Shimada, and Craig Morris, eds., pp. 3–14. Tokyo: University of Tokyo Press.

Nelson, Ben A.

1991 Ceramic Frequency and Use-Life: A Highland Mayan Case in Cross-cultural Perspective. In *Ceramic Ethnoarchaeology*, William A. Longacre, ed., pp. 162–181. Tucson: University of Arizona Press.

Nicholson, G. Edward

1960 Chicha Maize Types and Chicha Manufacture in Peru. *Economic Botany* 14(4): 290–299.

Núñez del Prado Béjar, Daisy Irene

1975a El rol de la mujer campesina quechua. *América Indígena* 35(2): 391–401.

1975b El poder de decisión de la mujer quechua andina. *América Indígena* 35(2): 623–630.

Orlove, Benjamin, and Ella Schmidt
1995 Swallowing Their Pride: Indigenous and Industrial Beer in Peru and Bolivia. *Theory and Society* 24: 271–298.

Perodie, James R.
2001 Feasting for Prosperity: A Study of the Southern Northwest Coast Feasting. In *Feasts: Archaeological and Ethnographic Perspectives on Food, Politics, and Power*, Michael Dietler and Brian Hayden, eds., pp. 185–214. Washington, D.C.: Smithsonian Institution Press.

Pozzi-Escott, Denise, Marleni M. Alarcón, and Cirilo Vivanco
1998 Wari Ceramics and Production Technology. In *Andean Ceramics: Technology, Organization and Approaches*, Izumi Shimada, ed. Museum of Applied Science Center for Archaeology, supplement to vol. 15, pp. 253–281. Philadelphia: University of Pennsylvania.

Quilter, Jeffrey
1996 Continuity and Disjuncture in Pre-Columbian Art and Culture. *RES* 29/30: 303–317.

Ramírez, Susan Elizabeth
2005 *To Feed and Be Fed: The Cosmological Bases of Authority and Identity in the Andes*. Stanford: Stanford University Press.

Ravines, Rogger, and Fernando Villiger (eds.)
1989 *La cerámica tradicional del Perú*. Lima: Editorial Los Pinos.

Rice, Prudence M.
1987 *Pottery Analysis: A Sourcebook*. Chicago: University of Chicago Press.
1998 Ancient Andean Ceramic Production and Technology: A View from the Outside. In *Andean Ceramics: Technology, Organization and Approaches*, Izumi Shimada, ed. Museum of Applied Science Center for Archaeology, supplement to vol. 15, pp. 339–351. Philadelphia: University of Pennsylvania.

Rodríguez O., Gustavo, and Humberto Solares S.
1990 *Sociedad oligárquica, chica y cultural popular: Ensayo histórico sobre la identidad regional*. Cochabamba: Editorial Serrano.

Rostworowski de Diez Canseco, María
1977 *Etnia y sociedad: Costa peruana prehispánica*. Lima: Instituto de Estudios Peruanos.

Rowe, John H.
1946 Inca Culture at the Time of the Spanish Conquest. In *Handbook of South American Indians*, vol. 2. Julian Steward, ed., pp. 183–330. Washington, D.C.: Smithsonian Institution Bureau of American Ethnology Bulletin 143.

Ruiz, Hipólito
1998 [1788] *The Journals of Hipólito Ruiz*. Richard Evans Schultes, ed. Portland: Timber.

Rye, Owen S.
1981 *Pottery Technology: Principles and Reconstruction*. Washington, D.C.: Taraxacum.

Sabogal Weisse, José R.
1980 *La cerámica del Piura*. Quito: Instituto Andino de Artes Populares.

Scott, James C.

1985 *Weapons of the Weak: Everyday Forms of Peasant Resistance.* New Haven: Yale University Press.

1990 *Domination and the Arts of Resistance: Hidden Transcripts.* New Haven: Yale University Press.

Segura Llanos, Rafael

2001 *Rito y economía en Cajamarquilla: Investigaciones arqueológicas en el Conjunto Arquitectónico Julio C. Tello.* Lima: Fondo Editorial de la Pontificia Universidad Católica del Perú.

Shepard, Anna O.

1956 *Ceramics for the Archaeologist.* Washington, D.C.: Carnegie Institution.

Shimada, Izumi

1994 *Pampa Grande and the Mochica Culture.* Austin: University of Texas Press.

1998a Andean Ceramics: An Introduction. In *Andean Ceramics: Technology, Organization and Approaches*, Izumi Shimada, ed. Museum of Applied Science Center for Archaeology, supplement to vol. 15, pp. 1–19. Philadelphia: University of Pennsylvania.

1998b *Andean Ceramics: Technology, Organization and Approaches*, Izumi Shimada, ed. Museum of Applied Science Center for Archaeology, supplement to vol. 15. Philadelphia: University of Pennsylvania.

Sillar, Bill

2000 *Shaping Culture, Making Pots and Constructing Households: An Ethnoarchaeological Study of Pottery Production, Trade, and Use in the Andes.* BAR International Series no. 883. Oxford: British Archaeological Reports.

Silverblatt, Irene Marsha

1987 *Moon, Sun, and Witches: Gender Ideologies and Class in Inca and Colonial Peru.* Princeton: Princeton University Press.

Silverman, Helaine

1993 *Cahuachi in the Ancient World.* Iowa City: University of Iowa Press.

Simmons, Ozzie G.

1962 Ambivalence and the Learning of Drinking Behavior in a Peruvian Community. In *Society, Culture, and Drinking Patterns*, David J. Pittman and Charles R. Snyder, eds., pp. 37–47. New York: John Wiley & Sons.

Skar, Sarah Lund

1993 Andean Women and the Concept of Space/Time. In *Women and Space: Ground Rules and Social Maps*, Shirley Ardener, ed., pp. 31–45. Providence: Berg.

Spahni, Jean-Christian

1966 *La cerámica popular del Perú.* Lima: Peruano Suiza.

Specht, James

1972 The Pottery Industry of Buka Island, Territory of Papua, New Guinea. *Anthropology and Physical Anthropology in Oceania* 7: 125–144.

Stanish, Charles

1994 The Hydraulic Hypothesis Revisited: Lake Titicaca Basin Related Fields in Theoretical Perspective. *Latin American Antiquity* 5(4): 312–332.

Trawick, Paul B.

2003 *The Struggle for Water in Peru: Comedy and Tragedy in the Andean Commons.* Stanford: Stanford University Press.

Tringham, Ruth E.

1991 Households with Faces: The Challenge of Gender in Prehistoric Architectural Remains. In *Engendering Archaeology: Women and Prehistory*, Joan M. Gero and Margaret W. Conkey, eds., pp. 93–131. Cambridge: Blackwell.

Tschiffely, Aimé F.

1933 *Tschiffely's Ride: Ten Thousand Miles in the Saddle from Southern Cross to Pole Star.* New York: Simon and Schuster.

Tschopik, Harry

1946 The Aymara. In *Handbook of South American Indians*, vol. 2. Julian Steward, ed., pp. 501–574. Washington, D.C.: Smithsonian Institution Bureau of American Ethnology Bulletin 143.

1950 An Andean Ceramic Tradition in Historic Perspective. *American Antiquity* 16(3): 196–218.

Vázquez, Mario C.

1967 La chicha en los países andinos. *América Indígena* 27(2): 264–282.

Vlade, Bruce, and Isabelle C. Druc

1999 *Archaeological Ceramic Materials: Origins and Utilization.* New York: Springer.

Weismantel, Mary J.

1988 *Food, Gender, and Poverty in the Ecuadorian Andes.* Philadelphia: University of Pennsylvania Press.

1991 Maize Beer and Andean Social Transformations: Drunken Indians, Bread Babies, and Chosen Women. *Modern Language Notes* 106(4): 861–879.

Wiener, Charles

1993 [1880] *Perú y Bolivia, relato de viaje.* Translated by Edgardo Rivera Martínez. Lima: Instituto Francés de Estudios Andinos.

Wiessner, Polly

1996 Leveling the Hunter: Constraints on the Status Quest in Foraging Societies. In *Food and the Status Quest: An Interdisciplinary Perspective*, Polly Wiessner and Wulf Schiefenhövel, eds., pp. 171–191. Providence: Berghahn Books.

Williams, Jocelyn S.

2005 Investigating Diet and Dietary Change Using the Stable Isotopes of Carbon and Nitrogen in Mummified Tissues from Puruchuco-Huaquerones, Peru. Doctoral dissertation, University of Calgary.

9

Chicha Histories

Pre-Hispanic Brewing in the Andes and the Use of Ethnographic and Historical Analogues

Frances Hayashida

In "Cloth, Gender, Continuity, and Change," Elizabeth Brumfiel (2006) calls on anthropologists to question the seeming persistence of traditional technologies through time. Using the example of weaving in Mesoamerica, she notes that "continuities can mask differences" that tell us about weavers and the societies in which they lived.[1] These differences are revealed by carefully examining the history of seemingly timeless practices. Here, I follow Brumfiel's advice and explore the problem of discerning continuity and change in maize chicha production in the Andes.

Chicha is a particularly good candidate for this kind of examination. Like cloth in Mesoamerica, chicha continues to be produced in different areas of the Andes using "traditional" technologies. Similarities in brewing techniques across a broad geographic area strengthen the impression of great antiquity. Today, chicha is made primarily by women, and women (like the Inca's chosen women, or *acllacuna*) brewed in the past, suggesting organizational as well as technological continuities. Chicha's use for feasts, as compensation for work, in toasts with the living and the dead, as offering, medicine, food, and intoxicant is vividly described in historical and ethnographic accounts across a range of geographic and temporal settings. These accounts are a rich source of analogues for archaeologists interpreting the production and consumption of this quintessential Andean drink. How do we develop analogies in a way that allows us to see both change and continuity?

I began to consider these issues while visiting *chicherías* (commercial brewing establishments) in Chulucanas, a town in the Department of Piura on the north coast of Peru (Hayashida 2008). In Chulucanas, chicha is cooked, cooled, and fermented in large earthenware vessels closely resembling jars found at late pre-Hispanic north coastal sites. Women boil the chicha over wood fires, stir it with wooden paddles or lengths of split cane, cool and aerate it with big gourd dippers, and strain it through cotton cloth (Fig. 9.1a). In the late nineteenth century, Brüning (Schaedel 1988) documented many of the same steps that I saw in 2005 (Fig. 9.1b). Farther back in time, the late-eighteenth-century watercolors of north coastal life commissioned by Martínez Compañón (1978), the archbishop of Trujillo, depict scenes of chicha production (Fig. 9.1c) that, aside from the change in dress, could have been painted today in Chulucanas or Catacaos, another Piura center famed for its chicherías (Camino 1987). For the pre-Hispanic period, chicha production locations with many of the same tools and remains associated with modern north coastal brewing have been reported

A

B

C

Figure 9.1. Straining the *chicha* in 2005 in Chulucanas (Fig. 9.1a; photo by the author), in 1890 in Sechura (Fig. 9.1b; from Brüning 1989), and in the late eighteenth century on the north coast of Peru (Fig. 9.1c; from Martínez Compañón 1978). The persistence of some techniques contributes to the impression that *chicha* practices overall are timeless.

at Chimú (Moore 1981, 1989; Prieto Búrmester 2004) and Moche (Castillo Butters 2005; Chapdelaine 2001; Shimada 1994) archaeological sites.

At the same time that some brewing practices persist, there are also clear discontinuities. While women are the primary producers today, and were in the time of Brüning and Martínez Compañón, male and female brewers prepared chicha to be dispensed by north coastal lords (Rostworowski de Diez Canseco 1977: 144); men (or households of men and women working together) brewed in communities specializing in chicha production (Rostworowski 1989: 278–279);[2] a male *botiller* (brewer or brewing supervisor) was part of the royal entourage of Naymlap, the mythical founder of the Lambayeque dynasty (Cabello Valboa 1951: 327); and men who appear to be making or serving chicha are depicted in Moche (Shimada 1994: 223) and Chimú (Uceda 1997) artwork.

Today, while brewers in larger commercial establishments continue to cook chicha in pottery vessels, others have shifted to aluminum pots, which are sturdier and do not need frequent replacement. Cooking in metal pots also requires less fuel wood, an increasingly scarce and costly resource as coastal trees are cut down for local consumption but also to meet the charcoal demands of *pollerías* (the ubiquitous spit-roasted chicken restaurants) in cities throughout Peru.

Thus, traditional brewing involves more than the simple persistence of chicha pots and practices; instead, it represents a conscious choice by successful brewers, motivated by personal preference and perhaps consumer demand for authenticity (also see Perlov, this volume). Similarly, the decision to abandon tradition is inseparable from economic forces far beyond Chulucanas.

Below, I explore the application of analogues to pre-Hispanic chicha production and how we might evaluate continuity and change through time. First, I outline the ethnographic and historical sources on chicha production that inform interpretations of pre-Columbian production and how they have been used by archaeologists. Second, I discuss Stahl's (1993) critique of homogeneous analogical models that assume rather than question persistence. These models should receive particular scrutiny in areas subject to European conquest and colonization. In the Andes under Spanish rule, the brewing and consumption of chicha were transformed by the repression of drinking for ritual and social purposes and the simultaneous tolerance and even encouragement of commercial chicha production in cities, towns, and *tambos* (roadside inns). The disruptions of the conquest and subsequent changes in brewing illustrate the need for a historical understanding of analogue sources. Thus informed, we can then make comparisons between sources and the archaeological record, rather than simply projecting the present onto the past, to discern continuity and change. I close with a call for ethnoarchaeological research into chicha production to complement and augment existing analogue sources.

Sources of Analogues

Archaeological studies of chicha brewing focus on production technology and organization to understand the role of beer and the choices made by producers in their economic and social contexts (Castillo Butters 2005; Goldstein 1993; Goldstein, Coleman Goldstein, and Williams, this volume; Jennings 2005; Moore 1981, 1989; Morris 1974, 1979; Moseley et al. 2005; Segura Llanos 2001; Shimada 1994; Valdez 2002). Ethnographic and historical accounts from a range of times and places in the Andes are sources of analogues for production in the pre-Columbian past. They provide information on ingredients, pots, brewing equipment, production steps, yields, serving and drinking practices, labor inputs, and, less frequently, the composition and organization of producer groups. They also may describe the links of brewers to consumers, whether human or supernatural, living or dead, lords or commoners, farmers or city dwellers.

For example, from Spanish chroniclers and native Andean writers, we learn of the acllacuna, who were relocated by the Inca from their home communities to Cuzco and provincial administrative centers, where they made cloth and also brewed the massive quantities of maize beer consumed and sacrificed at state-sponsored feasts and ceremonies (Morris 1979). Colonial administrative records from the Peruvian north coast register the testimony of the leaders of specialist brewing communities, who claimed that they had no fields (Rostworowski de Diez Canseco 1989: 278–279) and dedicated themselves full time to beer making. The observation of the cleric Cobo (1990: 194), that the most common household objects were the pots and cups used for preparing and serving chicha, provides a rare glimpse of domestic production in the countryside, but just a glimpse, since few other details, such as location, technology, participants (men, women, children?), or other aspects of organization, are given. Colonial wills list the whole and fragmented pottery that brewers carefully curated and passed on to their heirs, while litigation records tell us who these brewers were, where they came from, and how they made a living in urban and rural settings (Garofalo 2001, chap. 2; Garofalo 2003; Mangan 2005, chap. 3).

Also helpful are the historical lexicons of Andean languages, which reveal brewing techniques and the kinds and classes of chicha produced (see also Goldstein, Coleman Goldstein, and Williams, this volume). For example, Muchik phrases recorded on the north coast of Peru by Brüning in the late nineteenth century indicate that brewers of that time sieved their chicha twice (a coarse sieving and a fine sieving), as they do today in Chulucanas (Schaedel 1988). The southern Peruvian Quechua in González Holguín's lengthy lexicon (1989: 18, 248) includes terms for chicha specialists ("Aka camayok: El que vende or haze açua"), for those who chewed toasted maize flour for wages ("Muccupuccuk. Los que se alquilan para mascar"), and for the action "to help to make chicha" ("Akausini. Ayudar a hazer la açua"). Additional terms describe different kinds of chicha, including two kinds of red ("Cculli aka. Açua tinta, o colorada" and "Chumpi aka. Bermeja"), a yellow ("Qqello aka. La amarilla"), and a settled or clear beer ("Chhuya aka. Asentada, o clara"). Bertonio's (1984) seventeenth-century Aymara speakers also described beer varieties, including an aged chicha (*llutapu, yanu yakusa*), which is notable, since most ethnographic accounts emphasize that chicha spoils (turns to vinegar) after a few days. Tschudi, who traveled throughout the Andes in the mid-nineteenth century, also reports on aged chichas and adds that they were fermented in tightly sealed buried jars (Tschudi 1918: 42).

The most explicit descriptions of brewing technology and the ones most relied on by archaeologists trying to identify brewing in the archaeological record derive from observations at chicherías, locations where chicha is brewed for sale. Chicherías originated in the sixteenth century, proliferating in Spanish cities like Potosí, Lima, and Cuzco, and can be found today in cities, towns, and rural settings in different parts of the Andes. Studies exist for the Peruvian north coast (Anonymous 1961; Camino 1987; Nicholson 1960; Velásquez Benites 1996), Cochabamba (Cutler and Cárdenas 1947), Cuzco (Muelle 1978), Arequipa (Nicholson 1960; Valdizán and Maldonado 1922), and Bogotá (Llano Restrepo and Campuzano Cifuentes 1994). Chicha is produced in other contexts (e.g., for purely household or ritual consumption), but the chicherías have drawn the interest and attention of travelers and researchers, perhaps because of their high visibility and accessibility. In some cases, the author does not explicitly state that the observations come from a chichería, but the context may be inferred from the scale and permanence of production or from other details. For example, in their oft-cited Cochabamba study, Cutler and Cárdenas (1947) do not identify their sources in the text, but many of their photographs are of chicherías. Like Cutler and Cárdenas, most observers of brewing technology do not provide much detail on the producers or their organization.[3]

Chichería descriptions that are rich in technical details but poor in cultural content have certain limitations as sources of analogues. Chicherías represent a small sample of potential production arrangements (commercial, usually larger scale), and even purely technical decisions are made in a cultural and economic context that is far removed from the pre-Hispanic societies we hope to understand.[4] The lack of cultural content in purely technical descriptions of chicha making contributes to the impression of brewing as a timeless practice.

Technical accounts are perhaps most useful for identifying the presence or absence of chicha production in the archaeological record. This is how both Moore (1989) and Segura Llanos (2001) use them; each constructed a careful list of the possible material correlates of each production step, then compared the list to what they found in their excavations at late pre-Hispanic coastal sites. In both cases, positive identification of chicha production was made on the basis of clear material evidence for several different production steps. Thus, the presence of large cooking or serving jars alone would be insufficient evidence for production.

The Direct Historical Approach and "lo Andino"

Beyond the recognition of the presence or absence of brewing in the past, what are the possibilities for understanding the social and political context of production and variability across space and time? Postconquest brewing analogues are applied to the pre-Columbian past through the direct historical approach, where history (the persistence of chicha production) and geography (the Andes) link sources (ethnographic and historical accounts) and subject (the archaeological record). But, as Stahl (1993), following Wylie (1985), has noted, the connections between source and subject need to be demonstrated rather than assumed (see also Robin 2002). Discussing applications of the direct historical approach, Stahl (1993: 246) observes that

> typically, archaeologists have drawn on any and all available sources (historic/ethnohistoric and ethnographic) for which there is a historical relation between the subjects of the sources. This allowed the researcher to combine insights drawn from a variety of spatial and

temporal contexts (i.e. observations from a variety of areas by early explorers, colonial officials, and recent ethnographers) and to conflate these into a single homogenized analogical model. However, we must confront the possibility that by conflating sources from widely separated temporal contexts and potentially collapsing variability into homogenized holistic models we build in assumptions of persistence.

In the case of the Andes, the risk of falling into this trap is particularly strong, given long-standing ideas about the integrity of Andean culture across space and time (the concept of "lo andino," or "Andeanness"). While some practices *have* endured and *are* found over a wide extent of the Andes (e.g., the use of chicha for offerings, the embodiment of supernatural beings in features of the landscape), even ubiquitous and enduring traditions have histories, and the task of the archaeologist is to define those histories, teasing out how and why practices originate and change through time and what those changes tell us about larger social processes. We should be able to distinguish empirically when practices really do persist, when continuity masks difference (i.e., when material correlation masks cultural change), but also when difference masks continuity (when cultural traditions persist under different material guises).

Brewing models based on assumptions of persistence potentially obscure these distinctions. One example is Jennings and Chatfield's (this volume) model of changes in brewing, feasting, and women's status from pre-state to state-level societies across the pre-Hispanic Andes. To reconstruct pre-state organization, the authors derive an analogy from contemporary chicha production in peasant households in the Andean highlands, where women produce chicha for home consumption using small pots that suffice for household needs. Pots of similar size, which were possibly used for chicha, have been found at pre-Hispanic households. For communitywide feasts today, the sponsor solicits chicha contributions from other households and incurs a debt that he repays in kind at a later date. This reliance on women's labor and brewing knowledge maintains or elevates women's status. The argument is made that individual households cannot host a feast alone and must rely on pooled labor because of the small size of their pots. Larger pots are too big for a woman alone to maneuver and are costly to manufacture, decreasing the likelihood that they will be made and owned by individual households.[5] Pre-Hispanic state administrators, however, had no such energy or cost limitations or reciprocal-labor obligations; they brewed in big pots and threw feasts on a regular basis. Thus, with the emergence of states, women lost much of their control over feasting and were disempowered.

While the identification of big patterns in the past is both desirable and necessary, the proposition that there is a pan-Andean relationship between gender, brewing, and status in modern peasant households that serves as a model for pre-state organization remains to be rigorously tested. The material correlation (of household pot sizes) may mask differences in the activities and status of women and men and in the organization of feasting across time (i.e., peasant communities have undergone centuries of change) and space (e.g., on the Peruvian north coast, as Jennings and Chatfield note, there is documentary and iconographic evidence for brewing by men). A culturally rich and historically informed understanding of chicha is possible only if we move away from the image of brewing as a timeless, pan-Andean practice and actively look for change and variation.

Selection and Application of Analogues

How do we move away from this image? Stahl (1993) suggests attention to both the *selection* of analogues and their *application* (i.e., both source and subject). Selection involves careful evaluation of the historical and cultural context of sources and their possible limitations and biases to determine their relevance (Stahl 1993: 246–250). Attention to sources also allows us to question rather than assume the persistence of traditions, thus avoiding the construction of "pastiche" histories that collapse variability (Stahl 1993: 249).[6] In the case of chicha we should ask, "What are the possible sources of change or disruption in brewing and drinking practices and their consequences?"

With regard to application, Stahl (1993: 250–253) notes that analogies should be comparative and not merely illustrative. An *illustrative* approach projects historical or ethnographic observations onto the archaeological past and uses continuity in some attributes to infer comparability in others. Such an approach precludes the possibility of identifying cultural change or forms that do not exist in the ethnographic or historical record. The alternative is to explicitly *compare* source and subject, paying particular attention to dissimilarities between analogues and the archaeological evidence, to allow recognition of cultural forms that do not have modern or historical correlates. In other words, instead of assuming continuity, we should be looking for possible discontinuities and what they can tell us about cultural change.

In the pages that follow, I begin to lay the groundwork for a comparative perspective by considering two analogue sources from the colonial period: descriptions of rituals in the Andean countryside and of chicherías in colonial cities. This discussion has two goals: first, to situate these sources in their historical and cultural context; and, second, to draw attention to potentially deep changes in chicha practices following the conquest that affect how we use colonial and later sources to reconstruct the pre-Hispanic past. As timeless as modern brewing might seem, it is in fact the product of centuries of change, including the disruptions of conquest and colonial rule.

Colonial Transformations

Following Wolf (1982), Stahl (1993) observes that careful scrutiny of sources is particularly important in nonwestern areas subjected to European conquest and colonization, where productive relations, demography, structures of authority, and ideas about gender and race were transformed. At the same time, colonized people maintained cultural traditions, at times modifying or disguising practices or beliefs to escape European notice or control. The production and consumption of chicha underwent radical changes after the conquest. We can see this in the efforts of extirpating priests to control chicha because of its centrality to Andean ritual practices, as well as in the commercialization of chicha in towns, cities and tambos, where its popularity crossed racial lines and where entirely new production arrangements emerged to meet the high demand.

The Extirpation of Maize Beer

> Who except the priests can rid them of their drunkenness, which creates, foments, and preserves their idolatry? (Arriaga 1968b: 137)[7]

From the time of the conquest, Spanish administrators and the church tried to eradicate the use of chicha for Andean social and ritual events. Drinking, particularly the heavy public drinking, or *borracheras*, that accompanied feasts, work parties, and religious ceremonies, was characterized as a threat to the social order and as promoting immoral behavior and leaving the Indians susceptible to the entreaties of "demons." The centrality of chicha in sacrifices to local and regional *huacas* (holy places and objects) and *malquis* (bodies of ancestors) made its eradication particularly important. Following the Taki Onqoy messianic movement of the 1560s,[8] which preached the revival of Andean gods and the defeat of the Christian god and Spanish colonizers, the jurist Matienzo (1967: 79–82) urged severe restrictions on public drinking. Following Matienzo, Viceroy Toledo recommended that lords found guilty of drunkenness should first be warned. A second offense warranted exile for two months, the third, loss of his right to hold public office, and the fourth, exile for six months and loss of salary. Further transgressions should result in permanent exile and loss of his post. For commoners, the first offense warranted a reprimand, and the second, twenty lashes. The hair should be shorn (a great humiliation) for the third offense, with exile and the loss of land and kin ties for the fourth offense (Arriaga 1968a: 239–240). Even earlier, there had been attempts to curb gatherings and drinking. For example, on the Peruvian north coast, the inspector Doctor Cuenca banned the serving of chicha by lords at their residences or during administrative tours, when they traveled with jars full of chicha to dispense to subjects. These restrictions undermined the authority of local lords, who complained that, without chicha, their subjects would not obey them (Ramírez 1996: 20–21; Rostworowski de Diez Canseco 1977: 122–123, 144; Rostworowski de Diez Canseco 1989).

Chicha preparation and drinking were particularly targeted in the campaigns of extirpation of the sixteenth and seventeenth centuries. The first campaign began in the 1560s, following the Taki Onqoy movement; the second began in 1610 and resulted in Arriaga's 1621 manual, "Extirpación de la idolatría del Pirú;" the third flourished under the guidance of Pedro de Villagómez, archbishop of Lima from 1641 to 1671 (Arriaga 1968 b; Duviols 2003; Mills 1997; Salazar-Soler 1993; Spalding 1984, chap. 8; Stern 1982, chap. 3; Villagómez 1919). Though reduced, extirpation efforts continued through the eighteenth century (Mills 1997).

Details on the role of chicha in local religious practices are particularly rich in the documents accompanying the second and third campaigns, which were focused on the Archdiocese of Lima.[9] By this time, large public festivals had been largely suppressed, but the huacas and malquis responsible for the well-being of *ayllus* (kin-based social groups) and communities and the abundance of fields and flocks continued to be venerated and fed through sacrifices, sometimes under the guise of celebrations for Catholic holy days. In a series of visitas and procesos, church inspectors used interrogation, deception, threats, and torture to identify the women and men who directed ceremonies and sacrifices, then collected and destroyed ritual objects and punished those who would not collaborate or repent, saving the harshest treatment for those who had relapsed. Punishments included public humiliation, flogging, forced service to the church, dispossession of lands, banishment, and imprisonment in the Casa de Santa Cruz in Lima (Duviols 2003: 32–33, 462–466).

From the observations of the extirpators in the Archdiocese of Lima and the confessions they extracted, we learn of chicha's role in ritual life. Arriaga (1968a: 209) writes that "the principal offering, the best and most important part of Indian sacrifices, is chicha. By it and with it the festivals of the huacas begin, because of it they happen, and with it, they end. It is everything."[10]

Chicha was often accompanied by other offerings such as llamas, guinea pigs, silver, blood, coca, llama fat, special ears of maize, certain seeds or fruit, feathers, *mullu* (spondylus), *paria* (cinnabar) or other mineral powders, and *sancu* (balls of cornmeal) (Arriaga 1968a: chap. 4). Chicha was poured or sprinkled onto the huacas, offered to the dead (both recently departed kin and the long dead and carefully tended malquis), and consumed by ritual specialists and general participants alike in vast quantities at festivals, at times accompanied by music and dancing.

Arriaga (1968a: 206) identifies the chicha specialists of the coast as men, and those of the highlands as women. Chicheras (female brewers) are named and denounced in a number of the proceedings from Lima's archdiocese (Duviols 2003). Each was dedicated to preparing the chicha used for sacrifice and consumption at the ceremonies for a particular malqui or huaca. Some of the women are described as virgins (Mills 1997: 43, 44), while married women were expected to abstain from sexual relations with their husbands at times when they chewed maize for ritual chicha (Arriaga 1968a: 210). Where age is specified, some chicheras are described as older, while others are listed as young girls (e.g., those who brewed for Coya-huarmi, a huaca in the form of a *cantarillo*, or pottery jar, and dressed as a woman [Duviols 2003: 609]); in one case, an older woman worked with a young apprentice (Mills 1997: 44). For certain occasions, the chicha was not made by specialists. Instead, the priest in charge of the ceremony ordered or requested a contribution of chicha as well as other offerings from the ceremony participants (see, e.g., Duviols 2003: 495, 499).

Different kinds of chicha were prepared for distinct purposes. Arriaga (1968a: 209) describes a potent chicha called *yale*, made of malted and chewed maize mixed with powdered *espingo*,[11] which was prepared on the coast from Chancay to the south. Priests poured some over the huaca and consumed the rest, and it made them "act as if mad" (Arriaga 1968b: 41). Chicha of the sierra was sometimes made from maize grown in fields dedicated to the huaca or malqui. It was prepared "strong and thick, like *mazamorra* (porridge)" and was called *tecti* (Arriaga 1968b: 41–42). The huaca Libiac Cancharco received offerings of chicha mixed with crushed shell, together with blood offerings and other food (Mills 1997: 68). A white chicha (*chicha blanca*) called *cocoasua* was prepared from the first ears of corn harvested from a maize field and offered in sacrifice to the *ydolos* (religious images) and malquis, before the other ears could be consumed (Duviols 2003: 355). In Quipan, near Canta, the brewer devoted to the principal huaca made chicha from a special black maize grown on the huaca's fields (Mills 1997: 43). A divination ceremony held in San Pedro de Hacas (Cajatambo) to determine if the following year would be poor or prosperous required, among other offerings, *llollo asua*, a chicha with an oily layer on top ("hecha de mucho mais y tiene ensima como aseite que dicen ñabiyoc chicha con ojos" [Duviols 2003: 359]). In Pachangara (Cajatambo), chicha poured into an elaborately dressed and decorated large jar (*tinaja*) known as the huaca Tinlla Cocha, reportedly turned colors, forming an "arc like a rainbow on its surface" (Mills 1997: 58). By drinking this transformed chicha, residents gained the strength to sow their fields and ensured a successful harvest.

Extirpation manuals provided inspectors with guidelines for examination and interrogation, disposal of collected ritual objects and malquis, and punishment. In his list of questions for a "sorcerer or any other Indian who reveals or gives information about huacas,"[12] Arriaga (1968b: 117) instructs examiners to "ascertain which sorcerers have charge of festivals and fasts and have the chicha prepared" (Arriaga 1968b: 121).[13] After the interrogations, huacas, malquis, and personal ritual objects were collected and publicly burned. Items included the cups (*vasos*), precious-metal drinking vessels (*aquillas*), and gourd containers (*mates*) used to give food and drink to the huacas, as well as the pots in which they made tecti or chicha for the huacas, and the jugs (*cantarillos*) in which they carried it (Arriaga 1968a: 254). The ashes and objects that would not burn were thrown away where they would never be found, for even broken and burned remains would be retrieved and venerated (Arriaga 1968a: 254). Following the destruction of the huacas and malquis, accused "sorcerers" (the ritual specialists) were publicly humiliated and made to renounce their teachings. To close the ceremony, extirpators announced the regulations against further idolatrous behavior and punishments for transgressors (Arriaga 1968a: 275–277). These included orders against drunkenness and chicha made of *jora* (malted maize) as the "most efficacious means of destroying idolatry and wiping out the drunkenness of the caciques as well as that of the rest of the Indians" (Arriaga 1968b: 170).[14] Drunkenness during festivals, including those to celebrate the planting of fields, justified severe punishment. The production of tecti and sancu were also banned. Local priests were responsible for monitoring behavior and meting out punishment.

The extirpation accounts provide a glimpse of the intensity of colonial eradication efforts, as well as of the tenacity of ritual practitioners in the face of repression. This resistance is apparent in the need for reinspections and in the particularly strong punishments meted out to "repeat offenders." But the persistence of chicha in the archdiocese cannot be interpreted as the simple continuation of pre-Columbian practices. Although chicha was not eradicated, the vigilance of the priests no doubt resulted in the loss of some forms of brewing knowledge and practice, or their conversion (e.g., the possible substitution of other substances for chicha) to escape the notice of the church.

The Commoditization of Maize Beer

They make each year in this villa [Potosí] such a vast quantity of chicha . . . that it seems an impossible thing to imagine. (Descripción de la villa y minas de Potosí [1965]: 380)[15]

While religious repression transformed chicha practices in rural contexts, the commercial success of maize beer in colonial Andean cities wrought different but equally profound changes in production and consumption. In these contexts, maize beer changed from *aka* or *asua* (the Quechua terms) to *chicha* (the name introduced by the Spanish), from indigenous to colonial, and from gift or offering to commodity (Cummins 2002: chap. 9; Mangan 2005: 82). A boom in brewing and drinking accompanied the growth of urban centers, and chicha was available both from street or market vendors (*gateras*) and taverns (chicherías). While town councils and ecclesiastical authorities periodically attempted to restrict availability, the overwhelming popularity of maize beer and the income generated from sales, rental of tavern properties, and taxes precluded its strict control. Histories of Cuzco and Lima by Garofalo (2001, 2003) and Potosí by Mangan (2005) highlight the new roles that chicha and its producers and vendors played in colonial social life and economies. Maize beer changed from a ceremonial and ritual drink consumed by Andeans to a profitable, intoxicating refreshment enjoyed by the many and ethnically diverse inhabitants of colonial cities.

The city of Potosí was founded with the discovery of the productive Cerro Rico silver mine in 1545. Here, chicha began as an indigenous drink consumed by the masses of *mita* laborers assigned to the mines,[16] but by 1570, it had crossed racial and ethnic lines to become the favored drink of Indians, Africans, and Spanish workers and of their mixed-race (*casta*) descendants (Mangan 2005: 77, 102–103). In 1603, residents of Potosí reportedly imbibed 1.6 million bottles of maize beer, far outstripping wine consumption (Mangan 2005: 83).

The chicha was made from flour milled from maize grown in the agriculturally rich Cochabamba and Tomina regions (Mangan 2005: 30). An effort by the town council in 1604 to curb drinking by controlling the maize supply backfired when creative brewers turned to wheat flour as their base (Mangan 2005: 76). Alarmed by the threat to the valued bread supply, the council reversed its decision.

The earliest producers at Potosí were likely indigenous women accompanying their husbands to the mines to fulfill their mita duties. Their children made *muku*, the chewed and salivated-on morsels of maize flour used to trigger fermentation in batches of beer (Mangan 2005: 81). While this division may represent the continuation of a pre-Hispanic division of household labor, it might also be interpreted as a survival strategy by families facing new economic pressures.

By the beginning of the seventeenth century, Andean women continued as vendors and brewers in the *rancherías* (indigenous neighborhoods) surrounding Potosí, but in the city center, the trade was dominated by Spanish tavern owners, including many women (Mangan 2005: 84–90, 185). These women were not the elite of Potosí, but rather, those who used the money to "make ends meet" and to complement income from other activities such as washing, sewing, or sales of other products (Mangan 2005: 86). They themselves did not brew, but rather, employed indigenous women who needed the work to pay or cancel debts or to meet tribute payments (Mangan 2005: 86–87). Tavern owners provided flour and payment to contracted brewers in exchange for finished jugs of chicha (Mangan 2005: 84).

A few indigenous women were vendors and hired others as brewers (Mangan 2005: 87–88); there is also an example of an African slave who brewed and sold chicha, as well as a free mulatta who operated a chichería, though African participation was lower than in Lima (discussed below) (Mangan 2005: 83). A few indigenous men participated in the chicha trade of colonial Potosí, either as assistants or partners of their wives, or as brewers or vendors.

In contrast to Potosí, there were more opportunities for indigenous women in Lima to work independently as brewers and vendors and to operate their own taverns (Garofalo 2001: 116–144). Some chicheras worked alongside their husbands; others were single or widowed, or their husbands lived and worked outside of Lima. Brewers had their own equipment, and they obtained maize from the market or from husbands who cultivated fields nearby or in the sierra. The most successful ran their own taverns and worked with their families or had close ties with Indian communities. The poorest were those producing or selling chicha for others; these could become ensnared in debt to tavern owners. In Lima, Afro-Peruvian women also brewed and sold chicha, perhaps drawing on African beer-making traditions (Garofalo 2001: 124–130). They also produced *guarapo*, a fermented drink made from the sweet sap of maize stalks, and chicha with sugar; the latter, which did not use chewed grain, was preferred by Spaniards as being "cleaner" (Garofalo 2001: 129).

Striking examples of changes in brewing and serving also come from the rural areas surrounding Lima. Spanish authorities required chicha in tribute, which was then used to compensate agricultural workers in lieu of other payments (Garofalo 2001: 131–133). In addition to maximizing profits for the authorities and depriving workers of the resources needed to survive in the colonial economy, these practices distorted the pre-Columbian practice of serving chicha in exchange for labor, which was embedded in the complex exchange of goods and services between lords and subjects. Local lords challenged these demands in court, eventually winning their lawsuit. They continued to serve chicha to their subjects in exchange for labor in the fields, but they also operated taverns to provide income that benefited their households and perhaps their communities.[17]

The participation of indigenous lords in the chicha industry of Cuzco was even more pronounced, reflecting their continued affluence and influence after the conquest (Garofalo 2003). From the 1640s, with the collapse of the mita labor system and the influx of immigrants seeking work,

Cuzco's elites, both Indian and Spanish, established profitable chicherías, hiring indigenous women and men to produce beer. Smaller independent chicherías were established by skilled indigenous women, but their success depended on their ability to draw on networks of kin and other artisans to acquire, through inheritance or credit, the necessary equipment and ingredients to start their own business. Other women labored as employees, and the best enjoyed relatively high status and pay, comparable to that of other artisans in the city. As in Lima and Potosí, many others worked to cancel debts. This last group included men, though they seem to have been restricted to certain tasks such as gathering fuel, hauling water, and grinding *wiñapu* (germinated maize kernels).

The large scale of chicha production in Cuzco was accompanied by a greater degree of task specialization (Garofalo 2003). Thus, *wiñaperas* sprouted and malted maize (a procedure similar to the specialized chewing of maize flour seen in Potosí), others were hired to cook but not to vend, while men provided labor for specific tasks. Garofalo (2001: 173–175) observes that tavern owners may have encouraged specialization to prevent employees from mastering all of the different steps and possibly forming their own, competing, chichería. The desire of tavern owners to monopolize brewing is also seen in the lack of *curaca* (local lord) support for commoner Indians attempting to participate in the trade (i.e., they did not guarantee the work contracts of other Indian brewers). Cuzco provided fewer opportunities for commoners to establish their own small chicha businesses than did Potosí or Lima.

This summary of chichería history in Potosí, Lima, and Cuzco illustrates the different ways in which chicha became commercialized in the colonial Andes. Chicherías did not represent the simple transfer of indigenous brewing to colonial cities, but instead, involved a complete change in the meaning, production, and distribution of maize beer. Chicha was a colonial drink associated with Indians but produced and consumed across racial and ethnic lines. Production was divorced from relations of reciprocity and sacrifice and linked instead to concerns about profits, credit, and debt. These changes affected the organization and technology of production, as brewers from a variety of backgrounds (skilled and unskilled, immigrants from throughout the Andes, women and men, Andean, African, and Spanish) and technological traditions were drawn into the trade, as recipes became shaped by urban tastes, as brewers acquired their maize, muk'u, and wiñapu from the market rather than from local fields, as the brewing process became specialized by task, and as (at least in Cuzco) large operators attempted to squeeze out competitors.

Discussion

There are marked discontinuities in chicha production from pre-Hispanic to modern times which should be considered in the application of historical and ethnographic analogues to the pre-Columbian past. Here I have focused on the effects of two colonial phenomena: the extirpation of idolatry and attempts to eradicate chicha for ritual purposes; and the origins and growth of chicherías. A more complete assessment would include equal scrutiny of other colonial processes and events and a review of earlier and later periods. For example, we should critically assess the applicability of Inca sources to non-Inca or pre-Inca practices. The Inca insistence on feasting and ceremonial hospitality as part of strengthening the empire (Hastorf and Johannessen 1993; Morris 1979) and the massive sacrifice of chicha in state ritual created new patterns of chicha production and consumption and ideas about the beverage. Some practices, which we see as deeply and universally Andean, may in fact have been introduced to parts of the empire by the Inca or adopted under Inca rule.[18]

My point is not that there has been so much change that it is impossible to use analogues, but rather, that we should use them in a historically informed way that allows us to see and understand variation and change through time. Returning to Stahl's suggestions, we may use analogues to make comparisons rather than simply to illustrate the past as we look for points of difference and similarity that allow us to identify practices that may no longer exist and thus to perceive change through time.

In his study of chicha production at the Chimú provincial administrative site of Manchan on the north coast of Peru, Moore (1989) demonstrates how these comparisons might be made. In excavations of commoner households closely associated with elite compounds, chicha production remains were widely distributed. One occupation included a pit with dregs from a single brewing event that yielded more than 500 liters of beer, far beyond the volume consumed by a single household. Moore compares the archaeological evidence to three brewing contexts described in ethnohistorical accounts: (1) Inca-administered production by the acllacuna, the chosen women who wove and brewed for the state; (2) full-time production by specialist households of brewers noted in historical descriptions of the north coast; and (3) production by independent households that brewed and engaged in other activities for their own subsistence. The excavated contexts yielded remains for a variety of male and female activities (fishing, spinning, weaving), which rules out production by dedicated female brewers or by full-time brewing specialists. While the third scenario most closely matches the archaeological remains, the sheer quantity of chicha produced, and the location of the households at a provincial administrative center, suggests that the households were producing extra chicha as tribute for the Chimú, who in turn served it to workers or others in exchange for labor. In brief, Moore's comparison allows identification of a form of production for which there is no historical or ethnographic analogue.

An improved understanding of continuity and change in chicha production requires further strengthening of the comparative approach. As argued in this chapter, we can start by recognizing the historical and cultural context of our analogues. Brewing today is the result of centuries of change as traditions are created, altered, repressed, and perhaps revitalized in new forms. Chicherías are not living relics of the pre-Columbian past. However, together with historical accounts, modern brewing does provide information that can be compared and contrasted to the archaeological record. Archaeologists have come to rely on a handful of chicha brewing descriptions by botanists, cultural anthropologists, and travelers; explicitly ethnoarchaeological studies of maize beer production are surprisingly rare (Hayashida 2008). The ethnoarchaeology of chicha would ideally cover the full range of brewing arrangements (e.g., chicherías, household production, and the large-scale but temporary brewing episodes for feasts associated with religious festivals and work parties) and technologies (e.g., production steps and equipment, the use and significance of different ingredients and recipes) across a broad geographic area. Studies should include observations on local history, social significance, technology, economic realities, and the material correlates of brewing practices. This more holistic perspective logically includes situations in which "tradition" has been abandoned, in which metal pots and plastic bins have replaced pottery cooking and cooling vessels. While we tend to look for the most "authentic" brewing, we must recognize that material replacement, substitution, and innovation also took place in the past; study of these processes today (see, e.g., Allen, this volume, on the replacement of chicha by carbonated soft drinks, and Weismantel 1991) is essential to recognizing and interpreting the historical dynamics of brewing and drinking.

Notes

1. See also Kubler's (1985) essay on continuity and disjunction of form, meaning, and culture over time.

2. Note that Rostworowski (1989: 278–279) infers that only men were brewing in these specialized communities, basing her claim on the statement that the lord of the community identifies himself as the leader of the "yndios chicheros" and because of a statement in Arriaga (1968a: 106) that brewers on the coast (location not specified) are male and in the sierra are female.

3. One exception is Lupe Camino (1987), whose ethnography describes the importance of chicha in daily consumption, life-cycle rituals, and major community events, thus placing production within the larger context of the social life of Catacaos. She also includes the different economic arrangements of chicha brewers, distinguishing between small-scale producers, who brew on a rotating basis for their families and for sale out of their homes to neighbors; mid-scale vendors, who sell their chicha to workers in the countryside or in the nearby city of Piura; and "professional chicheras," who also brew in their homes, but on a larger scale for a fixed clientele as well as visitors drawn to Catacaos to sample its famous chicha.

4. The cultural significance of techniques and the necessity of situating producers within their social and historical context are widely addressed in the craft-production literature. See, for example, Costin and Wright (1998), Dobres and Hoffman (1994), Lechtman (1977), Lemonnier (1992), and Shimada (1999).

5. It should be noted that there are ways around these limitations: (1) multiple smaller vessels can be used, and (2) with dippers, the chicha can be transferred between vessels without moving the pots. In Chulucanas, transfers using gourd dippers are quite fast and are typically done by a single person, even with a large batch (more than 500 liters). There are, however, other labor bottlenecks when producing large quantities of chicha, as Jennings et al. (2005) and Hayashida (2008) have observed.

6. Anthropologists who study sociohistorical processes under colonial rule may similarly collapse sources to create a composite, precolonial baseline that ignores variation across space and time. They thus create a generalized, often idealized, precolonial past that is then contrasted with the changes following European conquest and colonization (Brumfiel 2003; Stahl 1993).

7. Epigraph: "Pues quitalles las borracheras, que son las que crían, fomentan y conservan las idolatrías, si algunos lo han de hacer son las curas" (Arriaga 1968a: 258).

8. Even as early as the 1560s, the preparation and offering of chicha to the huacas may have been much reduced. One of the claims of the Taki Onqoy followers was that the huacas "wandered through the air, thirsty, and dying of hunger because the Indians no longer sacrificed to them or offered them chicha" (Stern 1982: 55).

9. Duviols notes that *visitas* and *procesos* (inspections and proceedings) were also carried out in the regions of Cuzco, Arequipa, Trujillo, Ayacucho, Charcas, and

Atacama (2003: 29–30), and efforts to thwart Andean religious practices were not limited to formal extirpation campaigns.

10. "La principal ofrenda, y la mejor, y la mayor parte de sus sacrificios es la chicha; por ella, y con ella comienzan todas las fiestas de las huacas, en ella median, y con ella acaban sus fiestas, y ella es el todo" (Arriaga 1968a: 209).

11. *Nectandra* sp., the seeds found in pre-Hispanic burials on the north and central coast, may have had an analgesic or psychoactive effect (Montoya 1996).

12. "El hechicero y otro indio que se manifestare y diere noticia de las huacas" (Arriaga 1968a: 248).

13. "Que hechiceros tienen a su cargo echar las fiestas y ayunos y mandar hacer la chicha" (Arriaga 1968a: 250).

14. "[P]or ser como es el medio más eficaz para destruir la idolatría, quitar las dichas borracheras" (Arriaga 1968a: 276).

15. "Hácese cada año en esta villa tanta infinidad de chicha . . . que parece cosa imposible imaginar."

16. Mita was the colonial forced labor draft of Indian workers that was loosely based on the Inca system of rotating tributary labor.

17. See Stern (1995) for the complex ways that local ethnic lords involved themselves in the colonial market economy, weighing personal gain against the well-being of their subjects.

18. See, for example, Cummins' (2002) discussion of how the Inca manipulated the symbolism of chicha drinking cups.

References Cited

Anonymous
1961 [1720] Información anónima sobre la vida y costumbres del pueblo de Virú, Provincia de Trujillo, Departamento de la Libertad. Con un recetario criollo del maestro Barbero Don Feliciano de Bergara. Siglo XVIII. Año 1720. *Revista de Archivo Nacional del Perú* 25(1): 5–25.

Arriaga, Pablo José
1968a [1621] Extirpación de la idolatría del Pirú. In *Crónicas peruanas de interés indígena*, Francisco Esteve Barba, ed. Biblioteca de Autores Españoles, vol. 209. Madrid: Ediciones Atlas.

1968b [1621] *The Extirpation of Idolatry in Peru*, translated by L. Clark Keating. Lexington: University of Kentucky Press.

Bertonio, Ludovico
1984 [1612] *Vocabulario de la lengua aymara*. Cochabamba: Centro de Estudios de la Realidad Económica y Social.

Brumfiel, Elizabeth M.
2003 It's a Material World: History, Artifacts, and Anthropology. *Annual Review of Anthropology* 32: 205–223.

2006 Cloth, Gender, Continuity, and Change: Fabricating Unity in Anthropology. *American Anthropologist* 108(4): 862–877.

Cabello Valboa, Miguel

1951 *Miscelánea antártica: Una historia del Perú antiguo.* Lima: Universidad Nacional Mayor de San Marcos.

Camino, Lupe

1987 *Chicha de maíz: Bebida y vida del pueblo Catacaos.* Piura: Centro de Investigación y Promoción del Campesinado.

Castillo Butters, Luis Jaime

2005 Ideología, ritual y poder en la consolidación, colapso y reconstitución del estado mochica del Jequetepeque: El proyecto arqueológico San José de Moro (1991–2004). In *Programa arqueológico San José de Moro, temporada 2004,* ed. Luis Jaime Castillo Butters, pp. 11–81. Lima: Pontificia Universidad Católica del Perú. Electronic document http://www.tiwanakuarcheo.net/o index/pasjm ljc.html, accessed September 11, 2005.

Chapdelaine, Claude

2001 The Growing Power of a Moche Urban Class. In *Moche Art and Archaeology in Ancient Peru,* Joanne Pillsbury, ed., pp. 69–87. Studies in the History of Art, Center for Advanced Study in the Visual Arts. Washington, D.C.: National Gallery of Art.

Cobo, Bernabé

1990 [1653] *Inca Religion and Customs.* Austin: University of Texas Press.

Costin, Cathy L., and Rita P. Wright

1998 *Craft and Social Identity.* Archeological Papers of the American Anthropological Association, 8. Washington, D.C.: American Anthropological Association.

Cummins, Thomas B. F.

2002 *Toasts with the Inca: Andean Abstraction and the Images on Quero Vessels.* Ann Arbor: University of Michigan Press.

Cutler, Hugh C., and Martín Cárdenas

1947 Chicha, a Native South American Beer. *Botanical Museum Leaflets* (Harvard University) 13(3): 33–60.

Descripción de la villa y minas de Potosí, año de 1603

1965 In *Relaciones geográficas de Indias: Perú,* Marcos Jiménez de la Espada, ed., pp. 372–385. Biblioteca de Autores Españoles desde la Formación del Lenguaje hasta Nuestros Días, vols. 183–185. Madrid: Atlas.

Dobres, Marcia-Anne, and Christopher R. Hoffman

1994 Social Agency and the Dynamics of Prehistoric Technology. *Journal of Archaeological Method and Theory* 1(3): 211–258.

Duviols, Pierre

2003 *Procesos y visitas de idolatrías: Cajatambo, siglo XVII.* Lima: Pontificia Universidad Católica del Perú and Instituto Francés de Estudios Andinos.

Garofalo, Leo J.

2001 The Ethno-Economy of Food, Drink, and Stimulants: The Making of Race in Colonial Lima and Cuzco. Doctoral dissertation, University of Wisconsin.

2003 Bebidas incas en copas coloniales: Los curacas del mercado de chicha del Cuzco, 1640–1700. In *Élites indígenas en los Andes: Nobles, caciques y cabildantes
bajo el yugo colonial*, David P. Cahill and Blanca Tovías, eds., pp. 175–211. Quito: Ediciones Abya-Yala.

Goldstein, Paul

1993 House, Community, and State in the Earliest Tiwanaku Colony: Domestic Patterns and State Integration in Omo M12, Moquegua. In *Domestic Architecture, Ethnicity, and Complementarity in the South-Central Andes*, Mark S.
Aldenderfer, ed., pp. 25–41. Iowa City: University of Iowa Press.

González Holguín, Diego

1989 [1608] *Vocabulario de la lengua general de todo el Perú llamada lengua qqui-
chua o del inca*. Lima: Universidad Nacional Mayor de San Marcos.

Hastorf, Christine A., and Sissel Johannessen

1993 Pre-Hispanic Political Change and the Role of Maize in the Central Andes of
Peru. *American Anthropologist* 95(1): 115–138.

Hayashida, Frances M.

2008 Ancient Beer and Modern Brewers: Ethnoarchaeological Observations of
Maize Beer (*Chicha*) Production in Two Regions of the North Coast of Peru.
Journal of Anthropological Archaeology 27(2): 161–174.

Jennings, Justin

2005 La Chichera y el Patrón: Chicha and the Energetics of Feasting in the Prehistoric Andes. In *Foundations of Power in the Prehispanic Andes*, Christina A.
Conlee, Dennis Ogburn, and Kevin Vaughn, eds., pp. 241–259. Archaeological
Publications of the American Anthropological Association, vol. 14. Washington, D.C.: American Anthropological Association.

Jennings, Justin, Kathleen L. Antrobus, Sam J. Atencio, Erin Glavich, Rebecca Johnson, German Loffler, and Christine Luu

2005 "Drinking Beer in a Blissful Mood": Alcohol Production, Operational Chains,
and Feasting in the Ancient World. *Current Anthropology* 46(2): 275–303.

Kubler, George

1985 Period, Style, and Meaning in Ancient American Art. In *Studies in Ancient
American Art: The Collected Essays of George Kubler*, Thomas F. Reese, ed., pp.
395–405. New Haven: Yale University Press.

Lechtman, Heather

1977 Style in Technology—Some Early Thoughts. In *American Ethnological Society.
Annual Spring Meeting 1975. Proceedings*, pp. 3–20. Seattle: American Ethnological Society.

Lemonnier, Pierre

1992 *Elements for an Anthropology of Technology*. Anthropological Papers, 88. Ann
Arbor: Museum of Anthropology, University of Michigan.

Llano Restrepo, María, and Marcela Campuzano Cifuentes

1994 *La chicha, una bebida fermentada a través de la historia*. Bogotá: Instituto
Colombiano de Antropología.

Mangan, Jane E.
2005 *Trading Roles: Gender, Ethnicity, and the Urban Economy in Colonial Potosí.* Durham: Duke University Press.

Martínez Compañón y Bujanda, Baltasar Jaime
1978 *Trujillo del Perú.* Madrid: Ediciones Cultura Hispánica.

Matienzo, Juan de
1967 [1567] *Gobierno del Perú.* Travaux de l'Institut Français d'Études Andines, 11. Paris and Lima: Instituto Francés de Estudios Andinos.

Mills, Kenneth
1997 *Idolatry and Its Enemies: Colonial Andean Religion and Extirpation, 1640–1750.* Princeton: Princeton University Press.

Montoya, María
1996 Implicaciones del estudio de semillas rituales en la época prehispánica. *Revista del Museo de Arqueología, Antropología e Historia* 6: 203–219.

Moore, Jerry
1981 Chimu Socio-economic Organization: Preliminary Data from Manchan, Casma Valley, Peru. *Ñawpa Pacha* 19: 115–128.
1989 Pre-Hispanic Beer in Coastal Peru: Technology and Social Context of Prehistoric Production. *American Anthropologist* 91(3): 682–695.

Morris, Craig
1974 Reconstructing Patterns of Non-agricultural Production in the Inca Economy: Archaeology and Documents in Institutional Analysis. In *Reconstructing Complex Societies: An Archaeological Colloquium*, Charlotte B. Moore, ed., pp. 49–68. Supplement to the *Bulletin of the American Schools of Oriental Research*, no. 20.
1979 Maize Beer in the Economics, Politics, and Religion of the Inca Empire. In *Fermented Food Beverages in Nutrition*, Clifford F. Gastineau, William J. Darby, and Thomas B. Turner, eds., pp. 21–34. New York: Academic Press.

Moseley, Michael E., Donna J. Nash, Patrick Ryan Williams, Susan D. deFrance, Ana Miranda, and Mario Ruales
2005 Burning Down the Brewery: Establishing and Evacuating an Ancient Imperial Colony at Cerro Baúl, Peru. *Proceedings of the National Academy of Sciences* 102(48): 17264–17271.

Muelle, Jorge
1978 La chicha en el distrito de San Sebastián. In *Tecnología andina*, Rogger Ravines, ed., pp. 241–251. Lima: Instituto de Estudios Peruanos.

Nicholson, G. Edward
1960 Chicha Maize Types and Chicha Manufacture in Peru. *Economic Botany* 14(4): 290–299.

Prieto Búrmester, Gabriel
2004 Área 35: Ocupación doméstico/productiva chimú en San José de Moro. In *Programa arqueológico San José de Moro, temporada 2004*, ed. Luis Jaime Castillo Butters, pp. 140–154. Lima: Pontificia Universidad Católica del Perú.

Electronic document http://www.tiwanakuarcheo.net/0 index/pasjm ljc.html, accessed September 11, 2005.

Ramírez, Susan Elizabeth

1996 *The World Upside Down: Cross-cultural Contact and Conflict in Sixteenth-century Peru*. Stanford: Stanford University Press.

Robin, Cynthia

2002 Gender and Maya Farming: Chan Nòohol, Belize. In *Ancient Maya Women*, Traci Ardren, ed., pp. 12–30. Walnut Creek: Altamira.

Rostworowski de Diez Canseco, María

1977 Algunos comentarios hechos a las ordenanzas del Doctor Cuenca. *Historia y Cultura* 9: 119–154.

1989 *Costa peruana prehispánica*. Lima: Instituto de Estudios Peruanos.

Salazar-Soler, Carmen

1993 Embriaguez y visiones en los Andes: Los Jesuitas y las "borracheras" indígenas en el Perú (siglos XVI y XVII). In *Borrachera y memoria: La experiencia de lo sagrado en los Andes*, Thierry Saignes and Carmen Salazar-Soler, eds., pp. 23–42. La Paz and Lima: Instituto de Historia Social Boliviana and Instituto Francés de Estudios Andinos.

Schaedel, Richard P.

1988 *La etnografía muchik de las fotografías de H. Brüning 1886–1925*. Lima: Ediciones COFIDE (Corporación Financiera de Desarrollo).

Segura Llanos, Rafael

2001 *Rito y economía en Cajamarquilla: Investigaciones arqueológicas en el Conjunto Arquitectónico Julio C. Tello*. Lima: Fondo Editorial de la Pontificia Universidad Católica del Perú.

Shimada, Izumi

1994 *Pampa Grande and the Mochica Culture*. Austin: University of Texas Press.

1999 Pre-Hispanic Metallurgy and Mining in the Andes: Recent Advances and Future Tasks. In *In Quest of Mineral Wealth: Aboriginal and Colonial Mining and Metallurgy in Spanish America*, Alan K. Craig and Robert C. West, eds., pp. 37–73. Geoscience and Man, vol. 33. Baton Rouge: Geoscience Publications, Louisiana State University.

Spalding, Karen

1984 *Huarochirí: An Andean Society under Inca and Spanish Rule*. Stanford: Stanford University Press.

Stahl, Ann

1993 Concepts of Time and Approaches to Analogical Reasoning in Historical Perspective. *American Antiquity* 58(2): 235–260.

Stern, Steve J.

1982 *Peru's Indian People and the Challenge of Spanish Conquest: Huamanga to 1640*. Madison: University of Wisconsin Press.

1995 The Variety and Ambiguity of Native Andean Intervention in European Colonial Markets. In *Ethnicity, Markets, and Migration in the Andes: At the Cross-*

roads of History and Anthropology, Brooke Larson and Olivia Harris, eds., with Enrique Tandeter, pp. 73–101. Durham: Duke University Press.

Tschudi, J. J.

1918 *Contribuciones a la civilización y lingüística del Perú antiguo.* Vol. 1. Colección de Libros y Documentos Referentes a la Historia del Perú, 9. Lima: Imprenta y Librería Sanmartí.

Uceda, Santiago

1997 Esculturas en miniatura y una maqueta en madera. In *Investigaciones en la Huaca de la Luna 1995*, Santiago Uceda, Elías Mújica, and Ricardo Morales, eds., pp. 151–176. Trujillo: Facultad de Ciencias Sociales, Universidad Nacional de la Libertad.

Valdez, Lidio

2002 Maraynioc: Evidencias de producción de chicha en un establecimiento wari. *Gaceta Arqueológica Andina* 26: 69–86.

Valdizán, Hermilio, and Ángel Maldonado

1922 *La medicina popular peruana.* Lima: Imprenta Torres Aguirre.

Velásquez Benites, Orlando

1996 *Cultura, tradición e idiosincrasia del poblador piurano.* Trujillo: Facultad de Ciencias Sociales, Universidad Nacional del Trujillo.

Villagómez, Pedro D.

1919 [1649] *Exortaciones e instrucción acerca de las idolatrías de los indios del Arzobispado de Lima.* Colección de Libros y Documentos Referentes a la Historia del Perú, 12. Lima: Sanmartí.

Weismantel, Mary J.

1991 Maize Beer and Andean Social Transformations: Drunken Indians, Bread Babies, and Chosen Women. *Modern Language Notes* 106(4): 861–879.

Wolf, Eric

1982 *Europe and the People without History.* Berkeley & Los Angeles: University of California Press.

Wylie, Alison

1985 The Reaction against Analogy. *Advances in Archaeological Method and Theory* 8: 63–111.

10

Have a Drink

Chicha, Performance, and Politics

Mary Weismantel

In a photograph on the Internet, a skinny old lady from Peru holds an enormous glass tumbler in her outstretched hand. Peering amiably toward the camera from under a sweat-stained hat, she invites the viewer to have a drink. The liquid in the glass is opaque, rather dirty-looking, and topped with thick foam.[1] This is chicha, the traditional beer of western South America, and one of the most ubiquitous emblems of indigenous culture in Ecuador, Peru, and Bolivia.[2] Chicha shows up often in travelers' blogs about their South American adventures, or on sites run by tourist agencies. In pictures from the Andean highlands, like this one, the chicha being offered is made from corn and is served in a large, thick glass like those used for old-fashioned milkshakes, called a kero in Quechua. In the Amazonian lowlands, chicha is made from manioc, and the drinking vessel is a shallow bowl, sometimes quite large in size, which may be handmade of clay by local women. Typical photographs from Amazonia show carefully posed native men in full regalia drinking from decorated bowls, their faces painted and their heads crowned with feathers; much rarer are shots that show ordinary day-to-day consumption, in which the men and women wear T-shirts and polyester pants, and the chicha is stored in a plastic bucket.[3]

The notion of chicha as a symbol of native South America is not just a tourist cliché; it is forcefully promulgated by indigenous people themselves, for reasons of cultural pride, ethnic nationalism—and commerce. All these motivations make an appearance on the Web site OtavalosOnLine.com, a site maintained by Otavaleños, members of a Quichua-speaking group from highland Ecuador well known for their entrepreneurial savvy. Here, upcoming fiestas are promoted with photographs of women serving chicha. Their photos speak to two audiences at once, serving up nostalgia and news for the many Otavaleños living abroad and exotic appeal to tourists planning a vacation.

Chicha also serves more political ends. Bolivian populist parties used it in the late 1990s as a campaign ploy, producing posters depicting enormous *puñus* (the vessels in which corn beer is brewed) and events held in chicherías, the highland taverns where the beverage is brewed and served (Albro 2000). In Amazonian Ecuador in 1992, chicha played a role in a major event called the Caminata, one of a series of phenomenally successful mobilizations in which tens of thousands of indigenous people from all parts of the nation converged on the capital city to demand political representation, social justice, and the right to self-determination. Organizers' instructions for the fourteen-day march from the lowland province of Pastaza to Quito included a directive to "bring your own wrapped chicha" (Whitten, Whitten, and Chango 1997: 361).[4] This instruction had a pragmatic aspect, but it was also a self-conscious assertion of the potency of native culture, just like the directives to bring "musical instruments, including hand-coiled pottery cornets, drums, slit gongs, flutes, violins, and musical bows" as well as "lances, shoulder adornments, and headdresses, and come painted as warriors."

These examples—snapshots of western South America at the dawn of the twenty-first century—demonstrate chicha's enduring importance. Whether declaring war on the outside world or inviting it in for a party, native people use chicha to say, "This is our culture," and outsiders are quick to get the message—even if they express some ambivalence about the sanitary qualities of the messenger. One source of chicha's cultural potency is based in its antiquity, a claim amply affirmed by archaeological research and ethnohistorical documentation. As the chapters in this book attest, there is evidence of chicha making and consumption at many archaeological sites, making chicha one of the most substantial material forms of evidence for cultural continuity in the region.

But we need to be wary in asserting that chicha drinking constitutes an unbroken chain of cultural identity uniting the ancient past, the present, and the future. Merely documenting the presence of chicha in a past society does not demonstrate that this fermented beverage carried all of the cultural and political significance claimed for it today (Hayashida, this volume). Even in historical and contemporary times, chicha has not played a single, unifying symbolic role; instead, its meanings are fragmentary and even contradictory. Furthermore, the affection of Andean people for chicha no longer seems as unshakable as it once did. Despite its visibility on tourist blogs, the brewing and drinking of traditional chicha is on the wane (Allen, this volume), making assertions about its undying importance look more like invented tradition than lived reality.

These problems call into question the very definition of chicha. The word is associated in the anthropological literature with a particular complex of material forms, ingredients, and production techniques and their associated cultural meanings. But to a large extent, this complex of associations was created during a key period of modern intellectual history, the *indigenista* movement of the twentieth century. While its existence can be readily documented for the Inca Empire, once we move too far backward—or forward—in time, the connections begin to break down.

Today, many things called "chicha" bear little or no relationship to the processes of production that have historically given this word meaning. What shows up in the glasses of "chicha" enthusiastically brought to me by waitresses at Peruvian restaurants in the United States is not a thick peasant brew, but a sweet, watery pink substance reminiscent of Kool-Aid, made from an instant powder the main ingredient of which is sugar. Street vendors in the Andes sell this stuff by the glassful, and several Japanese Internet sites also offer it for sale, along with other adulterated Andean fare, presumably to meet the demand for all things Peruvian sparked by Japanese adulation for former president Alberto Fujimoro. Chicha—that opaque liquid thick with meaning—seems to be thinning out, turning into something insubstantial that carries evanescent echoes of the past, but no longer has the powerful presence it once did.

However, just as I was convincing myself that the connections between beer's ancient past and its lived reality were finally being severed in South America, I was confronted with a ceramic object that confounded this facile assertion. I was on the north coast of Peru in 2005, visiting Moche archaeological sites, and stopped at the workshop of a group of brothers who sell replicas of Moche ceramics to tourists.[5] Prominently displayed in their showroom was a brightly colored ceramic effigy that managed to combine all the ancient and modern meanings of South American beer in one figure—and that made me laugh out loud.

The little statue was a curious amalgamation of different time periods. The Moche period (AD 250–800) was represented by its face, which was modeled after the friezes at the nearby Huaca de la Luna—and by its body, which was distinctly phallic in form, like the infamous Moche "joke pots," which are effigies of human genitalia. But it was clearly modern too: after all, beer bottles also have a phallic shape—and this ceramic vessel had been made to look like a bottle of the local Pilsen Trujillo, right down to the carefully painted replicas of the label and cap. Rather than the glorious past, this was an effigy of the Moche present—in which enormous advertisements for this locally brewed beer are everywhere at the archaeological site, reminding visitors that the company is a major underwriter for the project.

This amusing little figurine reminded me not to be too literal in the search for continuities—and discontinuities—with the past. Historically, bottled beer was inimical to chicha: in the early twentieth century it competed ruthlessly with home brew in racially charged advertising campaigns that linked chicha to criminality and poor hygiene.[6] But here and now, an effigy of industrially produced beer had been made into the perfect fusion of two very different periods, the twenty-first century and the first millennium. And in the kero grasped in the little Moche beer man's outstretched hand, this figurine also incorporated ethnohistorically documented chicha rituals of the intervening centuries.

Like the women in Internet photos, he was performing the act that lies at the very center of chicha's signifying power: holding out a kero and inviting the world to have a drink. If we follow his lead and look for this particular action—the public offering and acceptance of a drink—rather than any particular ingredient or process, we too can find an elusive thread of cultural continuity that links the long-dead Moche to the industrially bottled beer being drunk by the archaeologists who are digging up their history. The proffered drink may also unlock the curiously ambivalent set of meanings that seems to surround chicha in all its many settings, from the Internet to the Amazonian rain forest to the highlands to the north coast.

The Multivocalic Drink

Chicha today is a multivocalic symbol: it speaks with many overlapping voices, with messages tailored to different audiences. In his classic work *The Forest of Symbols* (1970), Victor Turner finds this quality of multivocality to be what makes symbols work: rather then projecting a message that is clear, narrow, and specific—and that would be far more likely to alienate some viewers or participants—symbols project a diffuse web of related but distinct meanings. Each person—tourist or native, woman or man— responds to an individualized appeal; yet because others are also moved by the same symbol, this response is experienced as something shared and collective. Symbols thus bind individuals into a cohesive social whole and diminish potentially divisive differences.

Turner explored the work of symbols in a relatively homogeneous, small-scale society, but this multivocalic quality becomes even more important—and more difficult to achieve—in large, economically stratified, racially divided societies.[7] The brief glimpses of chicha drinking introduced above hint at the difficult symbolic work that home brew has to do in the contemporary Andes, a place where social divisions are sharp and potentially explosive. For indigenous people, chicha is a source of ethnic pride, but in tourist photos, it becomes a joke tinged with more than a little racial superiority. While foreign commercial interests promote powdered instant chicha as a novel commodity to be sold for profit, to the Ecuadorian marchers, it symbolized an ancient way of life dependent on rain-forest resources and indigenous autonomy and endangered by encroaching capitalist development. This particular contradiction is a peculiar artifact of our cynical, commercialized, and ambivalently multicultural present, but other, similarly contradictory, sets of ideas may be documented for earlier periods in chicha's modern history and in its colonial and prehistoric roles as well.

Some of this ambiguity arises from the nature of gifts, for to offer a drink is to offer a gift. A comparison of the photographs snapped by white photographers with those found on OtavalosOnLine demonstrates subtle differences in what—and how—this offer signifies. Both the Otavaleño and tourist photos show women serving beer. But in the tourist photos, the women are often dirty and old, and the tourists respond with humorous expressions of mild shock and distaste—"Look at the weird stuff they expected me to drink!" The indigenous photographers do not suggest anything laughable in the ancient tradition. No dirty old ladies here: the women are young, healthy, and well-scrubbed, dressed in brand-new versions of traditional outfits; and the chicha, too, is presented as tasty and appealing.

These photographs also introduce one of the most important social divisions configured through drink: gender. The usual gender formula is one in which indigenous women serve and men drink (Jennings and Chatfield, this volume); this is the implied gender configuration of almost all tourist photographs, even when the drinker is hidden behind the camera.[8] But one of the Otavaleño photographs offers a surprising reversal in which the brown hand of the photographer—presumably male—reaches out from behind the camera to offer a glass of chicha to a young woman serving food.[9] This unusual composition, in which a man offers a woman a drink, captures the more democratic meanings of chicha within rural communities, where the act of offering a drink is emblematic of the social bonds that connect individuals, families, affines, and neighbors (Allen, this volume).

In sum, chicha today carries meanings of gender, race, nation, and community—some of the most powerful identities we know. Drinking rituals play on the tensions within these identities, making social distinctions more visible while papering them over by insisting that everyone who drinks together belongs together. Furthermore, the offer of a drink begins with the most intimate and small-scale of relationships, those of family and friends, and then builds upon these to configure interactions that then take on larger political implications. This can be clearly seen in the context of contemporary Amazonian drinking parties, where gender is the pivot upon which an entire series of relationships—and conflicts—turn.

Amazonia, Twenty-first Century: The Drinking Party

Amazonia and its peoples are currently suffering the impact of rapid, uneven, and highly destructive modernization, but manioc chicha has nonetheless retained its importance in many places, as Michael Uzendoski discovered when he first began doing fieldwork in an Ecuadorian community that has converted to evangelical Protestantism:

> One afternoon . . . a woman came up to us with a large pot full of liquid and invited us to drink. The men . . . stopped [working] and waited for her to dip a bowl into the pot to serve the milky-white substance. One man was served. After the first bowl was finished, she then asked the same man to down another bowl. The process was repeated for each person. When it was my turn she said to me in an unemphatic tone, "Upi, cai asuara, asua Runa causaimi," which means "Drink this manioc beer, manioc beer is the life of the Runa people." (Uzendoski 2004: 883)

Despite their newfound commitment to Christ, these Napo Runa continue to attribute deep significance to chicha and to observe its attendant—and highly gendered—rituals.

Among the nearby Canelos Quichua, too, women define their social identity through chicha: not only because they drink plenty of it themselves, but because, as wives and mothers and hosts at fiestas, their primary role is to offer men chicha to drink—an offer which men should reciprocate with gifts of meat (Whitten and Whitten 2007). The dynamics of this gendered gift demonstrates chicha's double edge: through it, women offer men pleasure, but they also make a demand and even a threat. There is a coercive side to the proffered drink, for men cannot easily refuse it, however much they might wish to.

During large fiestas and small parties, these women brewers assume the role of *asua mamas*, or chicha mothers. One especially significant festival documented by ethnographers Norman and Dorothea Whitten begins with a ritual cry from the men: "Asua, asua, asua! Bring me asua, mama!" The women respond enthusiastically, bringing out "large (quart capacity or more) mucawas [serving vessels] brimming with asua," converging in twos and threes upon each drinker in turn. "The men drink and drink, first from one, then from another—taking in a half gallon mild brew with large gulps. If a man can't swallow it all he may blow out a cupful or more, in order to gulp more offered from another asua mama's bowl. Usually he can't drink it all down fast enough and then he gets the remainder from the bowl smack on his headdress as the 'chicha shampoo.' 'Jijijijijijiiii' cry the women as they rush back to the storage jars for more and more and more" (Whitten and Whitten 2007). "Jijijijijijiiii" indeed—one could also transcribe the sound as a laugh: "Hee hee hee hee" (Norman Whitten describes it as "a kind of wonderful musical laugh" that "goes up the scale and glissandos back down" [personal communication, 2007]). And the party was only beginning. The effect was generally one of exhilaration, but not without some ambivalence: this form of chicha drinking produces a euphoric hedonism that promotes social cohesion, but also the potential for social embarrassment inflicted by a woman on a man, a host on a guest. Later during the same fiesta, the women made a special point of drenching visitors who arrived in nice polyester clothing, as though for attending church, rather than in more traditional attire.

The ambiguities of chicha can also emerge in the aftermath, when guests accuse their hostesses of deliberately making them sick. These accusations become more serious when relations between two groups turn ugly and stories begin to circulate of women poisoning their guests. As the Whittens point out, many of the illnesses that attend drinkers at these ceremonies are accidental rather than deliberate, caused by imperfectly controlled fermentation processes that continue during parties that last over several days and tired and intoxicated hosts paying less and less attention to their brew.

But this chemical reality may be less important than the sociopolitical ends served by the accusation. The small-scale events that transform individuals from hosts and guests into suspicious antagonists are the building blocks of a larger social structure in which intragroup relations are constantly shifting from alliance to opposition and back again. Indeed, the drinking party is as ambiguous a symbol as chicha itself: an invitation can mark the cessation of hostilities between two previously hostile groups, but it may also provide the context in which long-simmering conflicts between friends erupt into open enmity—a process that begins with accusations about women and chicha.

According to the Whittens, the double meanings of chicha emerge again when Canelos Quichua women offer a drink to white outsiders. Beneath the appearance of rather obsequious cordiality lurk more ambivalent and even hostile messages concerning the destruction of rain-forest ecosystems that are lost on the recipients but fully understood by the giver and her community (Whitten and Whitten 2007).

The multiple meanings embedded in a woman's offer of chicha reinforce one another. It is because a woman offers beer daily to her husband, her father, and her brother that she uses it as a welcoming gesture to a guest. Similarly, the ambiguities, tensions, and conflicts that pervade relationships between the sexes, both in actual life and in a highly gendered cosmovision,[10] pervade every offer of chicha, even those made to a stranger. Submission and anger, pleasure and threat, even sustenance and poison are all potentials that lie within the *mucawa* filled with chicha.

In the highlands, chicha brewing is no longer a mundane household occurrence (Jennings and Chatfield, this volume), as it is among these Amazonians. Nonetheless, the woman offering chicha is also a potent, familiar, and multivalent image in the Andes, where the drink is associated with the commercial space of the tavern and the complexities of twentieth-century racial politics.

Cuzco, Twentieth Century: The Chichería

Although chicha drinking has declined continuously since Pizarro's arrival in 1532, the twentieth century was an important one in chicha's history, for it was then that educated citizens of the Andean nations began to appreciate its significance for the first time. The impetus was a proliferation of research by anthropologists, archaeologists, and ethnohistorians—and the poems, essays, and pictures produced by intellectuals and artists, who forged the mythology of chicha familiar to us today. At the heart of what we think we know about chicha lies a complex interaction between the everyday practice of chicha drinking, now and in the past; the research that has documented these practices; and the appropriation of that information to create new political and cultural symbols within the nations where chicha is drunk. The roots of chicha's power lie not only in local practices and traditional knowledge but also in the words of textbooks, the lyrics of songs, even the images on advertisements, all of which are familiar to every South American child of every race. It is in these texts and images, as well as in isolated jungle hamlets or highland villages where women still brew as their grandmothers did, that we can trace the modern history of chicha.

The image of the woman with a glass of chicha in her hand is part of this intellectual history. Every time someone snaps this scene, the photographer unwittingly follows a visual tradition that can be traced directly back to a specific time, and even to a particular person: Martín Chambi, one of the most important photographers of South America, and probably the greatest of all Native American photographers.[11]

Born to indigenous parents in a tiny highland community in 1891, Chambi learned to use a camera while working for a mining company and later migrated to Cuzco and opened a commercial studio. As a sideline to wedding and funeral photography, he began making postcards for the city's nascent tourist industry. It is largely thanks to Chambi that we recognize a certain set of iconic images, endlessly reproduced on postcards, travel posters, Web sites, and brochures, as "the Andes": the ruins of Machu Picchu, the lonely Indian playing a flute—and the woman with a glass of chicha (Chambi 1993; Ranney 1993; Weismantel 2001).

Chambi loved to photograph chicheras (women brewers) and chicherías. During his lifetime, Cuzco was filled with small taverns run by women who made corn beer in their home kitchens. In place of a sign, the chichera would hang a small flag outside her door, indicating a freshly brewed batch of chicha ready for drinking. The informality of this system lent itself to semiprofessional brewing: a woman could temporarily convert her house into a bar by hoisting a strip of cloth, and then take it down as soon as the chicha was gone.

It wasn't just the beer itself, but the intimacy, comfort, and informal conviviality of the chichería that gave a glass of chicha its special significance

(Perlov, this volume). In a stratified, often very formal, society marked by rigid social divisions, chicherías were one of the few places where Indian and white working men and intellectuals could be found together, presided over by the friendly but imposing figure of the chichera.

Chambi's choice of the chichería as subject matter was motivated by one of the most influential political, intellectual, and artistic movements of his day, *indigenismo*, which flourished in Latin American countries with large Native American populations, such as Peru and Mexico, between approximately 1920 and 1960. Cuzco was one its most active centers, where Martín Chambi's friends met regularly to affirm their belief in autochthonous culture, the defense of the Indian against injustice, and the glories of the pre-Columbian past.

No symbol was more important to the indigenistas than chicha. Its ambiguity was part of its appeal: through its rich history and multiple meanings, chicha could finesse the movement's internal fissures, which included conflicting racial ideologies and regional tensions (de la Cadena 2000). Native to the Andes, this corn beverage had nationalist appeal; and because it was the drink of the working man, educated writers and artists with socialist political convictions could make it into an emblem of class solidarity. The social space of the chichería also provided a place to celebrate the country's racially mixed, or mestizo, heritage—a tradition carried on decades later by the Bolivian populists who hold their rallies in chicherías.

Other indigenistas read other racial meanings into a glass of chicha. Rather than a celebration of mixture, they saw chicha as a symbol of pure Native American identity uncontaminated by Europeans; they did not look to the taverns in towns, but to the rural Indian communities, where chicha still held social and ceremonial significance. Martín Chambi's photographs document the continuity in vessel forms between the twentieth century and the Inca past: a smiling man in a poncho carrying an enormous storage vessel—an urpu or aríbalo (see Bray, this volume) on his back—or women toasting one another with keros.

Faced with a racist national culture that considered all existing native culture degenerate, the indigenistas championed chicha as material proof that the glorious Inca past had not been entirely eradicated. It could still be found in isolated places, and, if nurtured carefully and brought back into the center of Peruvian life, it could provide the seeds for a new society.

As can be seen by indigenous people's ongoing fight for basic human rights, these hopes have yet to be realized. Indeed, Peru's continuing ambivalence about its racial heritage can be seen in the new meanings that have accrued around the word *chicha*, which has come to signify a variety of cultural phenomena associated with nonwhites, such as the *cumbia*-inflected rock music produced by the children of highland immigrants to Lima (Bullen 1993). The meanings are generally negative: the term *prensa chicha*, or popular press, for example, connotes vulgar scandal-mongering rather than serious journalism (Cappelini 2005).

Nor has recent anthropological research endorsed indigenistas' romantic beliefs about peasant society. Peruvian intellectuals of the time saw chicha-drinking rituals as evidence of a form of indigenous communism that could provide a political model for the Andean nations. But as can be seen in Catherine Allen's lovely ethnography from the late twentieth century, *The Hold Life Has* (1988; see also Allen, this volume), the politics of chicha were not as democratic as the indigenistas wished to believe. Drinking rituals certainly embodied cultural and spiritual continuities with the past, as seen in the libations poured to pre-Hispanic deities such as the Pachamama. But while these ceremonies were far more egalitarian than in peasant communities elsewhere in the world—everyone gets a drink in turn, women as well as men—their structure nonetheless reinforced hierarchies of age, gender, and status. Drinking rituals in the Andes, says Allen, are asymmetrical by design (1988: 141; see also Anderson, this volume; Bowser 2004).[12]

Working-class taverns in the cities might be a better place to look for democratic virtues, for there relationships were more fluid, and migrants and urbanites seized the opportunity for forms of individual expression and social intercourse denied them elsewhere. But in tavern culture, too, contradictions abound. Consider, for example, the politics of gender. On the one hand, women served mostly male patrons, and as Marisol de la Cadena has pointed out, the enthusiasms of indigenista men look considerably less idealistic when one adds this gendered dimension of nonwhite women waiting on—and sometimes providing sexual services for—white men (de la Cadena 1998). At the same time, however, the chichería was a place where women could seek employment and so support themselves independent of husbands or male kin, and an ambitious woman could succeed as an independent entrepreneur (Perlov, this volume).

If we look farther back in chicha's history, these tensions between unity and division, hierarchy and equality become even more extreme. In the hands of an Inca lord, chicha could represent all of these, as well as both peace and violence: here, even more so than in Amazonia, the offer of a drink was both a gift and a threat.

1532: Gifts and Threats

A story about chicha. The date is 1532; the characters are Atahualpa, pretender to the Inca throne, and two Spanish conquistadors, de Soto and Pizarro. The teller of the tale (not recorded until 1570) is Titu Cusi Yupanqui, the only Inca to write his own version of the encounter between Europeans and Tawantinsuyu. According to Titu Cusi, "My uncle Ataw Wallpa . . . cordially received them and gave them each to drink, a drink that we drink, from a golden cup. The Spaniard, upon receiving the drink in his hand, spilled it which greatly angered my uncle" (2005: 135). This is the key incident described by Cummins in the opening chapter of his book on keros, *Toasts with the Inca* (2002: 1). In writings by Spaniards, there is no mention of these events; instead, the momentous event occurs later, when the Inca, offered a Bible, throws it to the ground. This incident has been repeatedly described as a moment of outrageous cultural sacrilege that precipitated immediate violence, setting off a chain of events that culminated in the downfall of the largest Native American empire in history. But as Cummins points out, the initial desecration involved a kero filled with chicha, not a book filled with words. According to Titu Cusi, when Atahualpa threw down the Holy Book, he was not motivated by incomprehension, but by a desire for retaliation. Having been "offended by the spilling of the chicha," he took the opportunity to respond in kind.

In this dramatic tale, Cummins captures all of chicha's political potency. Everything the Spaniard refused—the vessel itself, the liquid it contained, and the gesture of offering— constituted a highly condensed, multivocalic symbol representing entire realms of specialized craft production, religious life, and statecraft. The "golden cup" was an aquilla, a kero made of precious metal; such cups were, says Cummins, a "physical manifestation of Tahuantinsuyu's legitimacy" (2002: 59). The chicha it contained was corn beer, a liquid that embodied the fundamental agricultural and economic basis of the Inca state and of Andean society, refined into a highly exalted and specialized form. Since the chicha in it was offered by Atahualpa himself, we can assume that it was brewed not just by any women, but by the royal *acllacuna*, the highest order of the sacred "Chosen Women," one of whose tasks was to brew chicha for imperial use (see Goodman, this volume). These women and the products of their hands were so holy, says Garcilaso de la Vega (1966: 198), that the emperor himself "received them as sacred things, and he and his whole empire held them in greater veneration than the Greeks and Romans would have done if the goddesses Juno, Venus, and Pallas had made them."

The object was holy, and so was the act. The gift of chicha epitomized the rituals of state in Tawantinsuyu; toasts between lord and vassal carried all of the significance of a signed treaty among Europeans, or an Iroquois wampum belt such as the "Belt of Law." Indeed, one could write an entire history of Inca politics just by following each mention of chicha in the ethnohistorical documents: every time beer appears, something happens.

Early in imperial history, when Pachacuti's greatness became apparent and the other lords of Cuzco decided to pledge fealty to him, they began by brewing him great quantities of chicha (Betanzos 1996: 56). When Capac Yupanqui conquered the south coast lords, he "gave them golden qeros"; in the central highlands, Tupa Inca Yupanqui gave a defeated leader "some cups in which to drink" (Cummins 2002: 81–82). These gifts established the dependence of local men on their Inca overlord and put in place the ritual objects necessary for future interactions between the two parties. Imperial relations mirrored local-level politics: as Don Juan Puenape of Jequetepeque explained, without chicha the curaca could not govern (Netherly 1977: 216).

The importance of a leader's role as the ever-generous provider of chicha was underlined in the ritual in which the Sapa Inca, emperor of Tawantinsuyu, assumed the throne. Among the most sacred ritual artifacts given to the new king was a pair of golden keros, the *tupa cuxi*. According to Cummins (2002: 75,78), these keros represented the benevolent, peaceful, and productive aspects of the state, in contrast to the emperor's other royal accoutrements, which were in the form of weapons and signified his military might. But drinking chicha with one's lord was never an unambiguously pleasurable act, for generosity is, by its very nature, an exercise of power.

In interactions between victorious and vanquished military leaders, the hospitality of the conqueror was always accompanied with a threat. As Santillán explains, for those curacas who accepted defeat readily, "the Inca bestowed honors and gave cups of gold." And as for those who did not obey him of their own will, "he subjugated and forced them with complete rigor and cruelty to his will" (Cummins 2002: 85).[13]

In offering a glass of corn beer to a visiting stranger, then, contemporary Andean people revisit an act that is more than just traditional—and harmless—hospitality. To do so in Otavalo, reported to be the scene of an unbelievably bloody battle in which Inca forces slaughtered local residents without mercy, is to play with an especially powerful set of historical referents. These meanings are not always invoked by indigenous people today; indeed, a glass of chicha need not symbolize Inca heritage at all. The ritual of exchanging toasts, and the tradition of brewing beer, far predates Tawantinsuyu and belongs to every South American ethnic group as its birthright. Nonetheless, the Inca accounts bring to the fore the implicit meaning of all such rites, which is usually left unspoken: the ambiguity of the gift, which incurs debt and can inflict shame, guilt, and a sense of powerlessness, as well as bringing joy.

This dual characteristic was first described by Marcel Mauss (2006 [1924]), and its political implications were later developed by Karl Polanyi (2001 [1944]), who in turn influenced John Murra's (1975) analyses of Inca social and political organization. The Spanish were puzzled by tales of Inca conquest, which combined staggering cruelty with acts of seeming kindness and generosity—and, especially, with keros filled with chicha. These are, indeed, uniquely Andean tales. But ultimately, Inca reciprocity, with its combination of immediate generosity and threatened violence, simply plays out the political potential of the gift to its fullest extent. The kero filled with chicha is a particularly powerful—and powerfully ambiguous—gift, but not an atypical one.

When we try to follow the story of chicha back before the Incas, words disappear, and we are left with only the material record. This provides ample evidence for chicha production, as documented in this volume, and for chicha drinking rituals at Tiwanaku and elsewhere, in the form of elaborate keros decorated with religious and political iconography. Even where there are no keros, and so no direct formal links to ethnohistorically and ethnographically documented practices, other kinds of drinking vessels suggest rituals that were equally fraught with pleasure and risk for their participants. We can read something of these social dramas from the vessel forms even when archaeological contexts are largely absent, as is the case with Moche ceramics from museum collections.

Moche, First Millennium: Mouth to Mouth

Moche ceramics are well known as the most naturalistic of all ancient American art forms: museumgoers today enjoy the real-looking effigies of ducks and owls, manioc and squash, stoic prisoners and weary warriors. The best-known Moche ceramics are the bottles, with their distinctive stirrup spouts. But Moche potters also produced drinking vessels, some of which take the form of human genitalia: a man stroking an enormous penis as tall as he is, or a woman whose spread legs reveal an open vagina and an erect clitoris.

These would be startling objects even if they were simply visual images, intended only to be looked at. But even the most casual viewer cannot help but notice that they are not: these pots are made for drinking. The penis is a spout, and the vagina is the mouth of a chamber for holding liquid. In other words, these pots are designed to force drinkers to engage in acts of oral sex with the ceramic figures—thus bringing a new level of challenge to the act of accepting a drink.

As Susan Bergh (1993) has commented, the milky-white appearance of chicha, which makes it resemble semen, would only add to the sexual symbolism of these pots in action. Ethnohistorical data from the Huarochirí myths support the connection between chicha and male sexual fluids for the highlands and the coast (Salomon and Urioste 1991); in Amazonia, the Canelos Quichua associate it with female fertility and with women's bodies (Whitten and Whitten 2007). These associations would come alive if this sticky, opaque substance were allowed to flow in and out of bodies, human and ceramic.

Bergh and other scholars have been uncomfortable with the use of the term *joke pot* to describe these ceramics, arguing that, since we cannot guess the emotional states of ancient drinkers, the notion of a joke is too subjective. A better term, perhaps, would be to call large effigies of human genitalia that also serve as drinking vessels *performative*, for while we don't know if they literally caused laughter, they do have observable interactive and communicative functions that resemble the workings of a joke (Weismantel 2004). To deduce these uses is established archaeological practice where utilitarian objects are concerned; and like a tool or a weapon, the construction of a phallic joke pot sharply constrains the possibilities for how it can be handled and used, producing specific kinds of interactions and not others. From these constraints and possibilities, we can not only deduce the nature of the drinker's interaction with the vessel, but also hypothesize some aspects of the social contexts and attendant meanings of the act.[14]

Because these forms obligate the drinker to engage his mouth with modeled genitalia, and because that obligation is not immediately obvious when first presented with the vessel, but only becomes apparent as one grapples with it, these pots imply a performative scene that involves several actors: someone who presents the pot to the drinker; a drinker; and an audience of onlookers who wait to see how the drinker will perform. The form of the pot speaks to such a performance, just as a tool suggests cutting or digging or a weapon, acts of aggression. These pots, then, demonstrate the significance of the offering of the drink—and the acceptance of it—as dramatically as any of our other examples.

Furthermore, as was the case later in time, the political and performative aspects of Moche drinking were part and parcel of larger things. The sociality of the drink, and of the shared emotions it engenders, helps to reinforce awareness of powerful webs of social connection between and beyond individuals, encompassing the human, natural, and supernatural worlds. Amazonian drinking vessels link a female deity, women's bodies, manioc tubers, clay, the nutritive and soothing qualities of mother's milk, and the inebriating capacity of chicha; Inca keros linked maize, agricultural fertility, the power of the state, and the body of the king. Moche drinking vessels, too, took on additional meanings encoded in the iconography of their design—and in the liquids they could contain: chicha, water, and semen/breast milk/vaginal fluids, each of which could serve as a metaphorical replacement for the other.

As I have written about elsewhere (Weismantel 2004), the genital effigies were part of a larger group of ceramics, including effigies of anal and oral intercourse and of breast-feeding, that enact a very active sexuality that engages multiple bodily orifices and many different individual bodies. Rather than individual pleasure, these pots model social interaction; the visual focus is on the liquid fertility passed from one body to another, rather than on displays of naked flesh.

These social messages had larger ecological and religious connotations as well. As modeled by ceramic effigies of landscapes, the flow of liquid fertility ultimately encompassed mountains, agricultural fields, and, especially, the irrigation water that the Moche channeled from rivers into their fields, linking the human body with its flows of blood and semen to the flows of water down mountains and across the land—and into the agricultural crops from which chicha could be brewed.

In these ceramics, we have completely left behind the readily recognizable complex of artifacts and ingredients associated with chicha today: there are no keros; the beverage may not have been made of corn; and we do not know if the hands that held them were female or male. What we are left with is the use of drinking vessels to model a nested set of relationships, social, political, ecological and religious, that become physically embodied through the interaction of the hand, the mouth, the container, and the liquid. The flow of liquids between bodies—including rivers and mountains—

was enacted by drinkers who poured beverages from the ceramic bodies into their own. It is the physicality, sociality, and performativity of this medium for transmitting crucial cultural meanings—and, of course, the sometimes cruel interplay of pleasure and humiliation inherent in the offer of a drink—that remain constant over time.

Conclusions

Throughout its long history, chicha has demonstrated its symbolic potency. It often appears to make a single powerful statement, as in the gendered rituals of Amazonia, where the role of wife is symbolized by the bowl of chicha offered to a husband. But hidden behind these singular messages are equally significant tensions and ambiguities: Amazonian rites embody a peculiar mixture of obsequiousness and power; in the highlands, chicha symbolizes contradictory racial identities, indigenous and mestizo. In Inca political rituals where overlords drank with lesser lords, chicha reinforced the hierarchical relationship between master and vassal; but the moment in which the superior offered his inferior a drink was also an honorific one that created an important sense of shared membership in the imperial project. In the case of the Moche genital effigies, the construction of the vessel forces drinkers into positions not normally adopted in public; this particular potential for both personal pleasure and social pain offers an especially striking example of the inherent ambivalence in the offer of a drink.

In sum, chicha has consistently been used to express tensions between inequality and shared identity, as well as to embody qualities of the natural and supernatural world. These abstract principles take concrete and dramatic form in the movement of the drinking vessel from host to guest and back again. In the South American tradition, the drink is a gift—it's the woman offering you a brimming kero, not a can of beer you grabbed from the refrigerator when you were alone. Accustomed to individual consumption, we can easily miss this dimension of chicha drinking and so fail to incorporate the presence of other parties at the event in our analyses. These include not only the drinker and the person offering the drink, but also the audience that witnesses and interprets the interaction as well.

This performativity is perhaps most dramatically embodied in the Moche sex pots, but it emerges in each of the contexts explored in this chapter. In the staged photos taken by tourists, or the public consumption of chicha by political protestors, in Martín Chambi's photographs as well as the political dramas staged by Inca kings, this use of chicha to communicate meanings to third parties is a recurrent theme and highlights the sociality of the act of drinking.

The silly statue made by the brothers who live on the road to Moche may provide a guide for our study of chicha. This modern-Inca-Moche beer bottle made by self-appointed leaders of a north coast cultural renaissance reminds us that some incarnations of beer drinking may be rich with cultural significance while not conforming at all to our ideal of Andean chicha. In other words, our work may require an active imagination and the ability to enjoy a joke. Ambiguous, performative, and always political, the simple gesture of offering someone a drink has been fraught with cultural meaning from the eighth-century penis pot to the twenty-first-century tourist blog—and long may it remain so.

Notes

1. See http://www.culturexplorers.com/Pages/Destinations/Peru/photogallery/ Peru PhotoEnlarge 002.html, accessed March 5, 2006. This particular photograph is part of an extensive Web-based advertisement for a tourism company that sells trips to Peru, Mexico, Brazil, and Guatemala; the caption describes the woman as "my Quechua friend."

2. The term *chicha* also appears as a description of traditional beverages from elsewhere in South America, such as among the Mapuche of Chile or the Kuna of Panama, but this article concentrates on the fermented beverages of Amazonia and the Andes. See Goldstein, Coleman Goldstein, and Williams (this volume) on the word *chicha*, apparently a Caribbean term introduced into South America by early Spanish travelers, where it coexists with the Quechua term *asua*. Asua might be considered a more accurate term, but chicha has come to be the more widely known term among Spanish-speakers and in the scholarly literature and is the term that will be used here. See also Anderson, this volume, on the pre-Hispanic associations between vessel form and chicha in the southern highlands.

3. On the context and social meanings of ceramics for chicha consumption, see Bowser (2000, 2004), and Bowser and Patton (2004). An excellent series of photographs of Amazonian chicha production and consumption was available at http:// www.anth.ucsb.edu/projects/hbe/chicha.htm, as of June 16, 2008.

4. That is, chicha in the form of wrapped manioc mash, to which water could be added as needed.

5. I would like to thank Helaine Silverman, whose interest in tourism at archaeological sites prompted this stop.

6. See, for example, the poster in the on-line museum museovintage.com entitled "La chicha embrutece," in which chicha is associated with the figure of a mule—and a face with stereotypically African features.

7. Studies that employ modified versions of Turner's theory to look at such societies include Eric Wolf's classic study of the Virgin of Guadalupe in Mexico (1958); José Limón's (1994) famous essay "Carne, Carnales, and the Carnivalesque," on Texan Mexicanos; and my own analysis of *pishtaco* imagery in the Andes (2001).

8. Photos of foreigners of both sexes drinking chicha can be found on the Web, but most pictures are of men.

9. See OtavalosOnLine.com: http://images.google.com/imgres?imgurl=http://www.otavalosonline.com/pawkaraymi/2004/comida/mote%2520con%2520chicha.jpg&imgrefurl=http://www.otavalosonline.com/pawkaraymi/2004/comida/comida.htm&h=325&w=244&sz=50&hl=en&sig2=KwiqIque- cfTZHI9I6iYoA&start=50&tbnid=voDGL-VFL7CwmM:&tbnh=114&tbnw=85&ei=YotHROHVOcmMabSlsYcG&prev=/images%3Fq%3Dchicha%26start%3D40%26ndsp%3D20%26svnum%3D10%26hl%3Den%26lr%3D%26sa%3DN; accessed April 26, 2008.

10. See, for example, Reichel-Dolmatoff (1971).

11. For a fuller discussion of Martín Chambi, chicha, chicherías, and indigenismo, see my *Cholas and Pishtacos* (2001).

12. This contrasts to the coca ceremonies, which Allen found to be symmetrical.

13. Santillán (1563, in Jiménez de la Espada [1950: 46–47], cited in Cummins (2002: 85).

14. It is possible that these vessels were never actually used for drinking, since they were found in tombs, but if so, they nonetheless mimic drinking vessels.

References cited

Albro, Robert
2000 The Populist Chola: Cultural Mediation and the Political Imagination in Quillacollo, Bolivia. *Journal of Latin American Anthropology* 5(2): 30–88.
Allen, Catherine J.
1988 *The Hold Life Has: Coca and Cultural Identity in an Andean Community.* Washington, D.C.: Smithsonian Institution Press.
Bergh, Susan
1993 Death and Renewal in Moche Phallic-spouted Vessels. *RES: Anthropology and Aesthetics* 24: 78–93.
Betanzos, Juan de
1996 [1557] *Narrative of the Incas.* Translated and edited by Roland Hamilton and Dana Buchanan from the Palma de Mallorca manuscript. Austin: University of Texas Press.
Bowser, Brenda J.
2000 From Pottery to Politics: An Ethnoarchaeological Study of Political Factionalism, Ethnicity, and Domestic Pottery Style in the Ecuadorian Amazon. *Journal of Archaeological Method and Theory* 7(3): 219–248.
2004 The Amazonian House: A Place of Women's Politics, Pottery, and Prestige. *Expedition* 46(2): 18–23.

Bowser, Brenda J., and John Q. Patton

2004 Domestic Spaces as Public Places: An Ethnoarchaeological Case Study of Houses, Gender, and Politics in the Ecuadorian Amazon. *Journal of Archaeological Method and Theory* 11(2): 157–181.

Bullen, Margaret

1993 Chicha in the Shanty Towns of Arequipa, Peru. *Popular Music* 12(3): 229–244.

Cappelini, Mónica S.

2005 La prensa chicha en Perú. *Revista Chasqui*, no. 88. Http://chasqui.comunica. org/, accessed May 28, 2007.

Chambi, Martín

1993 *Martín Chambi: Photographs, 1920–1950*. Introduction by Edward Ranney and Públio López Mondéjar. Translated by Margaret Sayers Peden. Washington, D.C.: Smithsonian Institution Press.

Cummins, Thomas B. F.

2002 *Toasts with the Inca: Andean Abstraction and Colonial Images on Quero Vessels*. Ann Arbor: University of Michigan Press.

de la Cadena, Marisol

1998 Silent Racism and Intellectual Superiority in Peru. *Bulletin of Latin American Research* 17(2): 143–164.

2000 *Indigenous Mestizos: The Politics of Race and Culture in Cuzco, Peru, 1919–1991*. Durham: Duke University Press.

Garcilaso de la Vega, el Inca

1966 [1609] *Royal Commentaries of the Incas and General History of Peru*. Part One. Translated, introduction by Harold V. Livermore. Austin: University of Texas Press.

Limón, José E.

1994 *Dancing with the Devil: Society and Cultural Poetics in Mexican-American South Texas*. Madison: University of Wisconsin Press.

López Mondéjar, Publio

1993 The Magic of Martín Chambi. In *Martín Chambi: Photographs, 1920–1950*. Introduction by Edward Ranney and Publio López Mondéjar. Translated by Margaret Sayers Peden, pp. 13–28. Washington, D.C.: Smithsonian Institution Press.

Mauss, Marcel

2006 [1924] *The Gift: The Form and Reason for Exchange in Archaic Societies*. New York: Routledge.

Murra, John V.

1975 *Formaciones económicas y políticas del mundo andino*. Lima: Instituto de Estudios Peruanos.

Netherly, Patricia

1977 Local Level Lords on the North Coast of Peru. Doctoral dissertation, Cornell University.

Polanyi, Karl

2001 [1944] *The Great Transformation*. New York: Beacon.

Ranney, Edward
1993 The Legacy of Martín Chambi. In *Martín Chambi: Photographs, 1920–1950*. Introduction by Edward Ranney and Publio López Mondéjar. Translated by Margaret Sayers Peden, pp. 9–12. Washington, D.C.: Smithsonian Institution Press.

Reichel-Dolmatoff, Gerardo
1971 *Amazonian Cosmos: The Sexual and Religious Symbolism of the Tukano Indians*. Chicago: University of Chicago Press.

Salomon, Frank, and George L. Urioste
1991 *The Huarochirí Manuscript: A Testament of Ancient and Colonial Andean Religion*. Austin: University of Texas Press.

Turner, Victor W.
1970 *The Forest of Symbols: Aspects of Ndembu Ritual*. Ithaca: Cornell University Press.

Uzendoski, Michael A.
2004 Manioc Beer and Meat: Value, Reproduction and Cosmic Substance among the Napo Runa of the Ecuadorian Amazon. *Journal of the Royal Anthropological Institute* 10: 883–902.

Weismantel, Mary
2001 *Cholas and Pishtacos: Stories of Race and Sex in the Andes*. Chicago: University of Chicago Press.
2004 Moche Sex Pots: Reproduction and Temporality in Ancient South America. *American Anthropologist* 106(3): 495–505.

Whitten, Norman E., Jr., and Dorothea Scott Whitten
2007 Puyo Runa: Imagery and Power in Modern Amazonia. Urbana: University of Illinois Press.

Whitten, Norman E., Jr., Dorothea Scott Whitten, and Alfonso Chango
1997 Return of the Yumbo: The Indigenous Caminata from Amazonia to Andean Quito. *American Ethnologist* 24(2): 355–391.

Wolf, Eric R.
1958 The Virgin of Guadalupe: A Mexican National Symbol. *Journal of American Folklore* 71(279): 34–39.

Yupanqui, Diego de Castro [Titu Cusi]
2005 [1570] *Titu Cusi, a 16th Century Account of the Conquest: Instrucción del Inga Don Diego de Castro Titu Cusi Yupanqui para el muy ilustre Señor el Licenciado Lope García del Castro*. Introduction, Spanish modernization, English translation, notes by Nicole Delia Legnani. Cambridge: Harvard University Press.

Contributors

Catherine J. Allen is professor of anthropology at George Washington University.

Karen Anderson is a PhD candidate in the Department of Anthropology at the University of California, Santa Barbara.

Brenda J. Bowser is professor of anthropology at California State University, Fullerton.

Tamara L. Bray is associate professor of anthropology at Wayne State University.

Melissa Chatfield is a postdoctoral scholar at the Archaeology Center of Stanford University and a research associate of the Cuzco Archaeology Institute.

Robin C. Coleman Goldstein is a PhD candidate in the Anthropology Department at Northwestern University.

David J. Goldstein is visiting professor of archaeobotany at the Universidad Peruana Cayetano Heredia.

Melissa Goodman-Elgar is assistant professor of anthropology at Washington State University.

Frances Hayashida is associate professor of anthropology at the University of New Mexico.

Justin Jennings is senior curator of Latin American archaeology at the Royal Ontario Museum and associate professor of anthropology at the University of Toronto. He is the author or editor of many books, including *Finding Fairness: From Pleistocene Foragers to Contemporary Capitalists.*

Diane C. Perlov is senior vice president for exhibits at the California Science Center, Los Angeles.

Mary Weismantel is professor of anthropology and director of Latin American and Caribbean studies at Northwestern University.

Patrick R. Williams is associate curator of anthropology at the Field Museum of Chicago.

Index

Pages with *f* denote figures; pages with *t* denote tables.